PADRES
ESSENTIAL

PADRES ESSENTIAL

Everything You Need to Know to Be a Real Fan!

Bill Center

TRIUMPH
B O O K S
CHICAGO

Library of Congress Cataloging-in-Publication Data

Center, Bill.
Padres essential : everything you need to know to be a real fan! / Bill Center.
    p. cm.
ISBN-13: 978-1-57243-956-6 (hard cover)
ISBN-10: 1-57243-956-4 (hard cover)
1. San Diego Padres (Baseball team : National League of Professional Baseball Clubs)—History. I. Title.
 GV875.S33C46 2007
 796.357'6409794985—dc22
                                2007004140

This book is available in quantity at special discounts for your group or organization. For further information, contact:

    Triumph Books
    542 South Dearborn Street
    Suite 750
    Chicago, Illinois 60605
    (312) 939-3330
    Fax (312) 663-3557

Printed in U.S.A.
ISBN: 978-1-57243-956-6
Editorial production and layout by Prologue Publishing Services, LLC
Design by Patricia Frey
All photos courtesy of AP/Wide World Photos except where otherwise indicated

To the memory of Wayne Lockwood and Phil Collier
for years of devoted coverage of baseball in San Diego

Contents

Foreword

by Tony Gwynn

I'm a Padre.

I'm proud to say that...proud to say that I played my entire career with one team.

But my association with the San Diego Padres goes beyond the 20 seasons I spent in a variety of Padres uniforms.

I was a fan of the Padres long before I was a player.

My first trip to San Diego Stadium came in 1978 when I was a freshman basketball player at San Diego State. As a youth in Long Beach, I grew up a Dodgers fan...Willie Davis was my hero.

But shortly after coming to San Diego State, I started paying attention to the Padres, and in 1978 a group of friends and I shelled out 50¢ apiece to go sit in the bleachers and watch the Padres play the Cubs.

Those were great times. We'd buy the cheapest bleacher seats and start working our way forward through the stands. We'd make a game of seeing how long it would take us before we'd be sitting in the best seats behind home plate.

I remember going to see the Pirates play the Padres in 1979. I loved the way the Pirates attacked the ball. We snuck all the way around to seats right behind the Pirates' dugout when Willie Stargell came up late in the game. We were so close that we could hear the Pirates talking in their dugout. Then Stargell hit this ball to right center...the swing, the contact, the sound, and the sight of that ball taking off.

We were in awe. And we could hear the Pirates congratulating Stargell when he returned to the dugout. Pops!

To experience major league baseball live. It was the greatest.

When I first arrived in San Diego, I usually went to San Diego Stadium to see the other teams. But I saw the Padres so many times that I started to convert. They became my team. Like the Chargers and Clippers became my teams. I was a San Diegan.

Soon I began tracking the Padres. Dave Winfield. Randy Jones. Ozzie Smith. I was supposed to be there the day Smith made that great bare-handed stop on Jeff Burroughs, but I stayed home and saw it on television...I kicked myself for missing that one.

You knew back then that you'd become a Padres fan when you started looking at the paper each day to see how close they were to .500. That was always the key deal. You didn't think about them winning a title back then, but if they were .500, that was an achievement. I remember 1978, when the Padres did have a winning record for the first time. That was huge.

Back then, I didn't think much about ever playing for the Padres. I was playing basketball at San Diego State. Even when I started playing baseball for the Aztecs, I didn't think much about playing for the Padres.

Then, in 1981, I was offered a chance to be an extra in a Padres commercial they were filming at the stadium. I put on a Padres uniform for the first time. No. 15. I had my back to the camera in the commercial, but I was a Padre that day.

Four months later, the Padres drafted me. I remember trying on the uniform again. It felt good. It just felt like that's where I belonged.

The next 20 years produced so many memories.

When I was elected to the Hall of Fame earlier this year, so many of those memories were stirred. It was like I was reliving my entire career again.

So many great times, along with those bumps, in a road that are part of life. It's funny some of the things that stick out in your mind.

I remember the time I called Alicia from the road in 1983 while I was in a hitting slump. I asked her to try to tape some of my at-bats off the television so I could see what I was doing wrong. Anthony was a baby at the time, and Alicia had her hands full. But when I got home, Alicia had the tapes ready. What I saw helped turn my season around, and I was credited with being a pioneer in the use of videotape to study hitting. But it was Alicia who deserves credit. She got the whole thing rolling.

Then there was that early morning in 1998 when our bus driver got lost taking us to a hotel in Montreal. We had been driving in circles for what seemed like hours when Kevin Brown spotted this kid walking along the road. Brownie ordered the driver to stop, and we got this kid on the bus to direct us to our hotel. It turned out that it was about three blocks away. But as we got off that bus, every one of the players tipped that kid—$20, $50, whatever we had. I remember that kid standing by the bus and looking at that wad of bills. I always wondered how he explained all that money when he got home.

So many memories like that, as well as winning the National League pennants in 1984 and 1998. The memory of playing in Yankee Stadium in the 1998 World Series, visiting the monuments and homering off the façade in right field against David Wells.

And the memory of seeing my brother Chris get the hit at Dodger Stadium in 1996 that gave the Padres only their second National League West title.

To me, the memories are just as important as the milestones.

I don't remember the circumstances, but during my career I coined the phrase "We're the Padres" as a way of explaining some of the things the Padres did that couldn't be explained.

Sometimes the Padres way made you laugh. Other times it left you standing outside a stadium in the rain waiting for a bus. But the nuances that made us the Padres also gave us a special bond.

I feel honored to have played my entire career with the Padres. I feel honored that every one of my 3,141 hits came as a Padre. I am honored to be going to the Hall of Fame this summer as a career-long Padre—even though some of those yellow-and-brown uniforms, down to those brown cleats, were less than flattering.

The road wasn't always smooth with the Padres. The highs of 1984, 1996, and 1998 were counterbalanced by the "fire sale" of the early 1990s and those rumors from time to time that the team might be moved.

It was my hope that I would end my playing career in the new downtown ballpark. But the legal challenges that delayed construction for two years made that impossible.

Still, I'd like to think part of me is in PETCO Park—and part of the Padres' future as well as the past.

Like so many of my former teammates and the players who preceded us, "We're the Padres."

We always will be.

Introduction

The first time I viewed my friend's treasured baseball card, I did a double take.

John Grubb
Outfielder
Washington
National League

As colleague Wayne Lockwood and I looked at the card, we laughed. But it wasn't that deep, joke's-on-you kind of belly laugh. It was more of that sheepish, we-ducked-the-big-one-this-time relief type of chuckle.

There was only one small problem with that 1974 Topps card.

John Grubb didn't play for Washington of the National League. There was no Washington in the National League...at that time.

John Grubb played for the San Diego Padres—who would, probably, have been in Washington had it not been for the intervention of Ray Kroc, whose purchase of the Padres in 1974 saved baseball in San Diego.

Truth is, the Padres were out of San Diego in that dark winter of 1973–1974. The moving vans were actually packed with the Padres' equipment.

Because of that, the most important figure in Padres history will always be Ray Kroc. Without Kroc, Tony Gwynn would never have had 3,141 hits over 20 seasons as a Padre. Without Kroc, we would never have heard the sounds of AC/DC's "Hells Bells" greet the late-inning arrival of closer Trevor Hoffman at Qualcomm Stadium and

Long after the last Atlanta fan had departed Turner Field, the Padres returned to the pitching mound on October 14, 1998, to celebrate the team's second National League pennant. The Padres won the first three games of the NLCS en route to eliminating Atlanta in six games. NLCS Most Valuable Player Sterling Hitchcock is seated at the right. Club owner John Moores and wife Becky are standing behind Hitchcock. Tony Gwynn is at the upper left, standing next to Greg Vaughn, who hit a club-record 50 homers during the regular season.

then PETCO Park. Without Kroc, Padres fans would never have suffered through the losing seasons that made the nirvana of 1984 all that more special. Without Kroc, there would have been no need for John Moores and his vision for a downtown ballpark.

Without Kroc, there would be no need for this history.

Looking back, however, the winter of 1973–1974 was the most troubling time in the history of the San Diego Padres.

But it was far from the only bump in the road for a franchise that has taken a wild roller-coaster ride of highs and lows since being born a financially strapped expansion team in 1969.

The Washington crisis wasn't the only time there was talk of the Padres being moved. That was just the closest San Diego came to losing the team. And even when San Diego voted to build the Padres a baseball-only home in the heart of the city's internationally acclaimed downtown redevelopment district, legal challenges delayed construction for two seasons.

The Padres, however, have also taken their fans on rides down the face of some great waves.

Even the lovable losers of the Padres' early seasons had their moments. Nate Colbert launched bombs that would be tape-measure homers even by PETCO Park standards. Future Hall of Famers Dave Winfield and Ozzie Smith launched their major league careers as Padres. And who can forget those magical nights when Randy Jones fooled the likes of Pete Rose with his seemingly hypnotic low-speed sinker.

The Padres have always had their share of great players.

Topping the list, of course, is Gwynn—the only player voted unanimously into the club's Hall of Fame upon his retirement. In 2007 Gwynn will become the first lifetime Padre to enter the Hall of Fame.

Players like Jones, Winfield, Gwynn, Hoffman, and others—many more others than you would think—gave us hope and enjoyment.

But each highlight was shadowed by harsh reality. We should have learned our lesson on July 21, 1970. That was the night Clay Kirby no-hit the Mets through eight innings at San Diego Stadium, only to trail 1–0 thanks to an unearned run in the first inning. With two outs and no one on in the bottom of the eighth, Kirby's spot came up in the batting order. For some still inexplicable reason, manager Preston Gomez decided to send pinch-hitter Cito Gaston up in place of Kirby. Gaston struck out. The Mets scored two runs on three hits off reliever Jack Baldschun in the ninth.

Fact: the Padres have never had a no-hitter. Some fans believe it's the curse of Kirby.

Gomez, who had to be protected from several angry fans after the game, explained he was "trying to win" the game. Like that really mattered. Four of the Padres' first six editions lost more than 100 games, and the Padres were a decade old before they enjoyed a winning season.

Back then, there was almost as much entertainment off the field as on it. We could laugh at Ted Giannoulas masquerading as the famous chicken mascot. And there was "Tuba Man" Jim Eakle and his note-challenged band of quasi-musicians marching through the mostly empty grandstands.

Then along came McDonald's founder and baseball fan Kroc.

He not only saved baseball in San Diego, he gave the city's beleagured fans hope. In 1984 that hope turned into a fantasy season, although, sadly, Kroc passed away just before he could see his personal dream come true.

It went far beyond winning a first National League pennant. It was how the Padres won—returning home to Jack Murphy Stadium down 2–0 to the Chicago Cubs in the best-of-five National League Championship Series. No Padres fan will ever forget Steve Garvey's walk-off homer in the ninth inning of Game 4 to even the series.

Remember what happened the next day? Many Padres fans were just coming down off their Garvey high as the Cubs built a 3–0 lead behind Rick Sutcliffe. The Padres were apparently doomed. Sutcliffe hadn't lost a game since June and would eventually be presented the National League Cy Young Award.

But the Padres scored two runs in the sixth. And in the seventh...well, it seemed as if Kroc reached down from the heavens to intervene on the behalf of his beloved club.

Fan favorite Tim Flannery rolled a routine grounder toward Cubs first baseman Leon Durham. And the ball went right under Durham's glove. Before the inning was over, the Padres had four runs and their first National League pennant.

Did Kroc intervene from far above? The Padres faithful are believers.

But as much a high as 1984 was, it didn't push the Padres over the top. Things just don't work that way in San Diego.

The other shoe always seemed set to fall. The Padres seemed to do things in a way all their own. Gwynn had a phrase for it. "We're the Padres," Gwynn would say as a way to describe the countless bumps the Padres experienced along the way.

The glory of the 1984 season was followed by years of instability. The club was sold twice in a span of five years. The turmoil produced the "fire sale" liquidation of high-priced stars and another round of rumors about moving the franchise.

Enter John Moores, who bought the Padres in 1994 with a vision for the club and the city.

Moores believed the only way baseball would thrive in San Diego was in a baseball-only ballpark located in the heart of the city's revitalized downtown. And the only way to get public support for that project was to build a winner.

He handed the reins to general manager Kevin Towers and manager Bruce Bochy.

The 1996 team, led by National League MVP Ken Caminiti, claimed only the second National League West title in franchise history. Two seasons later, the Padres, led by pitcher Kevin Brown and Greg Vaughn's 50-homer season, won their second National League pennant.

That victory resulted in the vote to build the new downtown ballpark.

But like Gwynn has said so many times, "We're the Padres." Nothing comes easy. Legal challenges delayed construction, pushing back nirvana two seasons to 2004.

Then, the Padres moved into PETCO Park.

The next chapter had begun. No longer were there fears of San Diego losing the Padres. But some of the fun that came with hope was replaced with the pressure of expectations: build it and the players and wins will come.

The Padres opened PETCO Park with three straight winning seasons. In both their second and third campaigns, the Padres won the National League West title. In 2005–2006, for the first time in franchise history, the Padres advanced to the playoffs in back-to-back seasons.

The success came at a cost.

Weeks after the Padres were eliminated by St. Louis in the first round for a second straight season, the Padres allowed manager Bruce Bochy to move on to San Francisco after a record 12 seasons at the Padres helm.

Time for another era to dawn.

PADRES
ESSENTIAL

Millions Served

It would be easy to start a history of the Padres at the beginning.

The Padres were born as a product of National League expansion. Their first season was 1969. But that also seemed to be the Padres' beginning of the end—which apparently came on May 27, 1973.

That was the day that Padres founder and San Diego financier C. Arnholt Smith announced that he had reached agreement to sell the Padres to Washington, D.C., supermarket magnate Joseph Danzansky. The Padres would be moved to the nation's capitol after the end of the 1973 season...or before.

"I remember when the announcement came down," said then Padres infielder Dave Campbell. "The players all expected something like that could happen...probably would. But they were talking about the possibility of moving the team in the middle of the season.

"You can only guess the reaction."

In the city as well as the clubhouse.

Essentially, the Padres were dead in San Diego—the ultimate lame duck. The only question was when those moving vans packed with Padres equipment would head east from San Diego Stadium.

The Padres needed an angel. Actually, they needed an army of angels.

The first to appear was not a player or an owner. It was an attorney. As the Padres' moving day grew near, San Diego City attorney John Witt filed a lawsuit that started the reversal of history.

Witt was helpless to block the sale of the Padres to Danzansky. He was helpless to block the move of the team to Washington, D.C. But the Padres did have a 20-year lease for San Diego Stadium that extended through the end of the 1989 season.

Witt raised the question of how much the remaining 15 years of the Padres' lease was worth to the city of San Diego. And a judge ruled that if the Padres moved, the team could be liable for damages based on that lease. No exact dollar figures were announced. But the sums being tossed around made Danzansky blink. He backed out of his purchase.

The Padres hadn't been saved, but they had won at least a temporary reprieve. The National League decided it would operate the Padres in San Diego in 1974 while seeking either a new local owner or an outside owner willing to buy off the lease should the team be moved.

Over the next few months, prospective owners came and went. The plight of the San Diego Padres became a national story. Enter Ray Kroc. A lifelong baseball fan whose real dream was to own the Chicago Cubs, Kroc was cruising on his private yacht off Florida in the fall of 1973 when he saw one of the countless stories on the Padres in a newspaper.

He turned to his wife, Joan, and, out of the blue, said, "I think I want to buy the San Diego Padres." Her reaction: "Why would you want to buy a monastery?"

Thus began one of the great marriages in professional sports—Ray Kroc and the San Diego Padres.

Born in 1902, Kroc was a doer and a dreamer. His life was filled with ideas to become successful. Most didn't pan out.

"I got shot down and shot myself down countless times," he once said. "But failure doesn't stop you, it shapes you and makes you strive for the right idea."

Kroc was selling mixers in 1954 when he hit upon the "right idea" during a sales visit to a small restaurant in San Bernardino, California. Owned by brothers Dick and Mac McDonald, the take-out establishment featured a small menu, low prices, and friendly service.

Kroc soon entered a partnership with the McDonalds to expand and franchise their idea. Eight years later, after having bought out the brothers, Kroc headed an empire that already numbered 500 drive-through restaurants and had sold more than a billion hamburgers.

"Quality, service, cleanliness, and value," was the mantra of the ultimate salesman.

DID YOU KNOW ... That there have been only four ownership groups in Padres history? C. Arnholt Smith was the owner of the Padres from their birth as an expansion team in 1969 through 1974. Ray Kroc bought the team in 1974 and his widow Joan retained ownership when he died in 1984 through 1990. Tom Werner and 14 minority partners owned the Padres from 1990 to 1994. John Moores has owned the club since 1994.

"The first time I met Ray, I was blown away," said then Padres president Buzzie Bavasi. "He had this passion for life and a genuine love of people. He loved baseball. And he loved the city and the people of San Diego."

And they loved Kroc back.

Kroc endeared himself to Padres fans from day one. There were no heavy negotiations with Smith. They met for lunch and, at the end, Kroc said he wanted to buy the Padres. Smith responded that, although he didn't want to sell the club, the Padres were for sale.

Kroc asked the price. Smith said $12 million. "Deal," said Kroc.

Years later, Smith said he believed he had made a mistake by seeking what he believed to be fair market value. Smith believed that if he had doubled the price, Kroc still would have said, "Deal."

Kroc bought the Padres on January 25, 1974.

During a press conference to announce the sale, Kroc was bombarded by questions about the future of the Padres and his commitment. The media in San Diego had no feel for the outsider. When pressed about the financial viability of "his" Padres, Kroc fired that he would spend whatever was necessary to make baseball work in San Diego. "After all," he said, "what do I need with more money?"

Kroc wasted no time in winning over the hearts of Padres fans. Within days of purchasing the Padres, Kroc approved the contract of Willie McCovey. The slugger had already officially been acquired by the Padres, although his contract had been in limbo since a previously proposed sale of the Padres to Marje Everett, the owner of the Hollywood Park thoroughbred racetrack, fell through.

But the fans' never-ending love of Kroc was sealed on April 9, 1974. The club's home opener attracted 39,083. And Kroc scheduled time for himself after the eighth inning to go on the public address system to thank the fans.

However, the Astros were leading 9–2 in the eighth. A Padres rally died when Nate Colbert fouled out and Matty Alou, who had forgotten how many were out, wandered off the bag, and was doubled off first for the final out in the inning.

Kroc was steaming as he took the microphone. At first, he followed the script, thanking the fans and promising that better days were ahead.

Then...

"Fans, I suffer with you," said Kroc. "I've never seen such stupid ballplaying in my life."

The crowd still on hand erupted into cheers.

But the moment wasn't over. As Kroc was winding down, a streaker took off across the outfield grass at San Diego Stadium. Still clutching the microphone, Kroc shouted, "Get that streaker out of here! Throw him in jail!"

Kroc had instantly become a soulmate with long-suffering Padres fans. In the parking lot that night, fans stood around their cars reliving the events of the evening. The score? who cared...Kroc's one of us.

The players were not happy. The Padres issued a statement through player representative McCovey. "None of us like being called stupid," said Big Mac. "We're pros. I wish Mr. Kroc hadn't done that."

TRIVIA

Name the three Padres pitchers to win the Cy Young Award.

Answers to the trivia questions are on pages 219–220.

Over in the Astros clubhouse, Houston third baseman Doug Rader said, "Does he think he's in a sales convention dealing with a bunch of his short-order cooks?"

Kroc responded by staging Short-Order Cook's Night the next time the Astros visited San Diego. Rader filled his order by delivering the lineup card to home plate on a platter while wearing a chef's hat.

Baseball had become fun in San Diego. It became the thing to do. The 1974 Padres topped 1 million in attendance for the first time. The game could thrive in San Diego, though the fans' support of

Kroc—the 1974 attendance was an astounding 75.8 percent jump over the lame duck season of 1973—did not immediately translate itself into success on the field.

Try as he might, Kroc had a hard time immediately luring quality players to San Diego. Maybe it was those yellow-and-brown uniforms that made the Padres look like refugees from Sesame Street. Maybe it was the fact that the Padres were still the worst team in baseball. The Padres first season under Kroc produced the same 60–102 record as the last season before him.

Actually, the Padres' thin talent ranks got a major boost in a one-week span a half year before Kroc bought the team. Left-handed pitcher Randy Jones made his major league debut on June 16, 1973. And outfielder Dave Winfield arrived directly from the University of Minnesota campus on June 19.

The pair would become two of the greatest players in Padres history.

Jones, the diminutive sinker/slider specialist who turned deception into a form of art, would become both the Padres' first 20-game winner and Cy Young Award winner, in addition to becoming the first Padres player to single-handedly draw fans to Mission Valley.

Winfield, the first athlete ever drafted by all three major sports (baseball, football, and basketball) would eventually become the first player to wear a Padres cap in the Hall of Fame. In eight seasons with the Padres, Winfield hit .282 with 154 homers and 626 RBIs.

But at the dawn of the Kroc era, both Jones and Winfield were just getting their feet wet. And there wasn't much Kroc could do about 1974 after purchasing the team just three weeks before the start of spring training.

Although only three of 1973's Opening Day starters were still in the lineup a year later, the Padres were much the same the lovable lot of losers that almost earned one-way tickets to Washington.

One of the key figures in the Padres' plight was crowd-favorite shortstop Enzo Hernandez. Padres fans loved Hernandez because he represented all the club's problems rolled into one package. As a rookie in 1971, for example, Hernandez had 12 RBIs in 549 at-bats while committing 33 errors. In 710 games as a Padre, Hernandez had two homers and 113 RBIs. His career batting average: .224. His career on-base percentage: .283. He scored 241 runs in his Padres career against 119 errors. Still, Padres fans cheered every time public address announcer John DeMott opened the Padres lineup with "No. 11, ENNNN-ZZZZZO Hernandez."

Things changed ever so slightly in 1974 when Hernandez was dropped from first to eighth in the other. The newcomers included McCovey and Alou—who was sold to Japan within weeks of his base-running gaffe in the home opener—second baseman Glenn Beckert and outfielder Bobby Tolan.

The result could have been worse. The Padres would have lost 103 were it not for the greatest comeback in team history. On June 10, the Padres were trailing Pittsburgh 8–0 before scoring four runs in the eighth and five in the ninth.

"That season was terribly disappointing," said Jones, who established a franchise record with 22 losses despite a 4.45 ERA. The Padres scored two or fewer runs in 17 of Jones' losses and were shutout in seven of his starts. "The bottom line was that we had a lot of good hitters who just didn't hit that season."

As a team, the Padres batted .229 (the third-lowest mark in franchise history) and averaged 3⅓ runs a game. And they committed 170 errors.

There was one breakthrough of note. In his first full major league season, Dave Winfield hit .265 with 20 homers and a team-leading 75 RBIs. Only John Grubb (at .286) had a higher batting average among the regulars.

The next season marked one of the greatest individual single-season turnarounds in major league history. A season after losing 22 games, Jones became the franchise's first 20-game winner—and the first pitcher since the Cubs' Dick Ellsworth in 1962–1963 to go from a 20-loss season to a 20-win season.

Slowly, the Padres were making progress.

In his last year as the club's general manager, Peter Bavasi added free agents Gene Tenace and Rollie Fingers to the Padres in 1976 in addition to bringing in outfielder Willie Davis and third baseman Rader via trades.

The acquisition of catcher Tenace and relief pitcher Fingers from the Oakland A's was a major coup for the Padres. The pair had helped the A's to three straight World Series titles from 1972 to 1974. But their impact on the Padres was minimal, although Fingers led the National League in saves in both 1977 and 1978.

Randy Jones became the first of three Padres to win the Cy Young Award in 1976 with the greatest season ever by a Padres pitcher.

Jones posted a 22–14 record with a 2.74 ERA. He set club records for games started (40), innings pitched (315⅓), and complete games (25). Jones was 16–3 at the All-Star break. He was also named the National League starter for the All-Star Game, which he won.

Jones won 30 percent of the Padres' club-record 73 wins. And he should have won 30 games. He lost seven one-run decisions in the second half of the season—including two 1–0 games.

But Jones and the Padres paid too great a price for his 1976 season. By the end of the year, his priceless left elbow was pained. Jones needed off-season surgery to repair nerve damage apparently

More than two decades after his death, Ray Kroc remains one of the more popular figures in San Diego's history. An outsider when he bought the Padres, Kroc not only saved the team for San Diego, he created an aura around the franchise that remains today in the hearts of fans.

caused by the workload of his 1975–1976 marathon efforts (76 starts, 43 complete games, 600⅓ innings pitched).

Jones was never the same.

The 1977 season was one of great change for the Padres. Bob Fontaine was named the general manager, meaning a Bavasi—first Buzzie, then son Peter—wasn't at the Padres helm for the first time since the birth of the franchise. Fifty games into the season, Alvin Dark replaced John McNamara as the manager.

The Opening Day lineup included four players who were former first-round draft picks of the Padres—right fielder Winfield (1973), left fielder Gene Richards (1975), shortstop Bill Almon (1974), and first baseman Mike Ivie (1970)—who had been converted from catcher after experiencing problems tossing the ball back to the mound.

Richards, Almon, and left-handed starting pitcher Bob Owchinko all produced as prized rookies. Richards hit .290 and stole 56 bases, then a record for National League rookies. Almon hit .261 and was solid at short. And Owchinko was named the National League Rookie Pitcher of the Year off a 9–12 season and a 4.45 ERA.

But the key newcomer of 1977 was center fielder George Hendrick.

The Padres wanted a veteran back in the heart of the order and in the winter negotiated a blockbuster 3-for-1 trade with Cleveland. Only this time, it was the Padres giving up the three players—outfielder John Grubb, catcher Fred Kendall, and infielder Hector Torres—to land a superstar.

Hendrick delivered. Inserted into the cleanup slot in back of the emerging superstar Winfield (who made the All-Star team for the first time), Hendrick hit .311 with 23 homers and 81 RBIs.

"I thought that season we had one of the best 3-4 combinations in the game," said Winfield, who hit .275 with 25 homers and 92 RBIs, plus 104 runs scored.

The 1977 season set the Padres up for a banner 1978 season. In their 10th season—and fifth under Kroc—the Padres posted their first winning record (84–78), and San Diego Stadium played host to the 49th All-Star Game on July 11.

At that time in the franchise's history, the All-Star Game was the single greatest day in Padres history. Ray Kroc was given the honor of throwing out the ceremonial first pitch. Dave Winfield and Rollie Fingers were the Padres' representatives in the All-Star Game and both played prominent roles in the National League's 7–3 victory. Winfield, afforded the biggest ovation during pregame introductions, upped his All-Star Game average to .750 (he was 2-for-2 in 1977) with a hit and scored a run. Fingers, en route to his second straight National League Fireman of the Year award, pitched two scoreless innings.

There was a new attitude to the Padres in 1978. Roger Craig, the original pitching coach of the Padres back in 1969, took over as manager and became a calming influence. Nowhere was that influence more apparent than with the Padres pitchers, who were led by veteran Gaylord Jackson Perry. On January 25, 1978, the Padres packaged pitcher Dave Tomlin and $125,000 to acquire Perry from the Texas Rangers. A year earlier, Perry was 15–12 with a 3.37 ERA with the Rangers. But he was also 39 years old when the Padres acquired him.

"But some pitchers are ageless because of their style," Craig said years later with a grin. "They know how to do it."

Many people believed what Perry knew best is how to gain every edge possible—even if it included doctoring the ball. Did he or didn't he? The question that he even might, Craig believed, worked to Perry's advantage.

"If they think he is [doctoring the ball], all they are doing is putting doubt in their own mind," said Craig. "Doubt is a huge hurdle to overcome in this game. You need confidence to hit a baseball. If you've lost that confidence because you are wondering what is going on…well."

Perry and Craig seemed in perfect concert.

Perry went 21–6 with a 2.73 ERA and joined Randy Jones as the second Padre to win the National League Cy Young Award. He also became the first 40-year-old to win the Cy Young Award and the first pitcher to win the award in both leagues. And Perry was toughest at home, positing an 11–2 record in Mission Valley with a 1.75 ERA in 18 starts.

The 1978 season helped vault Perry to the Hall of Fame. In the season's final game, Perry made the Dodgers' Joe Simpson the 3,000[th] strikeout victim of his career. At the time, only Walter Johnson and Bob Gibson had more strikeouts than Perry.

"I thought Perry's '78 season with the Padres was a pitching masterpiece," said Craig. "Taken on its whole, it might have been one of the greatest efforts ever."

Perry wasn't the only future Hall of Famer making his debut with the Padres in 1978.

During spring training, the Padres decided to take a look at a 23-year-old shortstop named Ozzie Smith. The scouting report on Smith was that he couldn't hit enough to stay in the major leagues. But when the Padres took a look at his glove, the question became "Who cares?"

Smith wasted no time in becoming the "Wizard of Ahs." Playing behind Randy Jones on April 20, Smith dived to his left for a hard grounder off the bat of Atlanta's Jeff Burroughs. With Smith committed to his dive, Burroughs' smash hit a rough spot in the San Diego Stadium infield and took a wild hop. While in mid-air, Smith reached back with his bare hand and caught the ball. Then he scrambled to his feet and threw out Burroughs.

For a split second, Padres fans and players paused in disbelief. Then the park erupted into an ovation. Padres fans had one more piece of the puzzle to cheer.

The momentum of 1978 carried over into 1979 for only one player—Dave Winfield. The right fielder had one of the greatest all-around offensive season in Padres history.

Winfield batted .308 and led the National League with 118 RBIs and 333 total bases. He led the Padres in nine offensive categories including homers (34), runs scored (97), doubles (27), and triples (10). He became the first Padre voted into the starting lineup for the All-Star Game and finished third in the voting for the Most Valuable Player award.

But aside from Winfield and 12 wins from Perry, there was little to cheer in the 68-win campaign of 1979. Major changes were on the way. The most striking change came during the offseason when the Padres named broadcaster and former Yankees infielder Jerry Coleman their seventh manager.

Coleman had been the lead man on the Padres radio team since 1972. As a player, he had played on six World Series championship teams during a nine-year career with the Yankees. A decorated Marine fighter pilot in World War II and Korea—Coleman was the only major league player to see action in both wars—Coleman's only previous executive experience in baseball was as the Yankees' minor league director after his retirement as a player.

TRIVIA

What are the longest games in Padres history?

Answers to the trivia questions are on pages 219–220.

"When Ray Kroc and Bob Fontaine first approached me about managing, I laughed," said Coleman years later. "I didn't mean it to be disrespectful. I honestly thought they were having a little fun.

"Then I realized I was going to be managing the Padres."

Although Coleman had no past managerial experience, his Padres soon had his stamp. They were going to be fundamentally sound and aggressive. Pitching and defense became the Coleman mantra.

Coleman's Padres led the major leagues in stolen bases (a club-record 239) and became the first team to produce three players to steal more than 50 bases—Gene Richards (61), Ozzie Smith (57), and outfielder Jerry Mumphrey (52). Coleman's Padres set franchise records for plays made in the field and produced two Gold Glove winners (Winfield and Smith) for the first time in franchise history.

The season highlights included three straight shutouts pitched by Randy Jones and a third Fireman of the Year award in four seasons for reliever Rollie Fingers.

But, on July 7, the Padres made one of the biggest moves in franchise history. Bob Fontaine was fired as general manager and replaced by Jack McKeon. McKeon had a reputation for wheeling and dealing. He was proud of his "Trader Jack" persona. And he had a champion in club owner Ray Kroc.

"Mr. Kroc gave me one assignment," said McKeon. "Get me a winner. He wanted a championship. He set no boundaries. Mr. Kroc put the club in my hands. It was a huge responsibility. And I wasn't going to let him down."

Some of the forthcoming decisions had to hurt Kroc. After playing every game for Coleman in 1980 and hitting .276 with 20 homers and 87 RBIs, Winfield departed as a free agent, signing with the New York Yankees.

McKeon really started to roll during the first two weeks of December in 1981. On December 8, he acquired catcher Terry Kennedy and six other players in an 11-player blockbuster with the Cardinals that sent pitchers Rollie Fingers and Bob Shirley and catcher Gene Tenace to St. Louis. Most of the other six players McKeon acquired from the Cardinals would be used in later deals to bolster the Padres.

That same day, McKeon claimed outfielder Alan Wiggins from the arch-rival Dodgers in baseball's annual draft of unprotected free agents. In 1984, following a move to second base, Wiggins would become the lead-off hitter of the Padres' first National League champions.

TRIVIA

Barry Bonds holds the record for the most homers hit against the Padres with 85. Who is number two on the list?

Answers to the trivia questions are on pages 219–220.

A week later, McKeon traded Padres icon Randy Jones to the New York Mets. The message was clear. If Jones could go, anyone could go. McKeon was reshaping the Padres.

McKeon was busy right up to the season's first pitch. On March 31, he acquired pitchers Chris Welsh and Tim Lollar and outfielder Ruppert Jones from the Yankees for fleet out-fielder Jerry Mumphrey and John Pacella (who McKeon had acquired from the Mets for Jones). The following day, McKeon landed second baseman Juan Bonilla. The returns were not immediate in the strike-shortened season of 1981. Led by manager Frank Howard, the Padres finished last in both ends of the season.

Perhaps the shortened season gave McKeon more time to focus on the big picture. Because 1982 brought another wave of fresh faces.

The fiery and demanding Dick Williams replaced Howard as the manager. McKeon traded the slick-fielding Ozzie Smith to the Cardinals for fellow shortstop Garry Templeton, who would be the Padres captain in the pivotal 1984 season. And a young rookie out of San Diego State named Tony Gwynn would make his first appearance in a Padres lineup on July 19.

McKeon not only contoured the Padres lineup, he reshaped the club's home—which was renamed Jack Murphy Stadium in 1981 in memory of the longtime *San Diego Union* sports editor who was instrumental in the building of the stadium and the acquisition of the Padres and Chargers of the National Football League. The interior fence was installed. The distance to straight-away center was reduced from 420 feet to 405 feet. The power alleys came in around nine feet. And the height of the fence was halved to 8½ feet.

Gwynn wasn't the only prospect promoted by the Padres during the 1982 season. Right-handers Eric Show and Luis DeLeon and left-hander Dave Dravecky all pitched their first full seasons with the Padres.

The Padres finished with an 81–81 record—marking only the second time in franchise history that they didn't have a losing season. More important, they were still in contention for the National League West title until September 27—the deepest they had ever gone into a season as a contender.

The Padres were expecting much bigger things in 1983 after signing first baseman Steve Garvey as a free agent away from the hated Dodgers. And as Show, Dravecky, and Lollar were maturing as front-line starters, another young rookie named Andy Hawkins joined the mix.

But injuries slowed the Padres to a second straight 81–81 season.

The start of Tony Gwynn's first full season was delayed until June 21 due to a fractured wrist suffered in winter ball. Afrer a 12–5 start, Dravecky struggled in the second half of the season with a sore shoulder and finished with a 14–10 record.

The biggest injury was to Garvey, who on July 29 suffered a dislocated thumb while sliding into home during the first game of a doubleheader. Taken to Scripps Hospital in La Jolla, Garvey at first argued that doctors should tape the thumb up so that he could get back to Jack Murphy Stadium in time to start the second game. But X-rays showed Garvey's season was over. When he emerged from the hospital several hours later, his thumb was in a cast.

"It doesn't hurt," said Garvey. "But you can't imagine how much this hurts."

The injury stopped Garvey's National League–record consecutive-games streak at 1,207.

A day after the season ended, McKeon sat in his office and expressed disappointment in the Padres' 1983 campaign.

"But I think we are headed in the right direction," said the general manager. "The foundation has been poured."

The following season, the Padres would build a championship on that foundation. Kroc was ready to serve up a winner.

By the NUMBERS

8—Homers by Tim Lollar, the most by a Padres pitcher.

9—Pinch-hit homers by Jerry Turner, between 1977 and 1981, a Padres all-time record.

27—Club record steals without being caught by outfielder Jerry Mumphrey in 1980.

56—Stolen bases by Gene Richards in 1977 set a major league record for a rookie. Vince Coleman blitzed the record in 1985 with 110 steals as a rookie.

70—Hits by Jerry Turner as a pinch-hitter, the Padres record.

Finally, a Champion

The greatest season in Padres history started on the worst possible note. On January 14, 1984, Ray Kroc died—11 days shy of the 10th anniversary of his purchase of the team. Kroc was actively trying to improve his beloved team right up to his final hours. Two days before he died, Kroc approved the signing of free agent relief pitcher Goose Gossage.

"Ray's death was a blow to baseball in San Diego," Steve Garvey said several years later. "Ray was baseball to Padres fans. He saved their team. He dreamed their same dreams.

"Whatever Ray said was the word. Padres fans believed in all things Kroc."

Kroc's death not only stunned the city, it hit Padres players hard.

"I think it was toughest on the guys who should have been the most hardened...the veterans," said Garry Templeton. "The guys who had been around the longest knew best what Ray was about and what he thought of the Padres. We took it hard."

Five weeks before the start of spring training, the Padres had lost their soul. Padres players were talking about dedicating the 1984 season to the memory of Ray Kroc when the owner's widow stepped forward as the Padres new chairwoman. Joan Kroc promised San Diego that the Padres would continue on as a legacy to Kroc. And she dedicated the 1984 season to his memory and asked Major League Baseball for permission to put her husband's initials—RAK—on the left sleeve of the Padres uniforms.

"I was a newcomer compared to many of my teammates," said Tony Gwynn. "But I remember getting chills looking down at those initials anytime we won a close game. It affected all of us."

Years later, "On a Mission" became the Padres' motto. But that was truly the case in 1984.

"A baseball season is a long grind," said Garvey. "I can't tell you how many times in 1984 that we did think about Kroc, or how many times we did get a lift from the memory of the man's passion."

The '84 season of course resulted in the Padres' first National League championship. In fact, it resulted in the franchise's second winning season.

"Early in spring training, we set a goal for ourselves," said Gossage. "Whenever anyone even briefly lost sight of that goal, the rest of us reminded them."

Of course, 1984 didn't happen overnight. Kroc had been working on "my dream" since he bought the club. But his quest really picked up momentum when Jack McKeon became the general manager in 1980.

Piece by piece, Trader Jack rebuilt the Padres into a champion.

"And I mean piece by piece," McKeon once recalled. "Ray loved his players. He was loyal to them. Whenever we did anything, Ray was interested in what it would mean to the player, his teammates, and his family as well as to the Padres. But the bottom line was 'keep moving forward.'"

Shoving the Padres in the right direction was the role of manager Dick Williams—a taskmaster and disciplinarian.

As has already been mentioned, McKeon's overhaul of the Padres began with the 11-player 1980 trade that brought catcher Terry Kennedy to San Diego from St. Louis in exchange for pitchers Rollie Fingers and Bob Shirley and catcher Gene Tenace.

It was no fluke that Kennedy was McKeon's first building block.

"We felt we needed to start with a catcher who was going to be with us for a while," said McKeon. "We needed a catcher who would grow and develop with the young pitchers we had in the system."

Many moves were to follow. In 1980, the day after trading for Kennedy, McKeon selected outfielder Alan Wiggins from the Dodgers organization in the Rule V draft of unprotected minor lea-guers. By the start of 1984, Wiggins had been converted to a second baseman and was the Padres' leadoff hitter.

In 1981 the Padres selected University of Arkansas center fielder Kevin McReynolds with the sixth pick of the draft. Two rounds later,

Tony Gywnn was drafted out of San Diego State. In 1984 they were starting next to each other in the Padres outfield. The Padres also acquired right-handed pitcher Tim Lollar from the Yankees and left-handed pitcher Dave Dravecky from Pittsburgh for a minor league outfielder.

In 1982 Garry Templeton came from the Cardinals in an exchange of shortstops. St. Louis got Ozzie Smith, whose agent had reached a negotiations impasse with the Padres. McKeon also acquired right-handed pitcher Ed Whitson from Cleveland for pitcher Juan Eichelberger and first baseman Broderick Perkins.

TRIVIA

Who is the only Padre to be in uniform all five times the Padres have reached the postseason?

Answers to the trivia questions are on pages 219–220.

In 1983 McKeon signed Steve Garvey as a free agent. And in a three-way trade with Montreal and the Cubs, the Padres acquired first baseman Carmelo Martinez and left-handed relief pitcher Craig Lefferts from the Cubs while sending relief pitcher Gary Lucas to Montreal.

While Gwynn and McReynolds were the only homegrown regulars among the position players, most of the pitchers the Padres lined up for 1984 came out of their system, including starters Eric Show, Andy Hawkins, and Mark Thurmond.

Hawkins and Thurmond, respectively, were fifth-round picks in the 1978 and 1979 drafts. Show was drafted in the 18th round of the 1978 draft. Combined with Whitson, Lollar, and swingman Dravecky, the Padres had a formidable staff.

As spring training approached, the Padres were missing only two pieces of the puzzle. One was filled with the signing of Gossage as the closer. But McKeon and manager Dick Williams knew they needed a presence at third base, a position that had historically been—and still is—a problem for the Padres.

Days before the start of the season, the Padres traded surplus starter Dennis Rasmussen to the Yankees for Graig Nettles. It was a popular move with San Diegans and Nettles's new teammates. A native of San Diego and a member of one of the city's premier athletic families, Nettles had played basketball and baseball at San Diego High and San Diego State.

"I played my first full season in the majors the year the Padres were born," Nettles once said. "From 1969, it had always been my desire to play in San Diego."

Nettles was one of the top fielding third basemen in the game. He also hit for power, although his batting average had dipped in recent seasons with the Yankees.

"Graig brought so much to the equation," Gwynn said years later. "He had been around. He had played on some really good teams. He had been a Yankee, so he knew about playing under pressure. Nothing bothered him. I mean nothing. But he had this fire.

"He wanted to win. He didn't give a darn about what his average might be. He wanted to win. If you needed a homer to win a game, Nettles was the guy you wanted up there. I mean, he had to have ice water running in there."

So the Padres were set.

The keys on Williams's bench were versatile infielders Luis Salazar—who looked to be the Padres third baseman before Nettles was signed—and Tim Flannery. McKeon filled out the bench with free agents Kurt Bevacqua, Bobby Brown, and Champ Summers. The backup catcher was, at the time, a little-known second-year Padre named Bruce Bochy.

The Padres had a little bit of everything in 1984.

"I always thought it was a perfect mix," said McKeon.

There were seasoned veterans in Garvey, Nettles, Templeton, Kennedy, and Gossage. There were budding young stars in Gwynn and McReynolds. There was speed at the top in Wiggins. The rotation had ample live, young arms. And there was Gossage, again, at the back to put down the hammer.

"That was a fun club," said Gossage. "Everyone knew what they were expected to do. Everyone worked up to what was expected of them. Guys accepted responsibility. There was even some comic relief."

Gossage was speaking of the exploits of the young Martinez in left. The 23-year-old had never played anything but first base when Williams put him in left to start spring training. Once, Martinez was nailed in the chest by a line drive that he never saw coming.

"I stopped it from going to the wall," the lovable Martinez said of the play. "Mr. Williams warned me not to let the ball get through to the wall."

"It was one of his best plays of the season," said Templeton. "Altough it nearly killed him, Carmelo had the presence of mind to lean over, pick up the ball, and throw to second."

Dick Williams went with almost the same lineup every day: second base—Alan Wiggins; right field—Tony Gwynn; third base—Graig Nettles; first base—Steve Garvey; catcher—Terry Kennedy; left field—Carmelo Martinez; center field—Kevin McReynolds; and shortstop—Garry Templeton.

But the Padres were only a .500 team in mid-May and mired in fourth place when Wiggins stole a franchise-record five bases to lead the Padres to a 5–4 victory over Montreal that ended a seven-game losing steak.

"Wiggins was our trigger," said Gwynn. "Whenever he got on, good things happened. Because if he was on first, he was on second."

Gwynn hit over .400 in 1984 when Wiggins was on first. "I saw some great pitches," said Gwynn. "The pitchers knew if he stole second, he was going to score. I was just a kid. They were more concerned about Wiggins stealing second than they were with me. I learned a lot about hitting that year. I learned to think about what the pitchers were thinking about."

DID YOU KNOW . . . That on August 12, 1984, nine Padres and five Braves were ejected from a game that turned into a running brawl that included six connected incidents? It started when Braves pitcher Pascual Perez hit Padres leadoff man Alan Wiggins with the first pitch of the game. Three Padres pitchers tried unsuccessfully to hit Perez before Craig Lefferts succeeded in the eighth. There were two bench-clearing brawls. The Padres ejected were manager Dick Williams; coaches Ozzie Virgil and Jack Krol (who were acting managers when they were ejected); pitchers Ed Whitson, Greg Booker, and Lefferts; plus position players Champ Summers, Bobby Brown, and Graig Nettles. The nine ejections in a single game remain a Padres record.

TRIVIA

What two pitchers share the record for Opening Day starts?

Answers to the trivia questions are on pages 219–220.

On June 9, the Padres routed Cincinnati 12–2 to move into first in the National League West. They were never again headed.

The Padres play in late July was near perfect. On July 27, Kevin McReynolds became the first player in seven seasons to homer into the second deck at Jack Murphy Stadium, leading the Padres to a 7–3 victory over Houston.

The following day started the greatest four-day run of pitching in Padres history. Eric Show, Tim Lollar, Dave Dravecky, and Mark Thurmond threw four straight shutouts for the only time in franchise history.

Show and Lollar started the run with 1–0 and 9–0 wins over Houston. Dravecky followed with a one-hit, 12–0 shutout of the Dodgers—the lone hit being a seventh-inning double by Bill Russell—the ninth one-hitter in Padres history. Thurmond closed out the run with a 1–0 win over the Dodgers.

One of the biggest games of the season came on September 5 when the Padres rallied from a 7–0 deficit to defeat Cincinnati 15–11 behind McReynolds's 5-for-5 night.

Just over two weeks later, the Padres clinched their first National League West title. On the afternoon of September 20, behind Lollar's three-run homer, the Padres defeated San Francisco 5–4 to clinch a tie for the title. The players then adjourned to Gossage's home to watch that night's game featuring second-place Houston. When the Astros lost, the Padres clinched the title.

"That was one of the greatest parties I've ever attended," said Nettles. "Early on, we were paying attention to the game. Then guys started talking about Kroc. I didn't know the man that well. But from the way people talked about him, you knew he was special. Then it got crazy."

Among the late arrivals was Joan Kroc, the kind, gentle, and stately widow of the franchise's savior. Joan Kroc is remembered almost as fondly as her beloved husband in San Diego. During her later years, Mrs. Kroc became the leading supporter of many of the city's charities. But on this night, she wasn't so stately.

"I have seldom enjoyed anything in my life as much as being part of that winning night," she later said. "It was the greatest. And to hear the players talk about Ray the way they were. It was so special."

As the evening progressed, the party moved from the front of the television to the deck surrounding Gossage's pool. Soon, everyone started jumping into the pool. Standing next to the pool in an exquisite gown was Mrs. Kroc.

Here, the story follows several different paths. Did Gossage pull Mrs. Kroc into the pool as he claimed years later? Did she jump? Did she fall? Whatever, she landed in the pool.

"I jumped," she would say later. When asked, Gossage would grin. "I'm keeping my mouth shut," Gwynn would say years after the party.

"Here's what happened," Gossage finally admitted in 2007. "Joan reached out to shake my hand and I pulled her into the pool."

"The best thing about clinching when we did is that we had plenty of time to recover," said Terry Kennedy. "And we needed all of it."

Although Gwynn won his first batting championship with a .351 average, the Padres scored few individual highs in 1984. Wiggins scored a then-club record 106 runs and led the National League with his 70 stolen bases. But no one hit more than 20 homers or won more than 15 games. No hitter drove in 90 runs.

"Every day, it seemed to be someone else, which I thought turned out to be one of the best parts of 1984," said Garvey. "We didn't have one or two guys. We had about 20."

Garvey led the Padres with 86 RBIs, which was the lowest total by a Padres team leader in a non-strike season since 1976. McReynolds and Nettles shared the home-run lead with 20. Martinez's 28 doubles were the most by a Padre. And Show was the lone Padre to win 15 games. But as a staff, Padres pitchers led the National League with 17 shutouts. The glue was Gossage, who had 25 saves, 10 wins, and a 2.90 ERA.

"He closed out the wins and won the games that were in doubt," said Garvey.

Dravecky was 9–8 with eight saves and a 2.93 ERA while making 12 starts and working 36 games in relief. Show was 15–9 with a 3.40 ERA. Thurmond (2.97 ERA) and Whitson (3.24) both had 14–8 records. The team's ERA of 3.48 was at the time the third-lowest in franchise history.

Contrary to popular lore, the greatest single swing in team history didn't win the 1984 National League pennant. Steve Garvey's walk-off homer against Chicago in Game 4 of the NLCS merely evened the series at 2–2. But it seemed to change everything about the course of Padres history.

"I always thought defense was our secret weapon," said Gossage. "I don't think Garvey made an error all season." He didn't.

There were only two divisions in the National League at the time, and the NLCS was a best-of-five series. The Padres' opponents were the Chicago Cubs. The Padres would have the homefield advantage, although the first two games would be played at Wrigley Field in Chicago.

Things did not go well for the Padres in Chicago.

Cubs leadoff man Bob Dernier hit Eric Show's second pitch for a homer. It was the only run the Cubs would need, although Gary

Matthews and starting pitcher Rick Sutcliffe also homered in the Cubs' 13–0 blitz. The Cubs also won the second game, 4–2.

The Padres appeared dead. No team had ever rebounded from a 2–0 deficit to win a league championship series. To make matters worse, the plane chartered to ferry the Padres home to San Diego had mechanical problems. The return was delayed.

"I don't think our spirits could have been much lower," said Garvey.

Then the Padres' charter bus from Lindbergh Field turned into the parking lot of Jack Murphy Stadium.

"We were stunned," said Gwynn. "Usually when we returned home from trips, the parking lot would be dark. When we saw the lights were on, we wondered what was going on. Then we saw them."

The "them" was thousands of San Diegans who had turned out to welcome the Padres home. Some had planned to be in the parking lot all the while. Others turned out after hearing the Padres' plane was delayed and people were waiting in the parking lot.

"This became the place to be," said fan Mark Hopkins. "I happened to drive by the stadium, saw all the people, and decided to join in. And I was here sort of early."

The reception seemed to pump new life into the ballclub.

The following afternoon, cheered on by a crowd of 58,346 and paced by the pitching of Ed Whitson and a three-run homer by Kevin McReynolds, the Padres defeated the Cubs 7–1.

Following an off-day, the clubs met again on Saturday afternoon in what still ranks as the greatest game in Padres history.

Originally, Rick Sutcliffe was scheduled to pitch for Chicago. Acquired from Cleveland in June, Sutcliffe went 16–1 for the Cubs in the regular season. His series-opening win marked the second time he had beaten the Padres. But Cubs manager Jim Frey decided to save the Cy Young Award–winner for the decisive fifth game against the Padres—or, if everything went to plan, the first game of the World Series.

The fourth game match-up featured the Padres' Tim Lollar against Scott Sanderson.

The Padres' greatest game was also perhaps Garvey's greatest. In the third inning, his two-out, two-run double gave the Padres a 2–0 lead. He tied the game at 3–3 with a two-out single in the fifth. And he helped the Padres to a 5–3 lead in the seventh with another two-out single.

But the Cubs tied the game in the eighth. And in the top of the ninth, the Cubs loaded the bases with two outs before Craig Lefferts coaxed Ron Cey into an inning-ending grounder.

With one out in the bottom of the ninth, Tony Gwynn singled, bringing Garvey to the plate to face Cubs closer Lee Smith.

"As I'm standing at the bag waiting for Garvey to hit, I just had a feeling," said Gwynn. "Steve had been locked in. I don't know why, but I just thought..."

Garvey homered.

"I nearly fainted," said Gwynn. "Shock and jubilation. I didn't know if I was going to make it home. I was trembling. I can't imagine how Steve felt."

"It was an incredible feeling," said Garvey, who had hooked into a 95-mph Smith fastball, driving it over the fence in right center—the spot being marked in the future by Garvey's No. 6 on the wall.

"I hadn't hit many homers in 1984. But I got a good swing on a good pitch from one of the game's best. Truthfully, I couldn't believe it."

Garvey had hit only eight homers during the regular season. He believed he was still feeling the aftereffects of the thumb he dislocated in July of 1983.

Clearly, Garvey's walk-off homer was the single greatest shot in Padres history. But it didn't really win anything for the Padres. The homer tied the series at 2–2. And Sutcliffe would be starting for the Cubs the following afternoon. The odds were still on the Cubs side.

"But not the emotions and the momentum," said Gwynn. "We just felt we were going to do it."

Early on Sunday, however, it looked like the Padres would be going home.

DID YOU KNOW . . . That the Padres dropped the Swinging Friar mascot after winning the National League pennant in 1984? The Friar returned in 1996, leading the Padres to their next National League West title.

The Cubs took a quick 3–0 lead against Show. Meantime, Sutcliffe was brilliant. Through five innings, Sutcliffe had a two-hit shutout working. He still appeared to be in control in the sixth when the Padres cut the Cubs' lead to 3–2 on sacrifice flies by Graig Nettles and Terry Kennedy.

Then the Padres struck for four runs in the seventh against Sutcliffe.

It started with a walk to Carmelo Martinez, who was bunted to second by Garry Templeton. Hitting for relief pitcher Craig Lefferts, Flannery hit a sharp grounder to Leon Durham that shot through the first baseman's legs, allowing Martinez to score the tying run.

After Alan Wiggins singled, Gwynn came to the plate and rifled a liner past second baseman Ryne Sandberg that bounced all the way to the wall in right center. Flannery scored. Wiggins scored. And, how appropriate, Gwynn would score on a single by Garvey.

Goose Gossage—the last of four Padres relievers (Hawkins, Dravecky, Lefferts, and Gossage) who would shut out the Cubs over the final seven innings—would come in and get the final three outs of the 6–3 Padres victory. The Padres were National League champions for the first time since their birth—and for the only time until 1998.

And San Diego went berserk.

The Padres were headed to the World Series—and into a buzzsaw called the Detroit Tigers. Led by San Diego product Alan Trammell, the Tigers won the World Series in five games.

The Padres gained a split of the first two games played in San Diego, winning the second game on designated hitter Kurt Bevacqua's three-run homer. But the Tigers swept the three games played in Detroit, denying the Padres a chance to get the series back to Jack Murphy Stadium.

"I always thought if we could have won one game in Detroit and been playing the final two games at home, that it might have been like the Cubs series all over again," said Gwynn.

The World Series ended in one of the worst sports riots in American history. Supposedly celebrating Tigers fans ran wild in the streets of downtown Detroit. Cars were overturned in the streets and set afire. One person died. Nearly a hundred were injured.

Detroit police struggled to regain control. And the situation went from bad to worse as the Padres boarded their bus for the trip to the airport. Fearing what happened, Padres wives and other members of the club's traveling party had been escorted from Tiger Stadium well before the game had ended and were safe at the airport. But the players found themselves trapped at the heart of the chaos. Rioters were rocking the team busses.

"I was afraid," Gwynn said later. "I thought at one point they were going to turn the busses over. We had heard about them setting the cars afire. We didn't know where our families really were.

"A lot of us feared for the worst. The situation was totally out of control. Finally, the busses started to move forward. You could feel everyone breathe again."

Back in San Diego, the Padres were greeted by more than 25,000 fans at the stadium. There were only cheers, no burning cars.

"As we were getting off the bus, I remember Nettles telling me he wished we had won it for these fans," said Gwynn. "Graig didn't say a lot. When he said that, it sort of blew me away and got me thinking. I wanted to get back so fast. I was so young. I thought it would happen again and again. That I'd be back to the World Series."

He did return...14 years later.

Before the Beginning

Believe it or not, some Padres fans were not happy with the arrival of the major league Padres in 1969.

Yes, they were happy to have a National League team. But they did not believe—and probably rightfully so—that the expansion draft had given San Diego a team that was as good as the minor league Padres of the 1960s.

San Diego was the premier franchise in minor league baseball. In six seasons between 1962 and 1967, San Diego had won three Pacific Coast League titles and was robbed of another championship in 1963 when they finished a half-game out due to a rainout.

And the Padres were a bigger success off the field—almost annually leading the minor leagues in attendance. The minor league Padres' big boost came in 1958 when the club moved from their decrepit Lane Field home at the foot of Broadway downtown to picturesque Westgate Park in Mission Valley.

At the time, now bustling Mission Valley was still a bucolic blend of riding stables, resort hotels, and golf courses. Although Interstate 8 had cut the valley in half while running parallel to the San Diego River, a few dairies still operated on the fertile bottom land.

The major intersection in Mission Valley was where the east-west I-8 crossed the north-south freeway connecting downtown San Diego with the rapidly growing northern suburbs. Just northwest of the interchange, Padres owner C. Arnholt Smith decided to build a new home for the team he purchased in 1955. Smith was emerging as one of the rapidly expanding city's financial powers. His economic base was Westgate California Tuna Packing Company. But he also led San Diego's biggest local bank and had major real estate holdings.

At the time, the Padres and San Diego High were the major sports franchises in San Diego. And it appeared San Diego could lose the Padres. Although the Padres had won their first regular-season PCL title in 1954, attendance at the aging Lane Field was declining rapidly. Actually, the ballpark itself was declining rapidly. The combination of termites and the marine atmosphere from its immediate proximity to San Diego Bay were taking a toll on the largely wooden structure. Sections of the grandstands had to be closed off at various times for repairs. The owners of the ballclub, led by Bill Starr, had been rebuffed in at least three attempts to build a new ballpark in partnership with San Diego. At the same time, rumors were circulating that the major leagues would be heading toward Los Angeles and San Francisco—and that westward expansion would be the death knell for the already struggling PCL. If there was a major league team in Los Angeles, Starr feared the Padres would be cut off as an island away from the rest of any remaining PCL.

None of this deterred Smith. As soon as he purchased the Padres, he denied the persistent rumors of the Padres moving—or even folding—and started his own effort to build a new ballpark.

"We had no choice," Smith said years later. "Eventually, Lane Field was going to collapse. Probably sooner than later. It was in a dreadful state."

On February 27, 1957, amid ever-growing rumors that the Brooklyn Dodgers would be moving to Los Angeles, Smith broke ground on the Padres' new ballpark in Mission Valley.

Westgate Park was designed with an eye toward the future. Although it would open with only 9,000 seats, the new ballpark was engineered so that a second deck could be added. The capacity could be expanded to 35,000 or 40,000 seats. The park was also designed with a large and expandable parking lot that was designed to retain many of the trees that had been part of the old riding grounds. Although most of the traffic from Westgate Park would flow out onto an expanded Friars Road to the north, you could still exit toward the south across an old bridge that spanned the San Diego River and wound through a riding stable just to the east of the Town and Country Hotel.

But the construction of Westgate Park did not go smoothly—much like that of PETCO Park 4½ decades later. The decision by both the Dodgers and New York Giants to move to the West Coast in 1958 cast doubt upon the future of the Pacific Coast League. There was even talk of the Padres being shifted to the Texas League. Construction was delayed as the very future of the Padres was pondered. And with the delay came cost escalations. What had been a $1.5 million project shot up to more than $2 million.

TRIVIA

San Diego and Montreal were granted expansion franchises on May 27, 1968. On October 14 that year, the Padres stocked their team with 30 players from a major league expansion draft. Who was the Padres first pick?

Answers to the trivia questions are on pages 219–220.

Still, the Padres' new Mission Valley home opened in 1958. And it immediately became a focal point for minor league baseball—despite several notable problems. The dressing rooms were extremely inadequate. Both were constructed with only nine lockers, an error caused by the designer's view that the game was played by only nine players. And a corner of right field was actually below the water table of the nearby San Diego River, leading to perennial soggy conditions.

But the rest of the ballpark was as beautiful as it was functional—a single deck of seats beneath a cantilevered roof, a seven-foot berm beyond the outfield fences that could be used as patio seating for games that attracted overflow crowds, more grass seating areas down both foul lines, a wide concourse behind the grandstands.

"I loved playing at Westgate Park," said Tommy Helms, the Cincinnati second baseman who played on the Padres' 1964 PCL championship team. "Not only was it a beautiful site, it was a good ballpark. It had a great feel to it."

Over the years, Westgate Park became a guideline for other minor league parks as well as a number of spring training ballparks.

Well, not everything about Westgate Park was state of the art. When the park opened in 1958, Smith decided to test a new product being introduced by his tuna canneries—hot dogs made of tuna. "Tunies" lasted one season.

Later decisions proved to be much more productive—including the one in the early 1960s to align with Cincinnati at a time when the Reds were producing some of the top prospects in the major leagues.

The Westgate Park Padres won their first PCL title in 1962 with a lineup that included future major leaguers Tommy Harper, Chico Ruiz, and Jesse Gonder, who was named the Most Valuable Player of the PCL.

The lasting figure of that 1962 season, however, was the Swinging Friar logo that first appeared on Padres programs. In varying forms over the years, the Swinging Friar became—and remains—the club's trademark.

The 1963 Padres were expected to include an infielder named Pete Rose. But Rose jumped directly from Class A to the major leagues.

After missing the 1963 PCL title by a controversial half-game—a rainout was not made up—the Padres returned to the top of the league in 1964 with a roster far superior to many of those run out by those early editions of the National League Padres.

Among the Padres regulars were Tony Perez, Deron Johnson, Helms, Cesar Tovar, Art Shamsky, Gus Gil, Lee May, and Don Pavletich.

It was during the 1964 season that the seeds of major league baseball were first planted in San Diego. As the Padres topped 250,000 in attendance, there were rumors that the struggling Milwaukee Braves were considering relocating to San Diego. Plans were reviewed on expanding Westgate Park to 40,000. At the same time, a push was underway to build a multi-purpose stadium four miles farther east in Mission Valley. San Diego Stadium would be the new home of the San Diego Chargers and a lure for major league baseball.

On the field, the Padres shifted affiliations and became the Triple-A minor league club of Philadelphia. That association resulted in the 1967 PCL championship. That team was led by PCL Most Valuable Player Ricardo Joseph and included slugger Jim Gentile.

The following season marked one of huge changes for the Padres and San Diego. The land under Westgate Park was sold and became

Tony Perez reached the Hall of Fame as a slugger for the Cincinnati Reds. But before the major league Padres were born of expansion in 1969, Perez was a Padre and the MVP of the Pacific Coast League in 1964. Ted Williams and Bobby Doerr, who were teammates on the original Padres of 1936, also played for the Padres before Hall of Fame careers.

the northeast corner of what is now the upscale Fashion Valley Mall. The minor league Padres moved into San Diego Stadium. And on May 27, 1968, the Padres were awarded an expansion franchise for the 1969 season—at the end of the first century of baseball in San Diego.

The first recorded history of baseball being played in San Diego dates back to 1870. There might have been games played in San Diego before then, but there was no newspaper to record them.

DID YOU KNOW . . . That the original home of the Pacific Coast League Padres was Lane Field, located in downtown San Diego? The second home of the PCL Padres was Westgate Park in Mission Valley. The first home of the National League Padres was San Diego Stadium (also known as Jack Murphy Stadium and Qualcomm Stadium), three miles to the east in Mission Valley. The second home of the major league Padres is PETCO Park in downtown San Diego, which is within walking distance of the old Lane Field site.

During the early 20th century, San Diego became a regular stop for barnstorming teams of major league players who would play in California during the off-season to supplement their income. Walter Johnson celebrated his 20th birthday by making a cameo pitching appearance for the San Diego Pickwicks in 1907. The first visit by major league teams to San Diego came on November 10, 1913, when the New York Giants beat the Chicago White Sox in an exhibition on a ninth-inning homer by Chief Meyers. During the 1920s, Babe Ruth and Lou Gehrig made several visits to San Diego as the headliners on barnstorming teams playing in Balboa Stadium.

The first San Diego area player to grab national headlines was Clifford Carlton "Gavvy" Cravath, who was born just south of Escondido in 1881 and didn't reach the major leagues of the east until he was 27. Seven seasons later, Cravath set the single-season, major league home-run record, hitting 24 with Philadelphia in 1915. He also hit .285 and led the National League with a .393 on-base pecentage and 115 RBIs. Cravath would lead the National League in homers six times, and when he retired in 1920, his 119 homers stood as the major league career record. His single-season and career home-run records would be broken by none other than Babe Ruth. Cravath was a member of some of those barnstorming teams who visited San Diego almost annually.

By the mid-1920s, talk started of San Diego joining the Pacific Coast League. But it wasn't until 1936 that Bill Lane decided to move his Hollywood Stars south to San Diego. The announcement was accompanied by a contest to name the relocated team. "Dons" was the most popular name. But Lane rejected "Dons" because the nickname was already used by the University of San Francisco. Lane decided to go with "Padres," which was proposed by only eight fans in the city-wide contest.

Needing to find a home for their new club, the city worked with the Depression's Works Projects Administration to convert Sports Field—a harbor-front recreation complex used largely by the Navy—into a baseball ballpark. The budgeted cost—$20,000. Construction began on January 28, 1936, just over two months before the start of the season. Two short weeks later, all the concrete needed to support the new grandstsands had been poured, although near-record rains late in February delayed construction of the grandstands.

The Padres made their debut on March 31, 1936, defeating Seattle 6–2 before 8,178 sun-baked fans. Sun-baked because the roof wasn't yet finished. Neither were the ticket windows and club offices. Most of the construction would be completed while the Padres spent much of their first month on the road.

Some things, however, were never corrected.

Years later, surveyors discovered that in their haste to put in the field, workers had made the distance to first base at Lane Field only 87 feet. And the distance to the right-field foul pole was only 325 feet, not the posted 340.

Midway through their first season, the Padres signed a June graduate from Hoover High to give the Padres a hometown player to cheer. That player was Ted Williams.

In their second season, the Padres presented San Diego with its first championship team. Although they finished third in the PCL's final regular-season standings, the Padres won the Shaughnessy playoffs. Williams led the Padres with 23 homers and batted .291 with 98 RBIs.

The Padres' next PCL title didn't come until the 1954 season. And it didn't come until after the 168-game regular season ended with the Padres tied for first with the Hollywood Stars.

On September 14, 1954, Bob Elliott hit two homers and Bob Kerrigan scattered nine hits over as many innings to lead the Padres to a 7–2 victory over the Stars. Two days later, 35,000 San Diegans attended a victory parade through the heart of the city.

During their 33 seasons in the Pacific Coast League, the Padres had a number of notable players, starting with Williams and Bobby

Doerr. But perhaps the most significant was Johnny Ritchey. A native of San Diego, Ritchey caught for San Diego High and San Diego State. A member of one of the city's foremost athletic families—brothers Bert, Al, and Earl were also great athletes at San Diego High—Johnny interrupted his college career in 1942 to join the Army and serve in Europe. He returned to San Diego State in 1946 and turned pro in 1947.

But Ritchey was black. His only offer was with the Chicago Giants of the American Negro League. After hitting .369 with the Giants in 1947, Ritchey returned to San Diego. The Padres signed him, and in 1948 Ritchey broke the color barrier in the Pacific Coast League. He hit .323.

"I always thought the way it happened was perfect," Ritchey said of being the first black player in the PCL.

"San Diego knew me, and I knew San Diego. I had always moved around in San Diego without very many problems. The fans cheered me in San Diego because I was a San Diego player making good. That was more important to them than color. San Diego always supported their own.

"It was only elsewhere at times that I had problems. I loved being a Padre."

A Difficult Birth

On April 8, 1969, C. Arnolt Smith's dream of major league baseball in San Diego came true. The Padres debuted as part of baseball's 100th anniversary Opening Day and San Diego's bicentennial year.

"This is a great day for baseball and San Diego," declared Padres president E. J. "Buzzie" Bavasi—the man who was primarily responsible for major league baseball coming to San Diego.

Bavasi had used the personal equity he had built over 30 years as a Dodgers executive to sell baseball's skeptical owners on San Diego as a major league city. The owners didn't know Smith, but they knew and trusted Bavasi—which is largely why San Diego was granted an expansion franchise on May 27, 1968. Perhaps the wisest move made as the owner of the Padres was hiring Bavasi in 1967 to coordinate his bid for an expansion franchise.

And on a cool spring night in 1969, all the hard work bore fruit that tasted far better than expected.

The Padres defeated Houston 2–1 in their National League debut before 23,370 at San Diego Stadium. To third baseman Ed Spiezio went the honor of getting the Padres' first hit—a fifth-inning solo homer off Houston's Don Wilson in the bottom of the fifth. An inning later, right fielder Ollie Brown, the Padres' first pick in the expansion draft, drove in the winning run with a double. Right-hander Dick Selma scattered five hits and struck out 12 in a complete-game victory.

The Padres were off and running—and winning. The following two days saw left-handers Johnny Podres and Dick Kelley both pitch 2–0 victories over the Astros. After three games, the Padres were 3–0.

Then reality hit...hard. Over the next 159 games, the Padres would go 49–110 to finish 52–110.

TOP 10
Padres Career Wins

	Player	Career Wins
1.	Eric Show	100
2.	Randy Jones	92
3.	Ed Whitson	77
4.	Andy Ashby	70
5.	Andy Benes	69
6.	Andy Hawkins	60
7.	Jake Peavy	57
8.	Joey Hamilton	55t
	Bruce Hurst	55t
10.	Dave Dravecky	53

"I remember how excited the city was after that first series," Bavasi recalled years later. "Someone on the radio mentioned the possibility of San Diego winning the pennant. I didn't want to be the one to burst their bubble. I knew that was going to happen soon enough."

Establishing a foothold is difficult for any expansion franchise. But back in 1969, Major League Baseball made it as difficult as possible for the four new kids on the block.

At the same time that San Diego and Montreal were granted National League franchises, Kansas City and Seattle were added to the American League. And the talent pool was further drained by rules that allowed the established teams to protect most of their regulars.

"To be honest," said Bavasi, "what happened in that 1968 expansion draft opened the eyes of baseball for future expansion. The game realized it couldn't put new teams behind the eight-ball like they did the Padres and their expansion partners. We really had no shot at success for years."

And that was only one of the problems facing the Padres.

The owner of the minor league Padres since 1955, C. Arnholt Smith first thought about landing a major league team for San Diego in the 1960s when the Milwaukee Braves showed interest in the area. Smith's interest was buoyed by the fact that the minor league Padres had won three Pacific Coast League titles in the 1960s and paced the minor leagues in attendance.

The movement to bring major league baseball to San Diego snowballed when voters backed construction of a multi-purpose stadium in east Mission Valley. The stadium, which would seat 50,000 for baseball, needed a summer tenant.

But San Diego was off in a corner of the United States and was locked in on all four sides—the Pacific Ocean to the west, Mexico to the south, mountains to the east and Los Angeles and the entrenched Dodgers and Angels to the north.

Could San Diego support major league baseball?

Baseball was expanding at the time. But the game's powers had questions about the viability of baseball in San Diego, a city that was going through a major economic transition. San Diego was just shedding its image as a "Navy town."

Smith wanted to make a pitch for an expansion team, but he realized he needed an ally. So he recruited Buzzie Bavasi away from the Dodgers to put together San Diego's bid for an expansion franchise. Bavasi had baseball's ear. He had been a Dodgers executive for 30 years and the team's general manager since 1951. He had presided over the Dodgers' move from Brooklyn to Los Angeles in the late 1950s.

Buzzie knew the game, the market, and the problem. Did he have the answer?

"There were two hurdles to overcome," Bavasi recalled years later. "We had to sell the city. And we had to sell the ownership."

Smith was one of San Diego's emerging financial leaders, turning a tuna cannery into the cornerstone of an empire that included real estate and U.S. National Bank. But his pockets weren't nearly as deep as baseball hoped. When Smith and Bavasi went to baseball's expansion meetings in late May of 1968, Smith expected the asking price for a franchise would be $6 million. Instead, it was $10.2 million. In those days, the difference was a lot of money.

Smith was taken aback. But he charged ahead. And on May 27, 1968, San Diego's bid was accepted.

Almost as soon as San Diego was bestowed a club, Bavasi began encountering problems. Smith's financial empire was already developing cracks. Money would be scarce. And Smith shot down Bavasi's plan to launch major league baseball in San Diego with a totally fresh look. Bavasi wanted to change the name of the team. Not only did Smith want to retain the traditional "Padres" name, he wanted to outfit his club in his favorite color—Mission Brown.

"I couldn't move him," said Bavasi. "As it turned out, the name Padres won huge acceptance with the fans of San Diego over the years, but the team colors..."

The first baseball team to play in San Diego Stadium was the lame-duck minor league Padres of 1968. Eddie Leishman served as the general manager to both the Pacific Coast League team that was ending its run and the National League team that was preparing for its 1969 launch.

On August 29, 1968, Preston Gomez was named the first manager of the National League Padres. And on October 14, the Padres selected 30 players in the expansion draft. San Francisco outfielder Ollie Brown officially became the first Padre.

No Padres history is complete without a look at that draft. In order, following Brown, were:

2. Dave Giusti, right-handed pitcher (from St. Louis)
3. Al Santorini, right-handed pitcher (Atlanta)
4. Dick Selma, right-handed pitcher (New York Mets)
5. Jose Arcia, infielder (Chicago Cubs)
6. Clay Kirby, right-handed pitcher (St. Louis)
7. Fred Kendall, catcher (Cincinnati)
8. Jerry Morales, outfielder (New York Mets)
9. Nate Colbert, first baseman (Houston)
10. Zoilo Versalles, shortstop (Los Angeles Dodgers)
11. Frank Reberger, right-handed pitcher (Chicago Cubs)
12. Jerry Davanon, infielder (St. Louis)
13. Larry Stahl, outfielder (New York Mets)
14. Dick Kelley, left-handed pitcher (Atlanta)
15. Al Ferrara, outfielder (Los Angeles Dodgers)
16. Mike Corkins, right-handed pitcher (San Francisco)

17. Tom Dukes, right-handed pitcher (Houston)
18. Rich James, right-handed pitcher (Chicago Cubs)
19. Tony Gonzalez, outfielder (Philadelphia)
20. David Roberts, left-handed pitcher (Pittsburgh)
21. Ivan Murrell, outfielder (Houston)
22. Jim Williams, outfielder (Los Angeles Dodgers)
23. Billy McCool, left-handed pitcher (Cincinnati)
24. Roberto Pena, second baseman (Philadelphia)
25. Al McBean, right-handed pitcher (Pittsburgh)
26. Steve Arlin, right-handed pitcher (Philadelphia)
27. Rafael Robles, shortstop (San Francisco)
28. Fred Katawczik, left-handed pitcher (Cincinnati)
29. Ron Slocum, catcher (Pittsburgh)

We stop with the 29th round, because as the Padres approached their 30th and final pick, Bavasi turned to veteran baseball writer Phil Collier of the *San Diego Union* newspaper and asked the media to recommend a final pick.

Collier had been another instrumental figure in the arrival of major league baseball in San Diego. As Smith and San Diego began dreaming of a major league team in the early 1960s, Collier's newspaper assigned the writer to a year-round assignment in Los Angeles to cover the Dodgers and Los Angeles Angels. Collier's daily files introduced many of his readers to major league baseball and advanced interest in the game in San Diego. Collier's efforts earned him a spot in Baseball's Hall of Fame.

But in 1969, Collier and other members of the media had drawn up their own draft forecasts. So when the 30th round was set to begin, Bavasi asked Collier and the media to offer him a name.

Collier's nominee was outfielder Clarence "Cito" Gaston of Atlanta.

Gaston played six seasons with the Padres and spent a total of 11 seasons in the major leagues. In the Padres' second season, Gaston hit .318 with 29 homers and 93 RBIs. He still ranks among the Padres' career leaders in a number of offensive categories. Gaston is best remembered as the manager of the 1992 World Series champion Toronto Blue Jays.

"I have often wondered what would have happened to me if Phil Collier hadn't named me his pick," the late Gaston recalled years later.

The Padres and Expos took opposite approaches to the draft. The Padres concentrated on young players with an eye on the future. The Expos went for veterans. The teams finished with identical records in their inaugural seasons.

A scan of the Padres draft list will show a major omission.

San Diego didn't draft a third baseman. On December 3, the club completed its first major trade, acquiring Ed Spiezio from the Cardinals for Giusti. Later that month, the Padres acquired first baseman Bill Davis from Cleveland for Versalles, one of the few veterans San Diego had acquired in the expansion draft. A week before the start of the season, the Padres acquired catcher Chris Cannizzaro from Pittsburgh in a trade.

The Padres Opening Day lineup was:

1. Rafael Robles, shortstop
2. Roberto Pena, second base
3. Tony Gonzalez, center field
4. Ollie Brown, right field
5. Bill Davis, first base
6. Larry Stahl, left field
7. Ed Spiezio, third base
8. Chris Cannizzaro, catcher
9. Dick Selma, pitcher

Early in the 1969 season, the Padres traded their Opening Day starting pitcher Dick Selma to the Chicago Cubs in exchange for pitchers Joe Niekro and Gary Ross. The trade established something of a policy for the young Padres.

As soon as one of their pitchers started having success, Bavasi would find a way to trade the pitcher for prospects. Niekro was swapped later that season for Pat Dobson, who a year later was traded for pitcher Tom Phoebus and shortstop Enzo Hernandez.

Although there wasn't much to cheer in 1969, the Padres had two great series—the first against the Astros, and September 4 through 7 against the Dodgers.

The Dodgers had punished the Padres throughout the 1969 season. And after each lopsided win—the scores included 19–0 (the 49th and last shutout of Don Drysdale's career), 14–0, 11–0, and 10–1—a member of the Dodgers would throw salt on the wound by pointing out that no rivalry existed with the upstart Padres.

In early September, the Dodgers returned to Mission Valley expecting to pad their 9–2 margin over the Padres—as well as their lead in the National League West. So confident were the Dodgers that they checked into a Mission Bay resort and allowed the players to travel south with their families.

What followed can best be described as an ambush. The Padres won all four games. And one of the heroes was Al Ferrara, whom the Dodgers had given up on and left unprotected before the expansion draft.

Nicknamed "the Bull," Ferrara drove in all three runs in the Padres' 3–0 series-opening win with a double and a homer in support of Gary Ross. The following night, Ferrara—whose nickname had something to do with his defensive work—saved Niekro with a running catch in a 4–1 victory that included a homer by Nate Colbert. Ferrara had a run-scoring double in the Padres' third win on Saturday night. The Padres rallied for three runs Sunday to pull out a 4–2 win.

As far as the Padres were concerned, the rivalry was on. They had knocked the Dodgers out of first—and Los Angeles would never recover.

"That made the season for us and killed it for them," said Bavasi.

Offensively, the Padres were pathetic in their inaugural season with two exceptions. Ollie Brown batted .264 with 20 homers and 61 RBIs. And Nate Colbert, who replaced Bill Davis at first only weeks into the season, hit .255 with a team-leading 24 homers and 66 RBIs. But as a team, the Padres batted .225 and scored only 468 runs—marks that still stand as franchise lows. The Padres averaged 2.9 runs per game.

The young pitching was stronger than expected. Clay Kirby, who picked up the nickname "the Kid" after making his Padres debut in April at the age of 20, posted a 3.80 ERA but finished with a 7–20 record.

The 1970 Padres showed stunning improvement offensively. Led by Colbert's 38 homers and Gaston's 29 (en route to the first .300 batting average season in franchise history), the Padres hit a total of 172 homers that still stands as the franchise record.

Sixty-eight of those home runs came at San Diego Stadium, an amazing figure considering there was no inner fence at the time. The distance down both lines was 330 feet. It was 370 feet to the power alleys and 420 feet to straight-away center. And the outfield was bordered by a 17-foot-high wall.

"We didn't get any cheap homers," said Colbert, who hit 16 homers at home. "We didn't get any regular homers. Visitors would come in here, look at the walls, and faint."

On July 10, the Padres set a home-run record that stands to this day. Trailing the Dodgers 9–2, in the ninth inning, the Padres got four homers from Ivan Murrell, Ed Spiezio, Dave Campbell, and Gaston before Colbert lined out to the warning track to end a 9–7 loss.

The sophomore Padres scored 1⅓ more runs a game than the 1969 team.

But the 1970 season was most notable for three pitching feats. On June 12, Pittsburgh's Dock Ellis, who later admitted he was pitching on a drug-induced high, threw the first no-hitter in San Diego Stadium history. It wasn't exactly a classic. Ellis walked eight and hit a Padre. But there wouldn't be another no-hitter for 31 seasons in Mission Valley—although there would be two near-misses within the next six weeks.

Five days after Ellis's "gem," Ivan Murrell's seventh-inning single was the Padres' only hit against future Hall of Famer Bob Gibson of St. Louis.

Then came July 21 and one of the more infamous nights in Padres history. Clay Kirby threw no-hit ball for eight innings against the New York Mets. But due to an unearned run in the first, Kirby was on the short end of a 1–0 score as his spot in the batting order came up with two outs in the bottom of the eighth.

For some reason—which remains inexplicable to most Padres fans to this day—manager Preston Gomez decided to send up Cito Gaston to pinch-hit for Kirby. As 10,373 Padres fans booed, Gaston struck out.

Taken in the fourth round of the expansion draft, right-handed pitcher Dick Selma scored several firsts for the Padres. He started and won the Padres first game in the National League. Then he was moved in the Padres first regular-season trade, going to the Chicago Cubs for pitchers Gary Ross and Joe Niekro.

Reliever Jack Baldschun surrendered a single to Bud Harrelson, leading off the Mets ninth. The Mets would score two runs in the inning on two more hits.

As the game ended, several fans tried to get to Gomez in the Padres' dugout. Players and security intervened and ushered Gomez to the Padres' clubhouse, where he seemed surprised that there was a controversy regarding his decision.

"You play the game to win," said Gomez of his decision. "I have to pinch-hit there if we have a chance to win." Gomez said that if he were placed in the same situation again, he'd pinch-hit for Kirby.

Said Kirby: "I don't know, I don't know."

No Padre has yet thrown a no-hitter.

A year later, Kirby became the Padres' first starting pitcher to post a winning record, going 15–13 with a 2.83 ERA on a team that slipped backward to 61–100. He wasn't the only Padre pitcher to turn in a banner season.

Left-hander Dave Roberts posted a 2.10 ERA—still the lowest in franchise history—and finished with a 14–17 record in 34 starts. His reward was a postseason trade to Houston with the Padres getting infielder Derrel Thomas and right-handed pitcher Bill Greif in return.

But the ace of the Padres staff at the time was clearly the Kid, who came close to two no-hitters during a five-day span in 1971. On both September 13 and 18 he took no-hitters into the eighth. On September 13, he lost a 3–2 decision in Houston. Five days later, Kirby was working on a perfect game through seven innings before Willie McCovey homered in a 2–1 Padres victory.

Six days after that performance, Kirby pitched what many consider to be the greatest game in Padres history. He pitched 15 innings and struck out 15 Astros. But Houston won 2–1, six innings after Kirby departed in the longest game in San Diego Stadium history.

The 1971 season was marked by two other singular accomplishments. On June 23, veteran right-handed Bob Miller won both ends of a doubleheader against the Astros—marking the only time that would happen in team history. And on September 7, Leron Lee became the first Padre to have five hits in a game.

But 1971 was a flip-flop for the Padres. The same team that hit 172 homers in 1970 slumped to 96 in 1971. The run production fell by 195 runs.

Eleven games into the 1972 season, Don Zimmer replaced Gomez to become the Padres' second manager. But the fourth edition of the Padres continued to struggle at the plate while the team's ERA shot up more than a half-run a game.

The Padres' fourth season did feature several great individual performances and the emergence of the Padres' first headliner— Nate Colbert. Born in St. Louis on April 9, 1946, Colbert was a member of the Padres' expansion class of 1969. But when the Padres traded for the 6'7" Bill Davis, Colbert lost his spot in the starting lineup. After two weeks, however, it became clear to the Padres that Davis was a bust. On April 24, two weeks after turning 23, Colbert got his first start as the Padres first baseman and celebrated with a 430-foot, three-run homer.

In six seasons with the Padres, Colbert would hit 163 homers—a figure that still stands as the franchise record. And the inner fence wasn't installed at San Diego Stadium until after Colbert had departed San Diego.

"When I saw the inner fence later, I wondered how many more homers I might have hit," said Colbert, who was the Padres' lone representative in the All-Star Game in 1971, '72 and, '73. "The wall had to cost me at least 10 that one year."

That year would have been 1972 when Colbert hit 38 for the second time in three seasons.

The 1972 Padres scored 488 runs. Colbert drove in 111 of those—or 23 percent. He also hit 37 percent of the club's home runs. And he got 13 percent of his homers and 12 percent of his RBIs on one day—August 1, 1972—in not only one of the greatest performances in Padres history but one of the greatest in major league history. In a doubleheader at Atlanta, Colbert hit five home runs and drove in 13 runs. His five homers tied the major league record for a doubleheader established by his childhood hero Stan Musial on May 2, 1954—with an eight-year-old Colbert in attendance at Sportsman's Park. The 13 RBIs were a major league record that has since been equaled.

What Colbert remembers most about that August 1 doubleheader is that he almost passed on playing.

"I had been playing with a sore back for almost a week and it was getting worse," said Colbert. "I thought two games in the same day would make it worse. But when I took a couple swings in batting practice, it didn't feel bad at all, so I decided to play."

PADRES SUPERLATIVES

Padres National League Award Winners

Most Valuable Player (1)—Ken Caminiti (1996)
Cy Young Award (3)—Randy Jones (1976), Gaylord Perry (1978), Mark Davis (1989)
Rookie of the Year (1)—Benito Santiago (1987)
Manager of the Year (1)—Bruce Bochy (1996)
NLCS Most Valuable Player (2)—Steve Garvey (1984), Sterling Hitchcock (1998)

In the first game Colbert hit a pair of three-run homers in the Padres 9–0 win. In the second game, the 6'2", 209-pound first baseman hit a grand slam in the first, a two-run homer in the seventh, and a solo homer in the ninth.

Outside of Colbert, however, there was little to cheer about the Padres offense. The Padres hit .227 as a team.

Pitching again carried the team as far as it could go. All six of left-hander Fred Norman's six wins came on shutouts. Steve Arlin posted a 10–21 record despite having a 3.60 ERA. Clay Kirby was 12–14 despite a 3.13 ERA.

"Our starting pitchers deserved better," said Zimmer. "We just couldn't score runs, especially early in close games."

And the curse of Kirby reappeared on July 18.

Less than a month after throwing a one-hitter against San Francisco, Steve Arlin was working on a no-hitter against Philadelphia with two outs in the ninth. No one in Padres history has come closer to a no-hitter. And Arlin would get closer. He threw two strikes past Denny Doyle, at which time rookie third baseman Dave Roberts looked into the Padres dugout to see if Zimmer wanted him to back up into a normal fielding position because Doyle was no longer a threat to bunt.

But Zimmer decided he wanted to keep Roberts in against the speedy Doyle. Well, you can guess what happened. Doyle chopped what would have been a routine grounder over Roberts's head to ruin the no-hit bid.

Zimmer went to the mound to apologize to Arlin, who hadn't even been aware of where Roberts was playing.

"I've always felt terrible for that one," Zimmer said years later. "I was playing the percentages. I was worried about Doyle hitting a nubber. I messed it up."

Arlin finished the season as hot as any pitcher in Padres history. He allowed only 33 hits in his final eight starts. Only once did he fail to go the distance.

But the Padres did not finish strong. Smith's financial empire was on the verge of collapse. His U.S. National Bank was headed toward failure. The Padres were so cash-strapped that money was part of every trade they made. Rumors grew that the club was both for sale and headed out of town. Attendance sank. The Padres headed into the 1973 season as a lame duck.

The only relief was comic. Marching through the mostly vacant stands was a ragtag band led by a Marine Corps helicopter pilot named Jim Eakle. The "Tuba Man's" constant oom-pah was as bad as the play on the field, although it created chuckles rather than moans.

And there was a San Diego State student named Ted Giannoulas who climbed into a chicken suit at the request of a local radio station and became one of the most identifiable and entertaining acts in mascot history.

As horrible as the 1973 season was, two players who would become a major part of Padres history made their major league debuts within eight days of one another in June. Left-handed pitcher Randy Jones arrived on June 12. And on June 19, Dave Winfield came straight from the University of Minnesota to a spot in the middle of the Padres lineup.

By that time, however, the Padres had already been sold to Washington, D.C., grocer Joseph Danzansky. The club plunged into despair. Attendance dropped to 611,826—the second-lowest total in team history. And most of those who turned out were coming to say good-bye.

The bags were packed. Only a miracle would save the Padres.

Enter Ray Kroc.

Randy Jones

Randy Jones will forever hold a special spot in Padres history.

Tony Gwynn is the greatest player to wear a Padres uniform. Dave Winfield was the first player to enter the Hall of Fame wearing a Padres cap. But Jones...he's one of us.

"I think Randy Jones was the first Padre to develop his own following," said veteran Padres radio commentator Jerry Coleman. "People would come out just to see Randy pitch."

"I remember going to see Randy pitch when I was at San Diego State," Tony Gwynn once recalled. "It was like a happening. And you'd sit there in the stands thinking, 'I could hit that stuff.' He was throwing, like, 75 miles an hour.

"But you knew you couldn't. Pete Rose couldn't hit his stuff. Mike Schmidt couldn't hit his stuff. But he looked like the guy next door. And he was throwing just about as hard."

Intimidating, Jones was not. He stood 6' tall. He weighed 175 pounds. And the left-hander on his best day could power the ball to home plate at the dazzling speed of 85 miles per hour.

So what made him one of the most feared pitchers in the National League in the mid-1970s? Jones had a devastating sinker that he could throw with pinpoint accuracy. And he kept hitters off balance with a rhythm that moved games along at a rapid pace.

"When Randy was working, you could make dinner reservations for about 2½ hours after the first pitch," said Dave Winfield. "The seventh-inning stretch would be on you before you knew it."

"Get the ball, throw the ball," joked Jones of his work habits. "The slower I threw, the faster I worked. And I had a lot of help from my teammates. We went 1-2-3 a lot of times, too. It kept the game moving."

On one Sunday afternoon in Mission Valley, he shut out the Pittsburgh Pirates 3–0 in an hour and a half. Fifty-nine of his 68 pitches went for strikes. And on one mid-summer night, Jones worked his way through a game so fast that the postgame fireworks promotion started before it was dark.

"There were a lot of jokes about that," said Jones. "But at the time, I don't think the club was real happy. It was a huge fireworks production. Fireworks in daylight just don't carry the same impact."

Few players in Padres history have had the impact of Randy Jones.

Not that he had much impact at all when he first arrived in San Diego. A fifth-round draft pick in 1972 out of Chapman University, Jones had pitched less than a full season in the Padres minor league system when he was promoted to the major league club on his 23rd birthday—June 12, 1973.

However, he arrived in San Diego just two weeks after the announcement was made that the Padres were moving to Washington, D.C.

"It was a weird situation," said Jones. "I was so excited about being in the major leagues. But the mood in the clubhouse was strange. There were rumors that we might move even before the season ended. I didn't even know if I should rent an apartment."

And the way Jones started in the major leagues, there was a question if he needed to.

The first hit allowed by Jones was a home run to Willie Mays. Six days later, he gave up a three-run homer to Hank Aaron in the first inning of his first start.

"I figured I put the two best hitters in the game behind me," Jones joked years later. "With that start, maybe I was going to be a footnote on someone's Hall of Fame plaque.

"What I remember about Mays is that it was at the end of his career. And he hit a two-strike sinker harder than I'd ever had one hit.

By the NUMBERS **5**— Straight complete games for pitcher Randy Jones between May 12 and May 30, 1976. Jones' ERA during the club-record streak was 0.99.

The ball rocketed out of there. You know, at Shea Stadium, a real long hit ball sort of disappears beyond the lighted area. I remember that ball disappearing into the darkness.

"I was impressed."

Quickly, so were the Padres. Jones finished the 1973 season with a 7–6 record and 3.15 ERA in 19 starts.

But while 1974 was a banner year for the Padres, it was not for Jones. He became the third—and most recent—Padre to lose 20 games in a season. In fact, he set a club record with 22 losses.

And things got worse as the season progressed. Jones was 1–9 after the All-Star break to finish 8–22 with a 4.46 ERA.

"I experienced something in 1974 that I had never experienced before," said Jones. "I had always been a cocky pitcher. I always pitched with confidence, although I had always been the underdog because of my size and velocity.

"But I lost it in 1974. Everything got to me. I started reading the rumors in the newspapers and believing what I read. They probably weren't all rumors. They said I was going to the bullpen, that the Padres would trade me if there was a market. I did a job on myself.

"I spent that winter not only working on my pitches, but working on my outlook. I wasn't going to nibble anymore. If I got the ball again, I was going after them."

Jones' 1975 season represented one of the greatest reversals in major league history. The 22-game loser of 1974 became the Padres' first 20-game winner—and the first pitcher since Dick Ellsworth in 1962–1963 to go from 20 losses to 20 wins.

The picture of Jones's frizzy hair poking out from beneath his cap as he moved through his low-kick delivery became the Padres' unofficial logo. And his sinker-slider repertoire became a devastating 1–2 punch.

"One of the things I wanted to do going into the 1975 season was try to eliminate some of the chances I had at losing," said Jones. "If I allowed one less run a game, I thought it could make a big difference.

"And Tom Morgan made a big difference."

Morgan was the Padres' new pitching coach. He worked on Jones's mechanics in the spring of 1975, getting the pitcher to put more of his body into his pitches and use less arm motion. He also told Jones not to worry about the score when he pitched.

*Randy Jones didn't scare off hitters with velocity. "Frustration was my game,"
joked the sinker-baller who was the Padres' first 20-game winner and their
first Cy Young Award winner. Jones was also the Padres' first "attraction."
Attendance would spike on days he pitched, many fans turning out in wigs
celebrating his frizzy haircut.*

TOP 5

Padres Single-Season Complete Games

	Player	Year	Complete Games
1.	Randy Jones	1976	25
2.	Randy Jones	1975	18
3.	Dave Roberts	1971	14
4.	Clay Kirby	1971	13t
	Eric Show	1988	13t

The Padres had scored two or fewer runs in 17 of his 22 losses in 1974 and had been shutout seven times. In 1975, Jones did much more than knock a run off each outing. He dropped more than two runs. His ERA plummeted from 4.46 to a National League–leading 2.24.

Jones' other numbers were just as staggering. Eighteen of his 36 starts resulted in complete games. He tied Fred Norman's record with six shutouts. He was 11–5 at the break and had thrown two one-hitters to win a spot on the National League All-Star team.

At the All-Star Game in Milwaukee, Dodgers manager Walter Alston paid Jones perhaps the highest possible compliment when he called on the Padre to get the final three outs rather than his own closer, Mike Marshall. Said Alston, "Give me that curly little left-hander who gets everyone out."

It was against Alston's Dodgers on September 23 that Jones became the Padres' first 20-game winner.

Jones finished second to the Mets' Tom Seaver in the National League Cy Young Award voting.

And the best was yet to come.

In 1976, Randy Jones won the Cy Young Award to become the first Padre to garner any type of major honor.

Opening Day of the 1976 season also saw the start of the Randy Jones introduction. As Jones walked in from the bullpen after his pregame warm-ups, each section he passed rose to greet him with a standing ovation. By the time he reached the mound, the entire San Diego Stadium crowd of 44,278 was on its feet.

"I remember that by the time I reached the mound, I was shaking," said Jones. "A lot of players will tell you they can't hear the crowd. I heard that. I had never heard anything like that before."

Jones would hear it every time he pitched in San Diego. Every time he approached a start from the bullpen, the fans would rise one section at a time to applaud his approach. And every time he pitched, there would be thousands more fans in the stands than for most Padres games.

Randy Jones had become a happening. And 1976 would be a season-long celebration. Jones set franchise records—which still stand—for wins (22), starts (40), complete games (25), and innings pitched (315⅓).

Maybe one day another Padre might top his wins total. But his league-leading marks in complete games and innings pitched will likely stand as franchise records forever.

Jones was 16–3 at the All-Star break.

"Everything I had was working for me," said Jones. "It was really magical there for a while. I couldn't miss the strike zone. At the same time, I was throwing only good pitches in the zone. The sinkers that started in the zone were out of it at the hitter's zone."

Jones was regularly drawing crowds of 40,000. And the crowd would arrive early to watch Jones warm up and be in position to cheer him during his walk to the mound. Jones responded by going 13–5 at San Diego Stadium with four shutouts.

TOP 5

Padres Career Complete Games

	Player	Career Complete Games
1.	Randy Jones	71
2.	Eric Show	35
3.	Clay Kirby	34
4.	Steve Arlin	31
5.	Bruce Hurst	29

"He deserves everything that is happening to him," said Pete Rose, who grew so frustrated by Jones's pitches that he once took to hitting left-handed against the left-hander.

"I can't pick up anything he does," explained Rose. "And it's just not me. It's everyone in this league."

During the first half of the 1976 season, Jones matched a 63-year-old National League record held by the immortal Christy Mathewson by working 68 straight innings without issuing a walk. Strangely, Jones jumped ahead of San Francisco's Marc Hill 0-and-2 in the potential record-setting inning before walking him on four straight pitches.

"I was really goofy that way," said Jones. "I'd be in position to do something and I'd just lose it for a moment. But it worked the other way, too. There were times I'd be on the ropes and I'd just uncork a great pitch. Hitters would be saying, 'Where'd that come from?' just like I was saying, 'What happened?' on that walk to Hill."

Sadly, Jones's greatest season might have also done him in. In his 40th and final start, Jones felt a pop in his left elbow.

"It was like a rubber band unraveling," he said.

Jones was through for the game and the season. And a further exam by famed Los Angeles orthopedic surgeon Dr. Frank Jobe produced more bad news. Something was seriously wrong in Jones's elbow.

Thirty years ago, medical science involving the pitching elbow was far from being as advanced as it is today. Dr. Jobe couldn't determine if Jones's problem was nerve damage or a tear in the biceps

TOP 5

Padres Career Shutouts

	Player	Career Shutouts
1.	Randy Jones	18
2.	Steve Arlin	11t
	Eric Show	11t
4.	Bruce Hurst	10
5.	Andy Benes	8

tendon. A damaged nerve would regenerate itself. Exploratory surgery showed it was a nerve.

"After that, it came and went," said Jones.

"My sinker stayed sharp and actually got better. But I lost the ability to snap off my slider. It was the slider that set up the sinker. After that final game of 1976, I struggled.

"I was never the same. I had moments. I had great games. But it was never the same."

Jones admits he has wondered

TRIVIA

Who was the first Padre to lead the National League in earned-run average?

Answers to the trivia questions are on pages 219–220.

over the years if overwork played a role in his nerve damage. He had pitched more than 800 innings in a three-year span. He worked regularly on three days' rest and sometimes pitched on two.

"Does it really matter?" Jones asked recently. "I had two of the greatest seasons a pitcher could ever have. I wouldn't change a thing."

He wasn't done. After going only 6–12 with a 4.59 ERA in a 1977 season shortened to 25 starts by the surgery, Jones was 13–14 in 1978 with a 2.88 ERA in 36 starts, and 11–12 in 1979 with a 3.63 ERA in 39 starts. He threw 13 complete games in 1978–1979.

And in 1980, he set a Padres record—which was broken by reliever Cla Meredith in 2006—by pitching 30 straight scoreless innings while becoming the first Padre to pitch three straight shutouts.

"It was classic Randy," then Padres manager Jerry Coleman said of the shutout streak. "It was like we had turned the clock back to 1976. Everything was working again. It was beautiful."

Then it was gone. Jones lost his next seven starts.

And soon Randy was gone from the Padres. On December 15, 1980, general manager Jack McKeon traded the icon to the New York Mets for John Pacella and Jose Moreno.

As a Padre, Jones had compiled a 92–105 record with a 3.30 ERA during some of the club's toughest times. He remains the all-time club leader in innings pitched (1,765), starts (253), complete games (71), and shutouts (18). Only Eric Show, who pitched behind

TOP 5

Padres Single-Season Wins

	Player	Year	Wins
1.	Randy Jones	1976	22
2.	Gaylord Perry	1978	21
3.	Randy Jones	1975	20
4.	Andy Hawkins	1985	18t
	Kevin Brown	1998	18t

much stronger offenses and defenses, won more games as a Padre than Jones.

But Jones's attachment with Padres fans went beyond his statistics. Padres owner Ray Kroc was among the first to recognized that. Jones made $62,500 in 1976 en route to the Cy Young Award. After the season ended, Kroc gave Jones a $25,000 bonus—loose change considering the number of extra fans Jones put in the seats every time he pitched.

"I always felt I connected with the fans," said Jones. "Look at me, I was one of them...the guy next door pitching for the Padres. There was a picture taken once of me standing next to Dave Winfield. He looked like Hercules. I looked like your high school teacher.

"And I wasn't like Koufax, Gibson, or Carlton. People weren't saying, 'Wow.' It was more like, 'Did you see that?' with a grin. Fun times.

"I loved it...the games I'd play back and forth with the hitters. They'd try to get me to slow down. And I'd throw the second they stepped in the box. I didn't want to strike them out and make them look bad. I just wanted that ground ball.

"And the umpires loved me, particularly on hot days. Bruce Froemming once asked me on a sweltering night back east if we could move it along. I told him, 'How about 90 minutes?' He laughed. But I think we got out of there in less than two hours. As I was leaving the mound after the last hitter, the second base ump trotted past and said, 'Thanks, it's always a pleasure working with you.'"

Still is.

After Jones retired as a player, the Padres welcomed him back to their family.

A member of the Padres Hall of Fame, Jones has become an ambassador of Padres baseball. His Randy Jones' Barbeque is one of PETCO Park's favorite concessions. He has a nightly feature on the Padres radio broadcasts. He appears on the in-house pregame show before every game at PETCO Park.

Like Tony Gwynn, Jones has signed so many autographs, the value of his signature is almost nil.

"It's been quite a ride," Jones said of his career as a player/ambassador/commentator/restaurateur. "I'm flattered anytime someone approaches me."

Randy Jones was the first Padre whose deeds have been passed down from father to son and now grandson.

"One of the best things that happens to me," said Jones, "is meeting a man around 35 or 40 who has his son with him. And the boy will know who I am. Why? Because the grandfather took his son to see me pitch. And he's said something to his son."

Jones, Ray Kroc, and Nate Colbert were members of the inaugural class of the Padres Hall of Fame in 1999.

Jones's No. 35 is one of four retired by the Padres, and "Randy Jones 35" jerseys remain one of the best sellers in the Padres souvenir store.

"There's not a day that I don't feel honored," concluded Jones.

The same goes for Padres fans.

Winfield and Smith

In the summer of 2007, Tony Gwynn will go into the Hall of Fame as the first career-long Padre enshrined in Cooperstown. But he ispreceded by two players who began their careers as Padres—Dave Winfield and Ozzie Smith.

Although their stays were relatively brief in San Diego, both made their initial marks as Padres. And Winfield decided to enter the Hall of Fame wearing a Padres cap.

"I think you always have a special connection with that first team that gave you the opportunity," said Winfield, who returned to the Padres in 2001 as a vice president and senior advisor. That was the same year that Winfield was inducted into the Hall of Fame. Ozzie Smith was inducted a year later.

Winfield and Smith actually played together for three seasons with the Padres from 1978 to 1980.

Winfield gained free agency status after the 1980 season and signed with the Yankees that December. Smith was traded to St. Louis the following December in a multi-player deal that was basically a swap of shortstops. The Padres acquired Garry Templeton, who became instrumental in the Padres 1984 run to the National League pennant.

"It was an honor to be able to see those guys play," said Tony Gwynn, who was at San Diego State part of the time that Winfield and Smith were Padres.

Winfield was a first-round draft pick of the Padres in 1973. Smith was a fourth-round pick of the Padres in 1977.

Born in 1951, Winfield was a nationally known athlete even before the Padres drafted him. A native of St. Paul, Minnesota, the

6'6", 200-pound Winfield was a star of both the University of Minnesota's basketball and baseball teams.

In baseball, he led the Golden Gophers in both hitting and pitching and was the Most Valuable Player of the College World Series, although the Gophers blew a Winfield-created 7–0 lead in the title game and dropped an 8–7 decision to Southern California.

The drafting of Winfield created a whirlwind of speculation—he was the first player to be drafted by all three professional sports. Would he sign with the financially strapped Padres—who appeared to be headed to Washington, D.C., at the time of the 1973 draft—or would he opt to play in the NBA or the NFL?

And if he signed with the Padres, would it be as an outfielder or a pitcher? Winfield was given the choice, and he elected to play every day as an outfielder upon the advice of the scout who signed him. But he had one more request: Winfield wanted to have the chance to jump directly to the major leagues without spending a day in the minors.

"What did we really have to lose?" said Padres president Buzzie Bavasi.

Winfield arrived in San Diego on June 19, 1973. He singled in his Padres debut.

Dave Winfield might be the greatest all-around athlete ever to wear a Padres uniform. In the spring of 1974, because the club had a surplus of outfielders, he was given a trial as a shortstop. And John McNamara considered sending Winfield to the minor leagues.

"But it was clear to everyone that Dave belonged," said McNamara.

After hitting .277 with three homers and 12 RBIs in 141 at-bats in 1973, Winfield became a regular in 1974 and hit .265 with 20 homers and a team-leading 75 RBIs.

DID YOU KNOW . . . That the 1980 Padres were the first National League team ever to have three players with 50 or more stolen bases—Gene Richards (61), Ozzie Smith (57), and Jerry Mumphrey (52)?

And at the age of 23, Winfield became one of the first athletes to establish a charitable foundation. For the 1975 season, Winfield created the Winfield Pavilion out in right field behind his position. The Winfield Foundation gave thousands of underprivileged San Diego youngsters their first taste of Padres baseball. It also became the cornerstone for a number of other player-fueled charitable programs run by the Padres. Winfield's community work extended to literacy, health care, and substance-abuse programs.

On the field, Winfield was maturing into a superstar.

"He was the total package," said Randy Jones. "Hit for power as well as average. Run. Catch. Throw. He might have had one of the greatest arms I've ever seen...and accurate."

But the Padres put Winfield in a tough spot. Beginning in 1975, Winfield hit third and fourth in the Padres' order with little around to protect him.

"I hit a lot of pitcher's pitches," said Winfield, whose personal growth paralleled that of the Padres offense for the next several seasons.

In 1977, he set the stage, setting the Padres' record for runs scored (104) while hitting 25 homers with 92 RBIs. In 1978, Winfield hit .308 with 24 homers and 97 RBIs. People beyond San Diego were taking notice. Winfield finished 10th in the voting for the National League Most Valuable Player Award.

Winfield was set for a break-out season. It came in 1979. He again hit .308, but this time he had 34 homers and a league-leading 118 RBIs. Winfield also led the National League in total bases and ranked second in slugging percentage and third in home runs. He also won his first Gold Glove award and finished third in the MVP voting.

By this time, Winfield was looking to bigger and better things. And big-market teams were looking at Winfield, who would become a free agent after the 1980 season.

"I really wanted to play on a championship team as soon as possible," said Winfield. "And I wanted to see what I could do nationally with my foundation and charities."

The Padres couldn't keep him. After Winfield hit 20 more homers with 87 RBIs in 1980, he opted to sign as a free agent with the New York Yankees.

Dave Winfield went straight from the University of Minnesota campus to the Padres' starting lineup in 1973. In eight seasons with the Padres, Winfield hit .284 with 154 homers and 133 steals, and was named to four All-Star teams. Following a 22-year career, Winfield entered the Hall of Fame in 2001 as the first player wearing a Padres cap.

In 7½ seasons with the Padres, Winfield had hit 154 homers, driven home 626 runs, and hit .284. In 22 full major league seasons, his homer and RBI totals would treble while his average would remain constant.

Although Winfield was the first Padres player to be voted a starter for the All-Star Game in 1978, he said his most memorable

PADRES SUPERLATIVES

Rawlings Gold Glove Winners

Player	Number	Position	Years
1. Tony Gwynn	5	OF	1986–1987, 1989–1991
2. Benito Santiago	3	C	1988–1990†
Ken Caminiti	3	3B	1995–1997†
4. Dave Winfield	2	OF	1979–1980†
Ozzie Smith	2	SS	1980–1981†
Steve Finley	2	CF	1995–1996†
7. Mike Cameron	1	OF	2006

moment as a Padre came with the previous mid-summer classic. Winfield and relief pitcher Rollie Fingers were the Padres' representatives for the first All-Star Game played in San Diego.

"I remember the ovation when I was introduced," said Winfield. "It was loud and lengthy. I remember standing there wondering what it would be like if the Padres ever made the playoffs."

Too bad he didn't stick around for 1984.

While there is no doubt that the Padres would have been a better team with Winfield and Gwynn in the same outfield in 1984, it's not as sure that they would have been that much better at the time with Smith at short over Templeton.

Templeton became a catalyst for that 1984 team with the bat as well as the glove. No question that Templeton wasn't the fielder Smith was. But he might have been the right shortstop at the right time.

The Padres had no misconceptions about Smith as they scouted him at out-of-the-way Cal Poly–San Luis Obispo.

"Everyone agreed he had a great glove," said Bavasi. "But there were questions about whether or not he would ever hit. But the more you watched him play short, the less you cared about his hitting."

Since the Padres' birth, shortstop had been a cross between the butt of a joke and a black hole for Padres fans. The names read like a Who's Who of Forgettables—Rafael Robles, Jose Arcia, Tommy Dean,

Enzo Hernandez, and Hector Torres.

The fan favorite had been Hernandez, whose nightly introduction by PA announcer John DeMott became something of a pregame anthem: "No. 11...ENN-ZOHHHH Hernandez."

The "charge" call seemed to fire up everyone but Hernandez, who might have been one of the more inoffensive players in major league history. In 2,324 at-bats with the Padres, Hernandez had two homers, 113 RBIs, and 241 runs scored. He hit .224 with a career on-base percentage of .283. As a rookie in 1971, Hernandez had 12 RBIs in 549 at-bats—or one fewer than Nate Colbert had in his record-setting doubleheader the following season.

Oddly, the Padres finally seemed to solve their shortstop problem in 1977 with the arrival of Bill Almon, who in 1974 was the first player taken in the June draft. Almon hit .261 as a rookie with two homers and 43 RBIs—lofty numbers for a Padres shortstop. He did, however, commit 41 errors. But Almon was the shortstop—until the Padres got a look at Smith. Almost overnight, Almon became the Padres' third baseman.

With the glove, Smith was a nightly highlight show before there was such a thing.

"I must admit, I was in awe of what Ozzie did with the glove," said Roger Craig, the Padres' manager in 1978. "Some of it was amazing. Other plays bordered on the incredible."

It didn't take Smith long to make his mark. Two weeks into the season, the Wizard of Ahs made a play that stands as one of the greatest of his Hall of Fame career.

Atlanta's Jeff Burroughs hit a hard, low liner toward center. Breaking on contact, Smith appeared in position to make what even then would have been an outstanding play. But as the ball kissed the infield dirt, it hit something and ricocheted in the opposite direction of Smith's dive. Somehow, Smith reached back with his bare hand, caught the ball, leaped to his feet, and threw out Burroughs at first.

"My dad still talks about that play," then–Padres third baseman Sean Burroughs would say years later. "He used to joke that he got robbed on the greatest play ever made by a shortstop."

Perhaps the most startling thing about Smith's rookie season is that he hit .258 with a team-leading 40 stolen bases. He also drove in

TRIVIA

Answers to the trivia questions are on pages 219–220.

Mike Cameron in 2006 became the ninth player in Padres' history to steal 20 bases and hit 20 homers in the same season. Who are the two Padres with two 20/20 seasons?

46 runs. Smith finished second in the National League Rookie of the Year voting.

Winfield and Smith also helped the Padres to their first winning season in 1978.

In four seasons with the Padres, Smith hit .231 with one homer and 129 RBIs. He also stole 147 bases and scored 266 runs. But there was no accounting for how many runs Smith had saved the Padres.

"Ozzie was the best weapon I've seen at shortstop," said veteran broadcaster Jerry Coleman, who also managed Smith in 1980. "He took runs off the board, which were just as valuable as runs you scored."

Smith's last years with the Padres were not happy. Demands made by his agent created a chasm between the club and its prized shortstop. At the same time, Templeton, considered one of the game's top offensive shortstops at the time, was wearing out his welcome in St. Louis.

Thus, the trade.

Jack McKeon was once asked to compare the merits of Templeton versus Smith.

"Well," said Trader Jack. "We won the pennant with Tempy."

No telling what the Padres might have done with Smith...and Winfield.

Tony Gwynn

It was a ritual played out before every game at Qualcomm Stadium.

Tony Gwynn would walk out of the Padres' dugout, spot a kid looking for an autograph, and sign his name to whatever was in the child's hand.

Within seconds, a crowd would descend upon No. 19.

"I'm never going to make a dime with my signature," Gwynn would say, the words punctuated by his trademark belly laugh. "I've signed so much stuff in my career that there's no market value. It's good."

Gwynn would reach over the cards in protective plastic jackets—the cards circulated by professional autograph seekers. Instead, he'd find the smallest, dirtiest hands in the crush.

"Give me the kid with ice cream on his face...that's my kind of fan," said Gwynn. "Give me the kid who has just brushed the dirt off his hands with his shirt. That's me."

Through the pile once came a small, dirty hand, clutching a battle-worn baseball. Gwynn reached for the ball and grabbed the hand.

"What kind of a ball is this?" said the eight-time National League batting champion as he burst into laughter. "This ball is so beat up, I can't sign it."

As the face across the rail started getting the look of dejection, Gwynn reached into his back pocket and pulled out an official National League baseball fresh from the box. And as he started signing the pristine ball, Gwynn looked at the boy and said, "Will you trade me your ball for this ball?"

The little fan was speechless. "You gotta tell me 'yes' or 'no,'" said Gwynn. "You gotta speak up for yourself." The boy hesitatingly said "yes." And Gwynn handed him both balls. "Put this one on your shelf," said Gwynn of the new ball. "Keep hitting this one."

"Keep Hitting" could have been the trademark for Anthony Keith Gwynn—the greatest of all Padres. In fact, the Hall of Famer is known as Mr. Padre. He should be Mr. San Diego.

"I can't think of anyone in baseball who has done more for a team and a city than Tony Gwynn," Greg Maddux once said while talking about Gwynn's contributions to San Diego, as well as the Padres.

"He is the face of baseball in San Diego."

Gwynn spent his entire 20-season major league career with the Padres. And when he retired as a player after the 2001 season, Gwynn returned to his alma mater as the baseball coach of San Diego State.

He is the Padres' career leader in most every offensive category.

Then you go to the big arena.

Gwynn shares the National League record with eight batting championships. He is a 15-time All-Star, a five-time Gold Glove winner, and the holder of seven Silver Slugger Awards.

His .338 career batting average is the highest in the major leagues since San Diego native Ted Williams retired. And on August 6, 1999, Gwynn joined the game's elite 3,000-hit club—on his mother Vendella's 64th birthday—with a single off the Expos' Dan Smith in Montreal.

But the numbers are only part of the Gwynn story.

Tony Gwynn is one of 17 players in major league history to devote an entire career of 20 or more seasons to one team.

"I think of all of it, that is the best part," Gwynn said shortly before retiring in 2001. "Twenty years, one team. I'm a Padre."

Through thick and thin.

Gwynn is the only Padre to have played on both the franchise's National League championship teams. He is the only Padre to have played on the first three division championship clubs.

And he was there for fire sales as well as pennants. He endured rumors of the Padres moving.

"The highs have been wonderful," said Gwynn. "So good that they make you forget the lows. But we've had lows."

Gwynn is laughing as he remembers.

TOP 10

Single-Season Hits

	Player	Year	Hits
1.	Tony Gwynn	1997	220*
2.	Tony Gwynn	1987	218*
3.	Tony Gwynn	1984	213*
4.	Tony Gwynn	1986	211*
5.	Mark Loretta	2004	208
6.	Tony Gwynn	1989	203*
7.	Tony Gwynn	1985	197†
	Tony Gwynn	1995	197††
9.	Steve Finley	1996	195
10.	Gene Richards	1980	193

* — Led National League. † — Tied for National League lead.

But some of the memories also hurt. His father, the late Charles Gwynn, became so disenchanted with the direction of the Padres—plus turmoil inside the club—in the early 1990s that he counseled his son to leave San Diego in the rearview mirror as soon as possible.

"At the time, my dad was probably right," said Tony Gwynn. "I know he was right. But I'm a thick-and-thin type of guy. If you don't want to leave when times are good, you shouldn't walk when things get tough. And things got tough."

Gwynn has the belly laugh working again.

"We were bad at times. Terrible. But we've been great at other times."

The great constant through all the Padres' ups and downs has been Tony Gwynn—although Gwynn believes the only constant was change.

The Tony Gwynn who first joined the Padres in 1982 was a stringbean whose game was hitting and speed. But he wasn't very good in the field. His first task was to turn himself into a "major league–caliber" outfielder.

"I took thousands of extra fly balls and made just as many throws," said Gwynn. "I wanted to turn myself into the best outfielder I could be."

There is—and will be—only one Mr. Padre. Tony Gwynn was elected to the Hall of Fame in 2007 with the seventh-highest vote percentage in history. Gwynn spent his entire 20-season career with the Padres, finishing with a .338 career batting average—the game's highest since the retirement of Ted Williams—and 3,141 hits.

As a hitter, Gwynn—with the help of wife Alicia—was a pioneer in the use of videotape to study pitchers as well as himself. And late in his career, at the urging of Williams, Gwynn changed again, adding a power stroke to his repertoire.

Of course, the left-handed Gwynn is best known for making the 5.5 hole famous. That is the lane between third base and shortstop—a slot that Gwynn regularly found with his ability to drive almost any pitch the opposite way.

"Tony grew with the franchise," former Padres manager and general manager Jack McKeon once said of Gwynn. "Then roles reversed. The franchise rode with Tony. He was the one thing Padres fans could count on."

"San Diego's ambassador of baseball," is how former teammate and Padres manager Bruce Bochy described Gwynn.

Contrary to popular belief, Gwynn was neither born nor raised in San Diego. He was born in Long Beach, California, on May 9, 1960, and graduated from Long Beach Polytechnic High in 1977.

It was actually basketball that brought Tony Gwynn to San Diego. He was recruited as a point guard by San Diego State and set the Aztecs' assist record en route to a spot on the 1981 All–Western Conference team alongside Danny Ainge.

After his sophomore season of basketball at San Diego State, Gwynn convinced his basketball coach to allow him to also play baseball. On the same June day in 1981, Gwynn was selected by both of San Diego's two professional teams. The Padres selected Gwynn in the third round. The NBA Clippers drafted Gwynn in the 10th round. It was the first time an athlete had been drafted by two professional sports on the same day.

Gwynn's first love was basketball, but not by much. And clearly not by enough to have him make a bad decision.

"I always felt baseball was my best chance," said Gwynn, although Paul Silas, the Clippers' coach at the time, believed Tony could play in the NBA. "The reason why he went lower in our draft is because he went higher in theirs," Silas once said of Gwynn's draft status.

Gwynn immediately signed with the Padres and quickly made his way through the Padres' minor league system. After winning

MVP honors on the rookie Northwest League, Gwynn finished the 1981 season with Double A Amarillo, where he hit .462 in 23 games. By the start of the 1982 season, Gwynn was already with Triple A Hawaii.

And on July 19, 1982—less than 14 months after his professional debut—he made his Padres debut. As soon as he arrived in San Diego, Gwynn was slotted into the No. 5 spot in the Padres' order and sent out to play center field.

Gwynn responded with two hits and a sacrifice fly in a 7–6 loss to Philadelphia at Jack Murphy Stadium. His first at-bat resulted in a sacrifice fly. His first hit was an eighth-inning double off Phils reliever Sid Monge. His second hit was a single. As he reached first after that hit, Gwynn was extended the greeting hand of a hitter named Pete Rose.

"As we were standing there at first, Pete told me the first year was all about learning," said Gwynn. "I never forgot that."

After the game, the 22-year-old Gwynn told the media, "It boggles my mind to think I've made it this soon."

What was to follow boggled everyone's mind. Gwynn went hitless in his second game. Then he launched a 15-game hitting streak, the longest by a Padre in 1982. Gwynn hit .289 over 54 games that season. He never again hit below .300.

But Gwynn's start with the Padres had a painful side. He broke his left wrist while diving for a ball on August 25. And he re-injured the wrist that December while playing winter ball in the Dominican Republic. The injury delayed the start of his 1983 season.

It was during a 7-for-59 slide late in July 1983 that Gwynn made one of the most pivotal decisions of his Hall of Fame career.

"We were on the road and I saw the game was going to be telecast back to San Diego," said Gwynn. "My wife and I had just gotten some video-recording equipment for our television. So I called Alicia and asked her to tape that night's game for me. We were headed home, and I wanted to see if I could spot something wrong with my swing if I spotted it on the tapes."

Gwynn did spot something. He was flying open on his swing. He made some changes based on the tape. That marked the start of Gwynn's ground-breaking videotaping program. At first, he was a lone wolf—carrying bulky equipment on the road as he built a personal library. Then the Padres joined in with a team-wide video program. Today, every team in the major leagues uses videotape.

"It was so basic when I started," said Gwynn. "I was at the mercy of what they showed on television. If the TV cameras caught a shot of me swinging, I had a piece of tape to work with. If they didn't, I didn't, and it was back to the drawing board. And most of the work was done by Alicia. She was taking care of the baby (Anthony, who is now a Milwaukee Brewer) and running to the tape machine when I hit. I'm sure she wasn't happy with the program at times. But she helped turn my career around. We were a team."

A team that was soon reaping dividends.

Starting August 11—or about three weeks after the taping began—Gwynn hit in 39 of 41 games, including a career-best 25-game hitting streak. He hit .333 from the start of August to the end of the season and finished with a .309 mark. The 1983 season marked the first of 19 straight seasons that Gwynn hit .300 or better.

But it was in 1984 that Gwynn really came into his own and helped the Padres to their first National League championship. In his

TOP 10

Single-Season Batting Averages

	Player	Year	Average
1.	Tony Gwynn	1994	.394*
2.	Tony Gwynn	1997	.372*
3.	Tony Gwynn	1987	.370*
4.	Tony Gwynn	1995	.368*
5.	Tony Gwynn	1993	.358
6.	Tony Gwynn	1996	.353*
7.	Tony Gwynn	1984	.351*
8.	Tony Gwynn	1999	.338
9.	Tony Gwynn	1989	.336*
10.	Mark Loretta	2004	.335

* Led National League

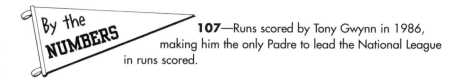

107—Runs scored by Tony Gwynn in 1986, making him the only Padre to lead the National League in runs scored.

first full season in the major leagues, Tony Gwynn hit .351 with a club-record 213 hits—winning the first of his batting titles.

"I was ready at the start of the 1984 season," said Gwynn. "I had become a confident player. I had improved a lot of things playing winter ball in Puerto Rico. And I knew we had a good team. I was ready."

The 1984 season marked the first of Gwynn's five 200-hit seasons. It marked the first of six times that he led the league in both batting average and hits. He finished third in the National League Most Valuable Player voting, won his first Silver Slugger award, and was named to his first All-Star team.

"I learned so much that season," said Gwynn.

Not all of it was good.

Gwynn's strongest memory from 1984 came from something said during the Padres' raucous celebration following their come-from-behind victory over the Cubs in the National League Championship Series.

"Someone in the clubhouse said: 'Nothing else matters now, we're in the World Series,'" recalled Gwynn. "Well, it did matter. The Tigers took it to us in the World Series. That statement would ring in my ears for the longest time. I don't know if we could have ever beaten the Tigers in the World Series. But we should have played better."

Gwynn honestly believed 1984 was the start of something big for the Padres. He was wrong. "I was naïve," he said.

The 1985 season was the first time Gwynn heard teammates criticize his conditioning. Gwynn was also hitting under .300 going into June. And as soon as he got hot, he suffered an injured wrist.

"It was a tough year," said Gwynn of 1985.

The next two years weren't much better. The 1986 season saw Gwynn hit only .296 over the last month of the season and finish third in a batting race he led much of the season. And although

Gwynn did win his second batting title in 1987 with a .370 average—the highest mark in the National League since Stan Musial hit .376 in 1948—the Padres came within three games of a 100-loss season.

"Offensively, I came into my own in 1987," said Gwynn, who became the first player in National League history to hit .370 and steal 50 bases in the same season. He had two .400 months, including a 44-for-93 June.

The Padres rebounded in 1988, and Gwynn won his third batting title, although his .313 average was the lowest winning average in National League history. Gwynn suffered two hand injuries during the season. The first required surgery during spring training to increase the movement in a tendon in his left hand. And, on May 7 in Pittsburgh, Gwynn sprained his right thumb when he fell hard on the artificial turf while trying to dodge a batted ball, forcing him to the disabled list for 21 days.

Gwynn won his third straight batting title—and his fourth in six years—in 1989. "More important to me, I felt I got my game back," said Gwynn, who went 6-for-8 in the final three games against San Francisco to edge the Giants' Will Clark by .003 for the batting title. "It was great fun the way it ended," said Gwynn. "Honestly, I would have been just as happy had Will won the title."

Gwynn's run of batting titles ended in 1990 with what Gwynn called a "miserable year."

In his second season with the Padres, first baseman Jack Clark charged that Gwynn was a "selfish" player. During a clubhouse meeting in New York in May 1990, Gwynn learned that more than half his teammates sided with Clark.

TRIVIA

Padres have won nine National League batting championships. Tony Gwynn won eight of them. Who was the Padres other batting champion?

Answers to the trivia questions are on pages 219–220.

"They blasted me, and I blasted them back," said Gwynn. "I had never been part of anything like that before and I was in the middle of it...the target. It ticked me off."

During the middle of the controversy, Padres general manager Joe McIlvaine told Gwynn that Tony and Clark couldn't co-exist on

TOP 38

Padres All-Star Game Selections

	Player	Position	No.	Starts
1.	Tony Gwynn	OF	15	12
2.	Trevor Hoffman	RHP	5	
3.	Dave Winfield	OF	4t	1t
	Benito Santiago	C	4t	3
5.	Terry Kennedy	C	3	1t
	Nate Colbert	1B	3	
	Bruce Bochy	Man., Coach	3	
8.	Steve Garvey	1B	2t	2
	Ken Caminiti	3B	2t	1t
	Randy Jones	LHP	2t	
	Goose Gossage	RHP	2t	
	Mark Davis	LHP	2t	
13.	Fred McGriff	1B	1t	1t
	La Marr Hoyt	RHP	1t	1t
	Chris Cannizzaro	C	1t	
	Cito Gaston	OF	1t	
	John Grubb	OF	1t	
	Rollie Fingers	RHP	1t	
	Gaylord Perry	RHP	1t	
	Ozzie Smith	SS	1t	
	Ruppert Jones	OF	1t	
	Dave Dravecky	LHP	1t	
	Garry Templeton	SS	1t	
	Roberto Alomar	2B	1t	
	Tony Fernandez	SS	1t	
	Gary Sheffield	3B	1t	
	Andy Benesv	RHP	1t	
	Steve Finley	OF	1t	
	Kevin Brown	RHP	1t	
	Greg Vaughn	OF	1t	
	Andy Ashby	RHP	1t	
	Ryan Klesko	OF	1t	
	Phil Nevin	1B	1t	

Padres All-Star Game Selections (con't)

Player	Position	No.	Starts
Rondell White	OF	1†	
Mark Loretta	2B	1†	
Jake Peavy	RHP	1†	
Preston Gomez	Coach	1†	
John McNamara	Coach	1†	

the same team. "The way it was said, I started thinking I was going to be traded," said Gwynn. "And it got to me. I couldn't get going."

Gwynn's .309 average was his lowest for a full season. And Gwynn was hurting physically as well as mentally. This time, for the first time, it was his knees—a problem that would follow him for the rest of his career. The cartilage under his left kneecap was wearing out. "I had a bald spot, bone on bone," he said.

Gwynn's knees hurt throughout the year. And dealing with Clark was painful. On August 15, 1990, Gwynn had reached the midpoint of his quest for 3,000 hits with a single off Montreal's Steve Frey. But exactly one month later, on September 15, Gwynn wasn't exactly crestfallen when he suffered a fracture to his right index finger while trying to make a catch at the wall in Atlanta. "Breaking the finger was almost a reprieve," admitted Gwynn of his season-ending injury.

Gwynn's 1991 season couldn't have started better. Clark was gone. "Jack didn't like the way I played, and I really didn't give a damn," said Gwynn. Plus, Gwynn became a 10-and-5 player—a 10-year veteran who had spent at least the past five years with the same team—meaning he couldn't be traded without his permission. His average shot up to .373, and he was voted to start in the All-Star Game. But Gwynn's left knee had taken a serious turn for the worse. Hitting only .243 after the break, Gwynn had arthroscopic surgery on the knee September 18, ending his season.

The 1992 season produced a watershed event for Gwynn that was nearly as important as his discovery of videotape. San Diego hosted the 1992 All-Star Game, and the featured guest was native son Ted Williams. Just before the game, Williams cornered Gwynn in the National League dugout.

"Ted got all over me," said Gwynn. "Right from the start, he jumped me. He looked at me and said, 'Tony, you're a big guy. You should be hitting for more power.'

"He's feeling my arm muscle. 'You've got muscle,' he's saying. He grabs my bat, 'Toothpick,' Ted says. He was really ragging on me. Then he got deadly serious. 'Tony,' Ted says, 'Major League history is made on the ball inside. Drive the inside ball.'

"He was fine with what I did with the outside pitches. But if they tried to bust me with an inside pitch, Ted said I should bust them back and drive the ball with power. Now he's telling me, 'Tony, I'm going to be watching...we're not through here.'"

Williams got Gwynn to thinking. But there was not much else he could do in 1992. For the third straight season, Gwynn finished the season on the disabled list. And for the second straight year, the season was cut short so that surgeons could cut on Tony's troublesome left knee.

But the worst was yet to come. Charles Gwynn passed away just days after discussing Tony's future with his son. "At the end of the season, I was really down," said Tony. "My dad sensed my frustration. Honestly, I was thinking about quitting. I was beginning to think my knee would never get better. And my dad didn't think the Padres

PADRES SUPERLATIVES

Most Seasons in Uniform

	Player	Manager	Coach	Total
1. Tony Gwynn	20			20
2. Bruce Bochy	5	12	2	19
3. Tim Flannery	11		7	18
4. Rob Picciolo			16	16
5. Trevor Hoffman	15			15
6. Greg Booker	7		7	14
7. Merv Rettenmund	2		11	13
8. Whitey Wietelmann			11	11
9. Garry Templeton	10			10

TOP 10

Career Hits with the Padres

Player	Hits
1. Tony Gwynn	3,141
2. Garry Templeton	1,135
3. Dave Winfield	1,134
4. Gene Richards	994
5. Phil Nevin	842
6. Terry Kennedy	817
7. Ryan Klesko	786
8. Nate Colbert	780
9. Benito Santiago	758
10. Bip Roberts	673

were committed to winning. He wanted me to keep playing and go to another team. I wanted to stay and maybe retire."

In the wake of his father's death, Tony reached an internal compromise. Stay and play. And he began putting the thoughts of Ted Williams into practice.

"That talk with Ted before the 1992 All-Star Game turned my career around," said Gwynn. "It changed the way I did things for the next nine years."

Nine of the greatest years in Padres history—starting with 1993. "That was the year I put all the information together...Ted's ideas, the video work, the batting practice. Even before spring training, I felt good about what I was doing. I had improved on everything. And the package was solid. I knew that a step forward in one area was a step forward elsewhere."

Gwynn hit .358 for the season. He had four games of five or more hits, tying a major league record shared by Ty Cobb, Stan Musial, and Willie Keeler. On August 6, he became the 193rd player in major league history to reach 2,000 hits with a single off Bruce Ruffin.

But the season ended just as had the previous three—with knee surgery.

PADRES
SUPERLATIVES

Silver Slugger Awards

	Player	No.	Pos.	Years
1.	Tony Gwynn	7	OF	1984, 1986–1987, 1989, 1994–1995, 1997
2.	Benito Santiago	4	C	1987–1988, 1990–1991
3.	Terry Kennedy	1	C	1983†
	Garry Templeton	1	SS	1984†
	Gary Sheffield	1	3B	1992†
	Fred McGriff	1	1B	1992†
	Ken Caminiti	1	3B	1996†
	Greg Vaughn	1	OF	1998†
	Mark Loretta	1	2B	2004†

However, the stage was set for the greatest run and greatest disappointment of Tony Gwynn's career—1994.

"I have never been locked in like that for an entire season," said Gwynn, looking back on 1994. "Too bad it ended like it did."

It wouldn't be surgery this time. It would be a far deeper cut to all of baseball—the strike that wiped out the last 50 games of the regular season as well as the playoffs and the World Series.

Gwynn was hitting .394 when play stopped on August 11. Had he had three more hits, Gwynn would have been at the magical .400 mark last achieved over a full season by Ted Williams in 1941.

"There's no doubt in my mind that had the 1994 season continued or resumed, I would have hit .400," says Gwynn, who was hitting .383 at the All-Star break before he went on a .423 run (47-for-111) over the last 28 games.

Gwynn's resolve had strengthened during the off-season because his weight, in the wake of three season-ending knee injuries, had again become an issue inside the Padres family. "I was going to show these folks that weight was not an issue even though they had made it one. I told myself, 'I'm going to have a good and healthy season.' Then came the strike."

Like all baseball players, Gwynn found the 1994–1995 off-season difficult. Players couldn't use club facilities because of the strike, which continued with no settlement in sight. "It really messed with my training and my head," said Gwynn.

What really messed with Gwynn's head, however, is what happened during the first round of batting practice once the strike was settled and spring training belatedly began. Gwynn had used only one bat during his aborted run at .400 in 1994. He labeled the bat "Nine Grains of Pain" for its unique construction.

"Best bat I ever had," says Gwynn. "It was perfectly balanced. The wood was perfect. Alicia wanted me to retire it after the 1994 season and mount it. But no, stupid me. Run it out there again in 1995. First round of batting practice, it breaks. I was worried it was going to be an omen."

It wasn't. Gwynn won his sixth National League batting championship and second straight—setting the stage for a great stretch run highlighted by a single hit by his brother.

Gwynn hit .353 in 1996 and won his seventh batting championship in 1996 as the Padres won their first National League West title since 1984. But Tony missed 46 games during the season.

On the penultimate day of the '96 campaign, Gwynn hit a two-run, two-out single in the eighth in Los Angeles to break a 2–2 tie and clinch the Padres a playoff berth. The following afternoon, however, it was another Gwynn, Chris, who hit a two-run, pinch-hit double in the eleventh to give the Padres a 2–0 win and the National League West title.

"When Chris hit that ball, my emotions soared," said Tony of the younger brother who had struggled to a .178 average during the season. "It was the best, the highlight of the year. Our dad had to be looking down with a huge smile on his face."

Many observers believe the 1997 season was Tony Gwynn's all-around best. At the age of 37, Gwynn posted career-highs in doubles (49), homers (17), and RBIs (119), and won his eighth (and last) batting title with a .372 mark. In fact, Gwynn, in his 16th season, became the oldest player ever to drive in 100 runs for the first time in a career. Gwynn batted an astounding .459 (67-for-146) with runners in scoring position and was 8-for-13 with the bases loaded. Tony also had the second (20 games) and third (19 games) hitting streaks of his career.

Aside from a bout of kidney stones, Gwynn was also healthy—for the last time in his career.

Gwynn believes the 1998 season was the most painful of his career. The heel problems that plagued him in 1996 returned. He spent much of the season trying to find a pair of shoes that would ease the pain stemming from an inflamed bursa sac. Finally, it was the Chargers' equipment manager, Sid Brooks, who came up with the answer—a pair of high-top cross-trainers outfitted with baseball cleats.

But the season climaxed with one of the greatest memories of Gwynn's career—opening the World Series at Yankee Stadium.

"When Yankees announcer Bob Sheppard announced my name in the lineup before the first game, I had chills," said Gwynn. "I rode the subway. I visited the monuments."

And he hit a two-run homer off the the second-deck façade in right off David Wells in the first game to give the Padres a short-lived 4–2 lead. "That homer," said Gwynn, "was the biggest hit of my career."

If not that hit, then the single that Gwynn hit the following August 6 in Montreal on the 64th birthday of his mother and the sixth anniversary of his 2,000[th] hit. No. 3,000.

"I hated that 3,000 hits became a publicity thing," said Gwynn, who also sort of hated that it happened in Montreal. It should have happened the previous homestand in San Diego.

"I needed 13 hits in that homestand to get 3,000 at home," said Gwynn. "I got seven. For the first time since 1986, I really gagged with the bat."

And if not in San Diego, Gwynn wanted number 3,000 to come August 5 in St. Louis. Gwynn got No. 2,999 in the same game that Mark McGwire hit his 500th homer.

As it happened, Gwynn remembers more of what happened after the hit than the single off Dan Smith itself. When he reached first, he was hugged by the umpire, former San Diego State teammate Kerwin Danley.

TOP 5

Sporting News All-National League Teams

Player	No.	Pos.	Years
1. Tony Gwynn	5	OF	1984, 1986–1987, 1989, 1994
2. Randy Jones	2t	LHP	1975–1976
Benito Santiago	2t	C	1987, 1989
Ken Caminiti	2t	3B	1995–1996
5. Gaylord Perry	1t	RHP	1978
Dave Winfield	1t	OF	1979
Mark Thurmond	1t	LHP	1984

"Out of the last 10 hits, number 3,000 was the easiest," said Gwynn. "I was calm in Montreal until I returned to the bench after the hit. I sat there for a moment, then it all hit me. The years to get there, my dad, my mom, who was there. Alicia and the kids. I got up and went up the tunnel and fell to my knees, crying like a baby. I can't remember ever crying more than I did that night."

Gwynn hit .338 in 1999, but he didn't have enough at-bats to qualify for a ninth batting title. And he would never come close again. His 2000 season ended after only 127 at-bats for an eighth round of surgery to his left knee.

While recuperating, Gwynn decided the 2001 season would be his last. But with whom? His contract with the Padres had expired. Cleveland and Kansas City sought Gwynn's service as a designated hitter in the American League. But at the last minute, the Padres came up with a one-year contract.

Gwynn would finish his career as a Padre. But his farewell tour would not be one of force. Throughout his career, Gwynn had had problems with his left knee and leg. In his 20th and final season, it was his good leg that failed him. On April 20, Gwynn suffered a strain deep inside his right hamstring while running out a double against the Dodgers. He missed most of the next nine weeks. And after he retired, Gwynn's right knee began to fail.

"That's been my foundation," Gwynn said looking down at a heavily bandaged right knee. "And now that's failed me, too."

Finally, Gwynn announced the obvious. Days after Cal Ripken announced that he would retire at the end of the 2001 season, Gwynn followed suit. From that point on, Gwynn was serenaded with cheers wherever the Padres played.

"I couldn't believe the fans' reaction," said Gwynn. "They even cheered me in Philadelphia...in Philadelphia. Everywhere we went, it was the same thing. I can't tell you how great that made me feel."

But the best was saved for last. On October 7, 2001, a capacity crowd at Qualcomm Stadium stayed around long after the final out of the season to bid Tony Gwynn a loving farewell. It was announced that night that Gwynn was headed directly to the Padres Hall of Fame. Five years later, the destination became Cooperstown.

TRIVIA

On April 3, 1987, what trio of Padres became the first players in major league history to open a game by hitting back-to-back-to-back homers?

Answers to the trivia questions are on pages 219–220.

They should let Greg Maddux deliver the introductory speech. Just before Gwynn's final season, Atlanta's trio of aces—Maddux, Tom Glavine, and John Smoltz—was asked how they pitch to Gwynn. Smoltz and Glavine laughed and deferred to Maddux, who had handcuffed Gwynn to the tune of .462 during his career.

"What do I do?" said Maddux. "Honest? If I throw it outside, he hammers it into the left-field corner. If I throw it inside, he pounds it to right. I just throw it down the middle and hope I hold him to a single."

Smoltz and Glavine had stopped laughing.

The Fall

The Padres went into the 1985 season favored to win their second straight National League West title.

In fact, it appeared general manager Jack McKeon had improved on the team that stunned the Cubs to win the National League pennant in 1984. Many observers believed the only thing the Padres lacked in 1984 was a first-rate starting pitcher.

McKeon filled that void by sending starting pitcher Tim Lollar, infielder Luis Salazar, and shortstop prospect Ozzie Guillen to the Chicago White Sox for number-one starter La Marr Hoyt. Hoyt was seen as the missing link. He would move to the top of the young rotation that included Andy Hawkins, Eric Show, Dave Dravecky, and Mark Thurmond.

"We were set," Tony Gwynn said, looking back on the spring of 1985. "I thought we were going to be around the top for years. We had a strong team in 1985, and there were a lot of good young players in the organization. "I thought we were at the start of a run."

Which stopped almost before it began.

On April 25, the Padres were preparing to open a three-game series at Los Angeles when a key member of the Padres turned up missing. Second baseman and leadoff hitter Alan Wiggins failed to appear at Dodger Stadium.

In 1984, Wiggins was the blasting cap at the top of the Padres' lineup. Although he hit only .258, he set franchise records with 70 steals and 106 runs scored and led the team with 75 walks. All told, he reached base more than 230 times.

But Wiggins was off to a horrible start in 1985. After 10 games, he had reached base only four times. He was hitting .054 after 37 at-bats. And on April 25, he disappeared. When Wiggins reappeared two days later, he was under the influence of drugs. Drugs had been part of Wiggins's past. Now they were back in his present. Which meant his future with the Padres was over.

Although Wiggins immediately entered a rehabilitation program, Padres owner Joan Kroc ordered the second baseman traded. He never played for the Padres again. And the Padres were never the team they were in 1984, although they hung around the top of the National League West through the first week of July.

Wiggins, a former first-round draft choice, was traded to Baltimore on June 27 for the proverbial "player to be named later." By that time, however, the damage to the Padres had been done.

"We didn't get over Wiggins, and we weren't the same team without him," said Gwynn. "Even in 1984, there were two Wiggins camps, players who liked him and those who didn't. Alan's problems in 1984 split the team.

"Wiggy and I hung together. When he disappeared, I took it hard. I never knew he had all those problems. He kept that part of his life away from me. I always wondered if I could have helped him had I known. But part of me also thinks Wiggy didn't want me involved to protect me. I loved the guy."

Wiggins wasn't the only problem splitting the Padres. The club started rebelling against the dictatorial rule of manager Dick Williams.

"The amazing thing about 1985 is that we stayed on top as long as we did," said Gwynn.

By the NUMBERS

1—Hit allowed by pitcher Jimmy Jones in his major league debut on September 21, 1986, defeating Houston 5–0.

7—Padres, plus manager Dick Williams, were named to the 1985 National League All-Star team.

22—Most Padres employed in a single game, on September 22, 1986.

34—Game-hitting streak for Benito Santiago in 1987, establishing major league records for a rookie and a catcher, in addition to setting the Padres club record.

At the end of June, the Padres were 15 games above .500 with a five-game lead in the National League West. Right-handed pitcher Andy Hawkins got off to an 11–0 start before he was slowed by a circulation problem in his right index finger. And over a two-month stretch through the All-Star break, La Marr Hoyt won 11 straight games.

But the Padres lost eight of 11 games on an eastern road trip just before the All-Star Game. By the end of the season, they would be only four games above .500 and 13 games off the pace.

The Padres had one last great moment—the All-Star Game in Minnesota. Seven Padres plus manager Dick Williams were part of the National League team. And Padres played prominent roles in the National League's 6–1 triumph. Five Padres started, including Hoyt, who was the game's Most Valuable Player. Padres catcher Terry Kennedy and first baseman Steve Garvey both singled home runs. Gwynn and third baseman Graig Nettles also started.

"But when it came time to get back to our normal work, we were done," said Gwynn. "I've never experienced anything like that season."

The Padres finished 83–79 and fell all the way from first to a tie for third in the National League West. On the plus side, the franchise, reaping the harvest of 1984, drew more than 2 million fans for the first time.

Following an off-season of confusion, matters really got bizarre. Dick Williams resigned as manager on the eve of spring training. The man who led the Padres to the 1984 National League pennant walked away.

"It was absolute turmoil," said Gwynn. "I go to report, and there's no manager. And 23 of the players are happy that Dick quit. It was like the winning side celebrating after a coup. Garry Templeton and I were not happy at all. But it was pointed out to us that we were in the minority.

"I can't say I was always happy to be playing for Dick Williams. He had a special way of pointing out your mistakes. He jumped all over you. But he forced you to be better. I learned a lot of baseball because of Dick Williams. I had to learn, because if I didn't he was going to bury me. A lot of players just couldn't handle that type of a

Steve Garvey spent the last five seasons of his distinguished major league career with the Padres. His No. 6 is retired thanks to that one historic swing of the bat against the Chicago Cubs on October 6, 1984.

man. Even then, the game had changed to a point where a tough ol' hombre like Dick had seen his time pass."

The Padres shifted gears. To replace the taskmaster Williams, the Padres hired the likable Steve Boros. "We weren't halfway through the season before players were griping about Steve," said Gwynn.

By this time, the Padres were in full plummet. The club that won 92 games in 1984 won only 74 in 1986. Nettles slipped to a .218 season. Staff ace Hoyt went from a 16–8 season with a 3.47 ERA to 8–11 with a 5.15 ERA in 1986.

And Hoyt's problems weren't restricted to the field. He had three drug-related encounters with authorities, culminating with an October 28 incident at the border. Hoyt was stopped by U.S. Customs returning from Tijuana. Stuffed in the groin area of his pants were 500 contraband pills ranging from sedatives to amphetamines.

Hoyt was done. So was Boros. And Joan Kroc wanted out.

Kroc's interest in owning the team her late husband loved was waning. Since 1985, son-in-law Ballard Smith had been running the Padres. But there was trouble inside the Smith marriage as well as the clubhouse. Led by Goose Gossage, players had rebelled against Kroc's decision to ban beer from the clubhouse.

Joan Kroc's interests were outside baseball. She became San Diego's leading philanthropist, supporting many of the region's leading charities and civic treasures.

"Mrs. Kroc was the kindest person I've ever met," said McKeon. "But she would never have owned a baseball team hadn't it been for Ray."

On March 26, 1987, Joan Kroc entered into an agreement to sell the Padres to George Argyros. Two months later, that sale was off. But Kroc was shopping the Padres, although it would take another three years to find what Kroc considered a suitable suitor.

Despite the instability at the top, general manager Jack McKeon kept searching for the missing pieces he believed would return the Padres to championship form.

"I never thought we were that far away," said McKeon.

The Padres might not be building a champion, but they were building a great farm system. John Kruk, who had been Tony Gwynn's rookie league teammate at Walla Walla, Washington, in 1981, reached the Padres in 1986 and hit .309 as a rookie. Also debuting in 1986 was right-handed pitcher Jimmy Jones, a first-round pick in 1982, who threw a one-hitter in his first game, a 5–0 victory over Houston on September 21.

And 1987 would see two more former first-round picks—outfielder Shane Mack (1984) and infielder Joey Cora (1985)—make their Padres debut.

But the rookie who electrified all of baseball in 1987 was Padres catcher Benito Santiago.

As well as the Padres had done in the draft, they were reaping even bigger rewards in Latin America, starting with the signing of shortstop Ozzie Guillen out of Venezuela in 1980. Santiago was the first of four future major league players the Padres discovered in Puerto Rico over a four-year span. He signed with the Padres as a free agent. The next year, the Padres signed another catcher out of

Puerto Rico—Sandy Alomar Jr. And in 1985, the Padres signed a pair of Puerto Rican infielders—Sandy's brother Roberto and Carlos Baerga.

Twenty-two-year-old Santiago was an immediate favorite with Padres fans in his first full year in the majors in 1987.

"Not everything he did was textbook," said teammate Tim Flannery of Santiago. "But he was dazzling. He was a different type of catcher—lean and athletic. And the fans loved how he would throw bullets to second with pinpoint accuracy from his knees."

A buzz would go through Jack Murphy Stadium whenever a fast runner reached base.

And toward the end of the season, Santiago put on one of the greatest hitting feats in Padres history. He hit in 34 straight games—the longest streak ever by a Padre, the longest streak ever by a catcher, and the longest streak ever by a rookie.

His streak appeared over at 32 games on October 1 when he was 0-for-3 against Cincinnati as he faced right-hander Frank Williams in his final at-bat. Santiago laid down a perfect bunt for a single. Did we mention Santiago could also run (he stole 21 bases as a rookie)? Although the Dodgers' Orel Hershiser put a halt to Santiago's streak, the catcher went 2-for-2 on the final day of the season to hit an even .300.

After the season, Santiago was a unanimous choice as the National League's Rookie of the Year—the only Padre to ever win the award.

"It was a magical year," Santiago said years later. "It was exciting for me because it seemed like I excited the fans. You know, we pumped it up, as they like to say."

There were some great highs to 1987. On April 13, the Padres scored a major league first when their first three hitters in the game—Marvell Wynne, Tony Gwynn, and John Kruk—homered in succession off the Giants' Roger Mason. The game happened to be the home opener, and the crowd of 48,686 went crazy. "The first was off a fastball, the second off a curve, and the third off a change-up," said Mason. "It's a good thing I don't have a slider."

"I looked at Tony and asked, where do we go from here?" said Kruk.

DID YOU KNOW . . . That catchers hold the two longest hitting streaks in Padres history? Benito Santiago set the Padres record, and the major league records for rookies and catchers with a 34-game hitting streak in 1987. In 1996, John Flaherty hit safely in 27 straight games.

Sadly, the answer was down. The Padres not only lost that game (13–6), they would lose 97 games in 1987.

The highlights to the 1987 season included Gwynn winning his second batting title with a .370 mark—the highest average in the National League since Stan Musial hit .376 in 1948—and Santiago and Kruk taking over at first base in June and finishing with a .313 average with 20 homers and 91 RBIs.

The Padres manager in 1987 was Larry Bowa, the fiery former National League infielder who had led the Padres Triple A affiliate at Las Vegas to the Pacific Coast League championship in 1986. Because Bowa was young and had worked with so many of the Padres' young prospects, general manager Jack McKeon believed Bowa was the perfect pick to replace Steve Boros.

He was wrong.

Players balked at many of Bowa's ideas, including the daily two-mile run to open spring training workouts.

"Some of the players who had gotten used to Steve Boros's easy-going ways were really intimidated by Bowa," said Gwynn. "He was a screamer. He was demanding. He managed just as he played the game, full throttle all the time. Playing for Larry was an experience. But he'd also do anything for you, although I don't think some of the players ever saw that."

There wasn't much time to see it. After the Padres got off to a 16–30 start in 1988, general manager McKeon fired Bowa (career managing record with the Padres 81–127) and replaced him with manager Jack McKeon.

"I answer only to one man, myself," joked McKeon.

And McKeon had some great answers for his boss.

Under McKeon, the Padres went 67–48 over the rest of the season—including 34–19 at home—and finished third in the National

That Dick Freeman has served two terms as Padres president? Freeman, who first joined the Padres as chief financial officer in 1981, was first named president in 1988 and oversaw two sales of the club. He returned as president and chief operating officer on October 1, 2002, with the opening of PETCO Park in 2004 being his prime responsibility.

League West. The Alomar brothers would both reach the major league team, where they would be under the watchful eye of their father, Sandy, who was the Padres' third base coach.

The season ended on a sour note, however. Midway through the 1987 season, Joan Kroc named former National League president Charles S. "Chub" Feeney the Padres' president. Although Feeney, who had previously spent 24 seasons guiding the fortunes of the New York and San Francisco Giants, was considered a knowledgeable baseball man, he became something of a lightning rod in San Diego.

Lightning struck Jack Murphy Stadium on September 24, which also happened to be Fan Appreciation Night. During the game, television cameras spotted several fans parading through the grandstands with a "Scrub Chub" sign. The cameras then turned to the press box and caught a very agitated Feeney reacting to the sign with a single-finger salute.

Among Joan Kroc's guests in the owner's box that night was San Diego Mayor Maureen O'Connor, who saw the incident and ratted out Feeney to the club owner. Feeney resigned the next day.

With Feeney gone, McKeon was pretty much in total control. Given a free hand to wheel and deal, Trader Jack wheeled and dealed. Some of McKeon's trades were truly huge. Most were controversial. In 1987, for example, he moved third baseman Kevin Mitchell, relief pitcher Craig Lefferts, and starting pitcher Dave Dravecky to division-rival San Francisco for third baseman Chris Brown and relief pitchers Mark Davis and Mark Grant. Davis won the National League Cy Young Award as a Padre in 1989. But Mitchell and Dravecky became keys for the Giants.

Some of his trades had a humorous side. On June 8, 1988, for example, McKeon acquired right-handed pitcher Dennis Rasmussen from the Reds for right-handed pitcher Candy Sierra. The Reds happened to be in San Diego at the time. All Rasmussen had to do was move from one clubhouse at Jack Murphy Stadium to the other. "Saved us airfare," said McKeon, "so we're dollars ahead." They also happened to be games ahead. Rasmussen went 14–4 with a 2.55 ERA in his last 20 starts with the Padres in 1988.

Just after the close of the 1988 season, McKeon acquired slugger Jack Clark from the Yankees for pitchers Jimmy Jones and Lance McCullers and outfielder Stan Jefferson. And in the following June, the Padres traded away another home-grown player (John Kruk) and utility infielder Randy Ready to acquire outfielder Chris James from the Phillies.

But the Padres' biggest acquisition going into the 1989 season was left-handed pitcher Bruce Hurst, who signed as a free agent. Hurst and Ed Whitson proved to be one of the best tandems in the National League. Whitson was 16–11 with a 2.66 ERA, and Hurst was 15–11 with a 2.69 ERA.

The Padres' 1989 season ended with one of the greatest stretch runs in franchise history. The San Diego that was 42–46 at the All-Star break went 47–27 in the second half of the season and 27–9 down the stretch—closing from being 10 games out to within three of the division-winning Giants.

The Padres were finally eliminated by Cincinnati on September 27 in one of their toughest losses of any season. The game was tied 1–1 in the thirteenth when the Reds' Eric Davis came to the plate with a runner on second and two outs. First base was open, and manager McKeon favored intentionally walking Davis—who already had 20 RBIs against the Padres that season—in favor of pitching to Todd Benzinger. But Padres reliever Calvin Schiraldi talked McKeon out of walking Davis—then gave up a decisive hit.

It was another Davis who made headlines for the Padres. Mark Davis became the third—and most recent—Padres pitcher to win the National League Cy Young Award. Working in 70 games, Davis had 44

TRIVIA

Who is the only Padre named the Most Valuable Player of the All-Star Game?

Answers to the trivia questions are on pages 219–220.

saves—one shy of the National League record at the time—with a 1.85 ERA.

The end of the 1989 season marked a number of turning points in Padres history. Popular infielder Tim Flannery retired as a player after 10 seasons with the Padres. Scheduled to become a free agent at the end of the season, Flannery announced his retirement two days before the season ended to guarantee that his entire career would be completed under contract to the Padres. Flannery's playing career with the Padres might be over, but his time with the organization was just beginning. Flannery spent seven seasons as the Padres' third base coach (1996–2002), then worked as a play-by-play radio broadcaster before leaving the organization after the 2006 season to follow long-time friend Bruce Bochy to San Francisco as a Giants coach.

A lot more change was to come.

In December of 1989, McKeon completed one of the more controversial trades in Padres history—sending brilliant young prospects Sandy Alomar Jr. and Carlos Baerga plus outfielder Chris James to Cleveland in a 3-for-1 deal for slugging outfielder Joe Carter.

Padres fans were also stung by the loss of Mark Davis just months after he won the Cy Young Award. Eligible for free agency at the end of the 1989 season, Davis was signed by the Kansas City Royals.

"I didn't want it to happen," Davis said later. "I wanted to stay with the Padres. But they never made a real offer. I think they had a lot of other things going on at the time."

That is an understatement.

The 1990 season would see the third transfer of ownership in the Padres history. Turmoil would follow.

Sad Sale

On April 2, 1990, an era ended for the Padres. Joan Kroc sold the team to Los Angeles television producer Tom Werner.

At the time, it was a sad day for the Padres—their fans as well as the players.

"Sometimes, things are special," first baseman Jack Clark said upon hearing the news. "They can't be replaced. And they're not supposed to be." And Clark had been a member of the Padres family for only one year.

Most members of the Padres were hoping that the deal would fall through, just as the 1987 sale to George Argyros had. They were hoping that Joan Kroc would again have a change of heart.

"I was really surprised when the announcement of the sale to Tom Werner was announced," said Tony Gwynn. "We knew the club had been for sale since the previous October. I just didn't think it would happen. But she had had enough."

The joy of 1984 was a distant memory.

Ray Kroc's widow had employed four club presidents, including two sons-in-law. Dealing with the drug problems of Alan Wiggins and La Marr Hoyt had taken a toll. So had the less-than-amicable departure of manager Dick Williams—some would call it a firing— in the spring of 1986. Then came Goose Gossage's suspension for his "insubordinate" comments following the clubhouse beer ban.

Those events triggered the sale to Argyros. But Kroc then had a change of heart after that sale fell through.

"I thought she was enjoying owning the club again," said general manager and manager Jack McKeon, who remembered a meeting Kroc held with the players in 1987.

TRIVIA

On August 6, 1992, these Padres set a major league record by hitting back-to-back homers in back-to-back innings. Who were they?

Answers to the trivia questions are on pages 219–220.

"We were struggling, and she came down and told the team she loved it and she was keeping it in the Kroc and San Diego family," said McKeon.

But Joan Kroc's last months with the Padres were spent trying to find a successor she believed was suitable.

"While I will be relinquishing ownership of the Padres, I will not be relinquishing my status as a loyal and enthusiastic supporter of this team," she said after the $75 million sale.

And Kroc believed she had found the right man in the 39-year-old Werner because 11 of his 14 minority partners were among San Diego's financial and civic leaders. What ensued, however, was five seasons of chaos until Werner's group sold to John Moores.

Werner did rebuild the Padres. Then he ripped them apart through the franchise's notorious "fire sale." He threatened to move the franchise. And he had Roseanne Barr sing the national anthem in probably the biggest single promotional mistake—and there have been many to choose from—in Padres history.

"He didn't exactly endear himself to the community," said Gwynn years later. "It was like we were off in some different direction every day."

Actually, the transition from Kroc to Werner's group had gone smoothly. Even though she had announced she was selling the Padres the previous October, Kroc approved the acquisition of free agents Jack Clark and Bruce Hurst, although the Padres did lose Cy Young Award–winning pitcher Mark Davis to free agency.

Sadly, Kroc's team also rubber-stamped one of the more controversial trades in Padres history. On December 6, 1989, McKeon, who had regained control of baseball operations in a power struggle with club president Dick Freeman, traded two home-grown prospects—catcher Sandy Alomar Jr. and infielder Carlos Baerga—plus outfielder Chris James to Cleveland for outfielder Joe Carter.

Baerga and Alomar would both go on to All-Star careers. Carter, meantime, would be moved again on December 5, 1990, going to

Toronto along with All-Star second baseman Roberto Alomar for Fred McGriff and shortstop Tony Fernandez.

In less than a year, the Padres had bid farewell to three-fourths of their coveted crop of Latin American finds. Almost two decades later, the Padres still haven't found their next Latin American star.

Meanwhile, Werner earned high marks off his first appearances in San Diego, which, like many communities, can be cool to outsiders. After all, his group included such local luminaries as Art Engel, Malin Burnham, Art Rivkin, Robert Payne, and Leon Parma.

Werner's share of the ownership package was 35 percent, which gave him the authority to make decisions. And he started making them shortly after the sale was finalized on June 15. Less than a month later, Jack McKeon turned over the managing reins to Greg Riddoch during the All-Star break. For McKeon, the second shoe fell days before the end of the season when he was fired as the Padres general manager.

Looking back, McKeon remains one of the more controversial figures in Padres history. He is credited for being the architect of the 1984 National League championship team. But McKeon's legacy includes later trades that stripped the Padres of much of their young home-grown talent in desperate—and eventually futile—attempts to land the Padres that one missing piece standing between them and a return to the playoffs.

Jack McKeon's 11-year reign as the Padres general manager was almost three times longer than any other man in the position until Kevin Towers started his ongoing run in 1996.

While Padres partisans were still digesting Werner's decision to replace McKeon as manager with Riddoch, Werner made a decision that haunted him throughout his ownership. To this day, it remains one of the more controversial moments in Padres history.

DID YOU KNOW . . . That the Padres removed brown from their uniform colors before the 1991 season, replacing it with navy blue?

Werner was a power in Hollywood. The Harvard grad from New York had made his fortune co-producing such television mega-hits as *The Cosby Show* and *Roseanne*.

Soon after Werner took control of the Padres, Roseanne Barr, the star of the nation's top-rated television show, asked Werner if she could sing the national anthem at a Padres game. Werner offered her the opportunity to sing the "Star-Spangled Banner" between games of a Padres-Cincinnati doubleheader scheduled for July 25 at Jack Murphy Stadium.

It wasn't until Werner offered Barr the invitation that he ran it past his underlings in the club's public relations and production departments. "Can she sing?" was one question raised. Another question is whether she would agree to tape the singing and lip-sync the finished product, which was the club's procedure for most singers.

Werner didn't know if she could sing. But he wasn't about to ask his star to lip-sync.

To make matters worse, as Barr prepared to sing the national anthem before a near-capacity crowd, a Padres player jokingly asked her if she was going to mimic baseball players and grab her crotch and spit on the ground. For some reason, that's what she decided to do—during her "rendition" of the national anthem.

Now, it's important here to understand San Diego. This corner of the United States grew and matured with the U.S. Navy. In addition to being one of the Navy's largest ports, San Diego County is home to two large Marine Corps bases and two Naval air bases.

No one recognizes this connection to the military better than the Padres, who have long hosted a contingent of Marine recruits for every Sunday afternoon game and have a number of military promotions—including a special Military Opening Day—throughout the season.

Against this backdrop, Barr began to sing into a microphone set up behind home plate. Actually, she started to scream what has conservatively been called the "Barr-Mangled Banner."

Shortly after she started, the crowd began to boo. She said she was trying to be funny. Few on hand found any humor in the performance. Even in the best of times, Barr didn't have the singing talent to pull off the national anthem. But as she plunged forward,

One member of the Padres entourage who never laid an egg was the Chicken. The club's unofficial mascot in the 1970s and 1980s became an ambassador to all of baseball. The man inside the suit is Ted Giannoulas, who began the gig as a promotion for a radio station while at San Diego State.

the boos grew in volume. Barr put her fingers in her ears and screamed louder. And the boos grew. And when she was finished, her coup de grâce was to grab her crotch and spit on the ground. What followed was the strongest reaction to anything in Padres history. This booing was ugly and menacing. Barr and her husband, Tom Arnold, were escorted from the stadium.

In his box upstairs, Werner was caught in a no-man's land. He couldn't criticize his star, but his customers wanted blood...well, at least an explanation. Werner hid from the media behind a locked door, sending out an underling to take the heat. The incident would haunt him throughout his ownership.

0—Padres who have pitched a no-hitter or hit for the cycle.

2—All-Star Games hosted by the Padres in San Diego in 1978 and 1992.

35—Homers by Fred McGriff in 1992, the only time a Padre has led the National League in homers.

But that incident wasn't the only bump in the road for the Padres in 1990. The Kroc-Werner transition season was filled with controversy, including a feud between the team's two offensive leaders, Tony Gwynn and Jack Clark.

The die seemed to be cast with the December 1989 decision to make the three-for–Joe Carter trade. McKeon's stubborn decision to trade both Sandy Alomar Jr. and Carlos Baerga created a rift, not only with the player-development side but with other players. "We had so many good young players who were traded away in about three years there," Tony Gwynn said years later. "You just can't give up your young players like that."

And Chris James was a catalyst in a clubhouse that had issues— most notably Clark versus Gwynn. The feud started when Clark openly charged Gwynn with being "a selfish son of a bitch." Clark proclaimed Gwynn was nothing more than a "table setter" and charged Gwynn with being "more interested in his batting average than if the team won or lost."

The problems began when Gwynn drag bunted one night with runners on first and second with none out.

"It was the way I learned how to play the game," said Gwynn. "The bunt was there. We had a shot at loading the bases with none out."

But Clark attacked the play and Gwynn. He claimed the only reason Gwynn bunted was to "protect his beloved batting average."

"There was a big meeting in New York in May," said Gwynn. "There were Clark guys and there were Gwynn guys. And there were more Clark guys than Gwynn guys. They blasted me and I blasted them back. And I said some things to Jack I probably shouldn't have said."

At one point in the meeting, Clark threw a soft drink across the clubhouse and charged that Gwynn got too much attention in the media for a player who didn't have that big of an influence on the outcome of a game.

"Once Clark brought that 'selfish' stuff to the surface, it became a very difficult year," said Gwynn, who began to believe it was his last season as a Padre, particularly after McKeon was replaced first as the manager and then as the general manager.

Gwynn finished with a .309 batting average—the lowest of his career. And the Padres went 40–52 from the end of June through the end of a disappointing season.

Disappointment was everywhere. Carter hit .232, although he did have 24 homers and 115 RBIs. Clark hit .266 with 25 homers, but only 62 RBIs. The unheralded hero of the season was the versatile switch-hitter Bip Roberts, who started games at six positions and hit .309 with 104 runs scored and 46 stolen bases.

The off-season brought considerable change, but it didn't involve Gwynn.

General manager Joe McIlvaine let Clark go to the Red Sox via free agency. And he pulled off a controversial blockbuster of his own—sending Joe Carter and Roberto Alomar to Toronto for first baseman Fred McGriff and shortstop Tony Fernandez. Carter and Roberto Alomar would become key players for the Blue Jays teams that won the World Series in 1992 and '93.

The Padres needed Fernandez because one of the club's cornerstone players retired at the end of the tumultuous 1990 season. Garry Templeton finished his 16-season career with 2,096 hits. A decade of that career had been spent with the Padres—much of it as the team captain—after he came from St. Louis in the 1992 trade for future Hall of Famer Ozzie Smith. Templeton's 1,135 hits are second on the Padres all-time list to Gwynn. Templeton, who hit .246 as a Padre, also ranks second to Gwynn among the franchise's all-time leaders in games played (1,286), at-bats (4,512), and doubles (195), and ranks sixth in both RBIs (427) and runs scored (430).

Perhaps because they lamented the loss of Smith, Padres fans never gave Templeton the credit he deserved. And while he didn't have the range, speed, or athletic ability of Smith at short, Templeton had one of the game's best arms and first-step reactions. Many observers of Padres history believe Templeton deserves a spot in the club's Hall of Fame.

Under manager Greg Riddoch, who is considered one of the game's premier instructors, the Padres of 1991 and 1992 emerged as one of the top offensive teams in the National League. Both editions finished third in the National League West.

Fred McGriff led the 1991 Padres with 31 homers and 106 RBIs. The following season, he led the National League with 35 homers and drove in 104 runs. Tony Gwynn batted .317 in both seasons.

Just before the start of the 1992 season, the Padres added one of the more potent bats ever to represent San Diego. The Padres sent three players to Milwaukee to acquire third baseman Gary Sheffield, who made a run at the becoming the first National Leaguer to win the Triple Crown since Joe Medwick in 1937.

Sheffield won the batting title with a .330 average. Not only was he, at 23, the youngest player to win the title since the Dodgers' Tommy Davis in 1962, he was—and still is—the only Padre other than Tony Gwynn to win the batting title. Sheffield also hit 33 homers to finish third (two homers behind McGriff) and was fifth in the league with 100 RBIs (nine behind the Phillies' Darren Daulton). Sheffield, who had hit only .194 in 1991 with the Brewers, finished third in the voting for the Most Valuable Player award.

"I think that team had the greatest 1-2 combination in Padres history and one of the best I've ever seen anywhere," said Tony Gwynn. "That team could bang."

"I would have matched the top of our batting order in 1992 with anyone's in baseball," said Riddoch. "Tony Fernandez and Tony Gwynn followed by Sheffield from the right side and McGriff from the left side. And Benito [Santiago] was so dangerous in the number five slot."

Inside the numbers were some amazing feats.

On August 13 and 14, 1991, Fred McGriff became only the fourth player in major league history to hit grand slams in back-to-back games. On August 6, 1992, Sheffield and McGriff hit back-to-back homers in both the first and second innings of a 7–5 victory over Houston.

The strangest part of the 1991 and 1992 seasons was the pitching. Left-hander Bruce Hurst and right-hander Andy Benes, the Padres' first-round pick in the 1988 draft, gave the Padres a potent 1-2 punch at the top of the rotation. The pair worked 444⅔ innings between them in 1991 and 448⅔ innings the following season.

In 1991, Benes was 15–11 with a 3.03 ERA and won 11 of his last 12 starts of the season. And Hurst was 15–8 with a 3.29 ERA. But 11 other pitchers made starts.

"Who knows what we could have done had we made the decision on Greg Harris earlier," said Riddoch.

The curve-balling Harris had been a reliever until the Padres promoted him from the minors in June and put him in the rotation. He responded with a 9–5 record and 2.23 ERA in 20 starts. And on August 10 and 15, he became the first Padres pitcher to win back-to-back 1–0 games. First he held Cincinnati to six hits, then he stopped Atlanta on three hits.

The Harris experiment worked so well that, in 1992, the Padres converted another reliever into a starter. Craig Lefferts responded with a 13–9 record and a 3.69 ERA. Hurst was 14–9 with a 3.85 ERA, and Benes was 13–14 with a 3.35 ERA.

"But we couldn't put together a complete rotation either season," said Riddoch, who was fired as the Padres manager on September 23, 1992, and replaced by Jim Riggleman. "If we could have found a fourth and fifth starter in either season, I think we would have won the National League West."

The highlight of the 1992 season came on July 14, when San Diego hosted its second—and most recent—All-Star Game. San Diego native and Hall of Famer Ted Williams escorted President George H. W. Bush to the mound to throw out the ceremonial first pitch.

TRIVIA

In 1991, Padres outfielder Darrin Jackson had 21 homers. How many RBIs did he have?

Answers to the trivia questions are on pages 219–220.

First baseman Fred McGriff, right fielder Tony Gwynn, and catcher Benito Santiago were starters for the National League. Third baseman Gary Sheffield and shortstop Tony Fernandez were also members of the National League team.

"All season, the mood was great," recalled McGriff years later. "We were so close. We were a pitcher or two away. And then we were all away."

Owner Tom Werner decided to cut his losses.

The best way to do that was slash payroll. The Padres would be sold off piece by piece—and then just sold.

DID YOU KNOW . . . That second baseman Roberto Alomar was the youngest Padre named to an All-Star Game when he was selected for the National League team in 1990 at the age of 22?

The Gang

At the end of the 1992 season, Padres owner Tom Werner decided to change course.

Not only had the contending teams he built fallen short, they had lost money. And his ownership consortium—now referred to as "the Gang of 15" by Padres partisans—didn't have the deep pockets of Ray and Joan Kroc.

Werner was trying to run the Padres as a business. And as a businessman, he was responsible to the bottom line and his partners.

The status quo was a no-go.

Suddenly, Werner started talking of San Diego as a "small market" team. He raised the possibility that the Padres could be moved—something San Diegans hadn't heard since Ray Kroc bought the Padres from founder C. Arnholt Smith in 1974.

"That put the San Diegans in the ownership group in a very uncomfortable position," said one of the local minority owners. "None of us wanted to be involved in the Padres leaving San Diego."

What was Werner to do? When revenue can't keep pace with expenses, the only solution is to cut expenses. In baseball, the biggest—and most controllable—expense is payroll.

Werner decided to reduce the payroll. Reduce? More like slash.

There were few signs of what was to come during the 1992–1993 off-season. General manager Joe McIlvaine even acquired another bat, obtaining Phil Plantier, who had played high school ball in San Diego County, from Boston for relief pitcher Jose Melendez. And days before the season began, the Padres swapped center fielders with Toronto, sending Darrin Jackson to the Blue Jays for Derek Bell.

However, the Padres had done nothing to treat the Achilles heel of 1991 and 1992—the starting rotation. And as Opening Day approached, staff ace Bruce Hurst was ailing. Opening Day starter Andy Benes would become the only pitcher to start in more than 25 games for the Padres throughout the disturbing 1993 season.

The Padres started slowly...and went downhill from there.

On June 9, Randy Smith was named the Padres general manager, replacing McIlvaine. The son of veteran baseball executive Tal Smith,

Gary Sheffield, shown here with childhood friend Darryl Strawberry, is the only Padre not named Tony Gwynn to win the National League batting title. Acquired from Milwaukee in a trade just before the start of the 1992 season, Sheffield batted .330 for the Padres with 33 homers and 100 RBIs and finished third in the MVP voting. He was traded to Florida the following June as part of the Padres infamous "fire sale." The little-known player the Padres got in return was Trevor Hoffman.

Randy Smith originally joined the Padres in 1984 at the age of 20 as an assistant in the scouting and player development department. Four years later, then–general manager Jack McKeon promoted Smith to be the club's scouting director.

Smith was considered one of the brightest young minds in baseball when the Padres made him the youngest general manager in major league history at the time. Smith knew what his role with the Padres would be. He was there to reduce the payroll. Werner wanted to eliminate San Diego's biggest salaries. Smith would be the hatchet man. The media would give the process a title that still sends chills along the spines of Padres fans: "fire sale." Smith would bristle at the term. Yes, his job was to reduce payroll. Most of the high-priced stars would be eliminated. But he didn't want to dismantle the ballclub.

"When you are going through something like we faced, your hands are tied to a point," said Smith. "But you are still trying to get the best players in return and rebuild with an eye for the future."

Given his marching orders, Smith did an exemplary job that helped position the Padres for a brighter future. But in 1993–1994, Smith was assigned the task of delivering a message no Padres fan wanted to hear.

Fifteen days after becoming the Padres general manager, Smith started the dismantling. The first to go was All-Star third baseman Gary Sheffield, who was hitting .295 with 10 homers in 68 games on June 24 when he was traded to the expansion Florida Marlins for three young right-handed pitchers—Jose Martinez, Andres Berumen, and a hard-throwing shortstop-turned-reliever named Trevor Hoffman. For his Triple Crown run in 1992, Sheffield had received a healthy raise from $750,000 to $3.11 million. Sheffield's trade to the Marlins immediately lopped $2.75 million off the payroll.

Next to go was All-Star first baseman Fred McGriff. He was hitting .275 with 18 homers and 46 RBIs in 83 games with the Padres when he was traded to Atlanta on July 18 for outfielder Melvin Nieves and pitcher Donnie Elliott—neither of whom ever did much in a Padres uniform. McGriff's trade to the Braves lopped another $4 million off the payroll.

Eight days later, Smith sent two-fifths of the Padres' rotation—Hurst and Greg Harris—to the Colorado Rockies for catcher Brad Ausmus and right-handed pitchers Andy Ashby and Doug Bochtler.

The immediate savings to the Padres of that trade was close to another $4 million—meaning Smith had cut almost $11 million from the payroll in just over his first month on the job. And looking down the road at the long-term implications of the contracts dumped, the savings topped $25 million.

But at what cost?

The Padres now stunk as a team. And the fans were turned off en masse. The 1993 Padres lost 101 games—a 21-game plunge from the previous season and San Diego's first (and only) 100-loss season since those hapless expansion Padres lost 100 or more games in four of their first six years.

And the Padres lost at the gate as well as on the field. Attendance fell by more than 400,000. An average of more than 5,000 fans were missing from Jack Murphy Stadium every night.

There was little to celebrate about 1993. Phil Plantier finished with 34 homers and 100 RBIs. And fellow newcomer Derek Bell hit 21 homers with 72 RBIs. Given the circumstances, Andy Benes had one of the stronger pitching seasons in Padres' history—going 15–15 with a 3.78 ERA. His win count represented almost a quarter of the Padres' total.

And there was Tony Gwynn. There was always Tony Gwynn. He hit .358 during a season that saw him record three milestones. On August 4, Gwynn had the only six-hit game of his career during a 12-inning, 11–10 victory over San Francisco. Gwynn had four games during the season with five or more hits, tying a major league record set by Wee Willie Keeler in 1897 and tied by Ty Cobb in 1922 and Stan Musial in 1948.

Two days later, Gwynn got the 2,000th hit of his career on his mother's birthday.

Gwynn fell short of another goal that season. Playing at home on June 10 against the Dodgers, Gwynn homered in the third inning, doubled in the fifth, and tripled in the sixth. Gwynn was a single shy of becoming the first Padre to hit for the cycle—one shot through the 5.5 hole. But with the Padres leading 11–2, manager Jim Riggleman

TRIVIA

What was the first spring training home of the Padres?

Answers to the trivia questions are on pages 219–220.

decided to give Gwynn a chance to rest his troublesome left knee. Riggleman was unaware that Gwynn had a shot at the cycle. Gwynn knew, but never mentioned it to the manager.

"I was only two years removed from the Jack Clark trouble," Gwynn said years later. "I was very aware of how I was being perceived by other players. That selfish thing bugged the heck out of me. What happens if I tell Rigs, 'Skipper, I have a chance at the cycle,' when he tells me I'm coming out of the game? It could have blown up in my face."

After the game, Riggleman apologized to Gwynn upon learning of the lost opportunity. "He got upset with me that I kept my mouth shut," said Gwynn. "Everyone thought it was Jim's fault. Then I started feeling bad for what I did to Riggleman. Sometimes, you just can't win."

Call it the hitter's side of the Clay Kirby no-hitter curse. No Padre has ever hit for the cycle.

"You know, I always believed it would happen for me," said Gwynn. "I never saw the cycle as being that difficult...that one day you'd get one if you continued to have success at the plate. The odds just had to say it was going to happen, right?"

Wrong.

Toward the end of his playing career, Gwynn and Hoffman were standing together in the corner of the Padres' clubhouse when they were asked about the fire sale of 1993.

"It was an extremely unsettling time," said Hoffman. "There was a lot of hostility from the fans to the players who came to the Padres as the replacements in the fire sale. And inside the clubhouse, you were always waiting for the next round of news. Everyone thought they were on the block."

PADRES SUPERLATIVES

Padres' Longest Hitting Streaks

	Player	Year	Games
1.	Benito Santiago	1987	34
2.	John Flaherty	1996	27
3.	Tony Gwynn	1983	25
4.	Bip Roberts	1994	23
5.	Bobby Brown	1983	21†
	Steve Finley	1996	21†
7.	Tony Gwynn	1997	20

Gwynn's locker at Jack Murphy Stadium was adjacent to the manager's office. "When it started, when we lost Sheff and McGriff, every time that phone would ring, you'd get chills. You'd instantly start looking around."

And as bad as 1993 was, 1994 was worse.

But this time, it had nothing to do with the Padres owners. The season stopped dead on August 12. The players walked out. And instead of starting to work on a solution, the two sides—the players and the owners—quickly polarized their positions. Not only was the regular season canceled, the World Series was scrubbed.

At the time of the strike, Tony Gwynn was three hits shy of being at a .400 pace—an average that no player had carried through an entire season since Ted Williams in 1941.

"I was naïve," said Gwynn. "I thought we'd be back."

The Padres were wrapping up a road trip as the strike approached. The players were uncertain as to whether or not the club would fly them home. When they reached the airport, they learned their plane had a flat tire.

"We sat there for six hours waiting for the plane to be fixed," said Gwynn.

The strike was the last straw for Werner and his partners. With most of the local minority owners wanting out of the program, Werner put the team up for sale. Who was going to buy a baseball team in the middle of the longest work stoppage in the game's history?

John Moores

Ray Kroc's game was hamburgers. John Moores's is computer software. But the two most successful owners in Padres history have much in common—both were self-made men with few pretensions from middle-class backgrounds. And like Kroc, Moores had a love of baseball. Which is what led him to discussions with Tom Werner in late 1994 about the purchase of the Padres.

The Harvard-educated Hollywood producer wanted out. The computer magnate in blue jeans wanted in. And Moores didn't need financial partners to pull it off.

"Having the chance to own a major league baseball team, that was a dream," said Moores after becoming the fourth and most recent man to control the Padres' fortunes in San Diego.

And like Kroc, Moores poured himself and his bankroll into the Padres. When pressure was needed, Moores could apply it with the best of them.

For the Padres to succeed, he said they needed a new ballpark. If it didn't happen, Moores said he would have to move the team. If it did, Moores was willing to make a decades-long commitment to San Diego. The result: PETCO Park.

"John is willing to take gambles," Padres general manager Kevin Towers said. "But when you present him an idea, you better be ready to back up your argument with facts."

Soon after taking over the Padres, Moores said his goal was to make the ballclub a success. "Does that mean winning?" someone asked. "With success comes winning," responded Moores.

John Moores was born on July 9, 1944. A native Texan, Moores attended public schools and married his childhood sweetheart at

Like Ray Kroc more than two decades earlier, self-made Texas software entrepreneur John Moores likely saved the Padres for San Diego when he purchased them on December 21, 1994. Under Moores, the Padres won the National League pennant in 1998 and built a new ballpark in the heart of San Diego's downtown redevelopment district.

the age of 19. Soon, the Moores were raising a family. John Moores worked full-time as a computer programmer while studying at night at the University of Houston.

Moores's knowledge of computers and software was not gained through formal education. "On the job experience," he jokes. "A lot of trial and error. You know how that works."

While working as an independent software consultant in 1980, Moores founded BMC Software, Inc. Huge company. John Moores was the firm's only shareholder and programmer. Working alone, Moores wrote the first of the series of software products that BMC marketed to improve mainframe computer operating system performance.

BMC Software rapidly grew and expanded its line of software products and services. Moores served as the CEO of the firm until

1987 and was the chairman of the board through 1992. To this day, Moores continues to apply his skill and knowledge to the development of computer software.

"I've always enjoyed helping people getting started," said Moores. "I know. Software is a tough business."

Which made him perfect for baseball.

Moores made his initial overtures about buying the Padres after the players went on strike in the late summer of 1994. There was no question that Werner's unwieldy team of 15 owners wanted out.

Moores finalized his purchase on December 21, 1994, while the players were still on strike. Moores came in with a plan and a strong team. During the purchase process, Moores came to the conclusion that the Padres needed a home to call their own. The city was just about to embark on a third expansion of then Jack Murphy Stadium that would stretch the capacity to almost 70,000 seats while fully encircling the field with grandstands.

"Baseball demands a more intimate setting," said Moores, who named Larry Lucchino the club president with the charge of developing a plan to build a new ballpark with community support.

Shortly after taking over, Moores began upgrading every aspect of the Padres' operation. And he wasted no time in addressing the biggest problem—the team on the field. Previous management had spent much of the previous two years dismantling the product through a process known to Padres fans as the "fire sale."

The club Moores bought was a shell of the team that posted back-to-back third-place finishes in the National League West in 1991–1992. The team Moores bought had lost 171 of their previous 279 games before going on strike. "The fans were not happy, that's one of the first things we realized during the negotiations. I knew that once the trade was finalized, we'd have to move quickly to win back the customers."

Moores did just that. He was now the owner of the "New Padres." And as soon as he took over control, Moores set his management team upon the task of improving everything the Padres did—from community involvement to softening the look of their Mission Valley home.

Exactly one week after Moores bought the Padres, the club completed the biggest—and one of the most important trades—in

PADRES SUPERLATIVES

Padres 20/20 Club

Player	Year	Homers	Steals
Dave Winfield	1978	24	21
Dave Winfield	1980	20	23
Joe Carter	1990	24	22
Derek Bell	1993	21	26
Steve Finley	1996	30	22
Reggie Sanders	1999	26	36
Ryan Klesko	2000	26	23
Ryan Klesko	2001	30	23
Mike Cameron	2006	22	25

Padres history. General manager Randy Smith completed a 12-player swap with the Houston Astros. The Padres got third baseman Ken Caminiti, shortstop Andujar Cedeno, first baseman Roberto Petagine, outfielder Steve Finley, pitcher Brian Williams, and a player to be named later (Sean Fesh) from the Astros in exchange for outfielders Derek Bell and Phil Plantier, infielders Craig Shipley and Ricky Gutierrez, and pitchers Doug Brocail and Pedro Martinez.

The trade would lay the groundwork for the Padres' rise to the top of the National League West in 1996. It started the momentum that resulted in the National League pennant in 1998. And that championship season resulted in the passage of the ballot measure that led to the construction of PETCO Park—the Padres' downtown home since 2004.

Moores's New Padres advanced quickly on a wide front. Improving the ballclub on the field wasn't enough. Moores wanted his club doing more in the community. Players were asked for ideas.

"Participation was encouraged," says Tony Gwynn with a respectful laugh. "The message was, 'We're moving forward with you or without you...and you're welcome to join us.' No one asked what would happen if we didn't. I don't think anyone wanted to know. So we all jumped in."

Moores, Lucchino, and community relations specialist Dr. Charles Steinberg addressed myriad issues. Nothing was overlooked. The Moores team extended open arms to everyone from the community to former Padres.

"Where we've been is part of the story of where we're going," said Steinberg. And the game's history became almost as important as Padres history. Over the past decade, Moores has become one of baseball's leaders in expanding knowledge and recognition of the game's Negro Leagues and the great players from a too-often-overlooked era.

The stadium was dressed up along with the team. Shortly after taking over the Padres, Moores and Lucchino took a "fan's-eye" tour of Jack Murphy Stadium. Too much concrete was the conclusion. "What is Southern California...palm trees," said Lucchino, who placed illuminated potted palms between the short fence and the towering walls beyond the outfield.

The palms changed the look of the stadium. "It became more like our home," said Steinberg. And Moores was just getting started. The information available on the scoreboards was expanded. So was the menu at the concession stands. The number of ushers was increased, and they became "greeters."

In the community, Moores, in 1995, established the Padres Foundation for Children, which helps fund programs in education,

SEASON OPENER

Major League Debuts

Player	Position	Year
Rafael Robles	SS	1969
Bob Davis	C	1973
Gene Richards	OF	1977
Ozzie Smith	SS	1978
Bip Roberts	2B	1986
Joey Cora	2B	1987
Josh Barfield	2B	2006

recreation, and health. That was also the year that the Padres launched the player-driven Padres Scholars program that, over its first decade, provided four-year college scholarships to more than 200 underprivileged and challenged students from San Diego County.

None of these improvements, however, were going to mean much if the Padres couldn't improve their on-the-field project. Smith was already at work. On October 21, 1994, Smith promoted third base coach Bruce Bochy—who had been with the Padres organization since 1983 when he arrived as a backup catcher—to succeed Jim Riggleman as the Padres manager.

It didn't help that Moores took over during difficult times. The strike that began the previous August 12 extended into the start of the 1995 season. Moores's debut was delayed. And when the Padres returned, the fans of San Diego—like those in the rest of baseball—didn't welcome their team back with open arms.

"Not only did we have to win games, we had to win the fans back," said Gwynn.

The 1995 Padres succeeded on both fronts. San Diego went 70–74 as the most-improved team in the major leagues.

Tony Gwynn won his sixth National League batting title with a .368 mark. Ken Caminiti hit .302 with 26 homers and 94 RBIs. Steve Finley batted .297 with 36 steals and 104 runs scored. And the Padres

PADRES SUPERLATIVES

First Overall Draft Picks Who Played for the Padres

Draft	Player	Pos.	Drafting Team
1970	Mike Ivie	C-1B	Padres
1972	Dave A. Roberts	3B	Padres
1974	Bill Almon	IF	Padres
1984	Shawn Abner	OF	Mets
1988	Andy Benes	P	Padres
1992	Phil Nevin	IF	Astros
2000	Adrian Gonzalez	1B	Marlins

tied a National League record set by the 1929 Chicago Cubs with nine grand slams.

In the meantime, John Moores expanded his role in San Diego beyond the Padres. Although he had no direct ties to San Diego State, Moores became a leading benefactor of Aztecs athletics, including paying for the construction of Tony Gwynn Stadium, the on-campus baseball facility.

Moores donated $21 million to the University of California–San Diego to establish the John and Rebecca Moores Cancer Center.

Over the years, John Moores has served as a regent of the University of California, a board member of San Diego State's Campanile Foundation, a trustee of the UC–San Diego Foundation, and a board member for the Scripps Institute of Oceanography and the San Diego Hall of Champions.

In March 2005, John Moores was named chairman of the board of trustees of the Carter Center—the international humanitarian organization founded in 1982 by former President Jimmy Carter and his wife Rosalynn. That was the same year that Moores was elected to a four-year term on Major League Baseball's Executive Council.

Trevor Hoffman

It was the early summer of 1993 when Tracy and Trevor Hoffman arrived in San Diego to a firestorm. Actually, it was a fire sale.

Despite back-to-back winning seasons in 1991 and 1992, the Padres hadn't finished higher than third in the National League West. Tom Werner and his 15-man ownership group was getting antsy. The Padres stumbled badly out of the gate in 1993. The owners were courting suitors, and the best way to make a struggling team attractive to prospective buyers was to cut the debt.

On June 9, 1993, 29-year-old Randy Smith was named the general manager of the Padres, becoming—at the time—the youngest man to hold that position in the major leagues. Smith's directions quickly became clear—trim the payroll. Two weeks after taking over, Smith pulled the trigger on the first trade of what became known as the Padres' "fire sale."

In an apparently one-sided deal of monumental proportions, Smith traded slugger Gary Sheffield—who had led the National League in hitting the previous season with a .330 mark—and a left-handed pitcher to Florida for a trio of young right-handed pitchers named Jose Martinez, Andres Berumen, and Trevor Hoffman.

Although it was an early shot in the fire sale—less than a month later, the Padres would trade 1992 National League home-run leader Fred McGriff to Atlanta and eventually would deal away front-line pitchers Bruce Hurst and Greg Harris—the "Sheffield trade" was viewed as a crime against the baseball fans of San Diego.

"I remember picking up the newspaper our first day in San Diego," Tracy Hoffman recalled years later. "We were public enemies. Trevor was hated."

Trevor Hoffman became baseball's all-time saves leader on September 23, 2006, when he recorded number 479 to pass Lee Smith. Hoffman is also the all-time leader with eight seasons of 40 or more saves.

It wasn't as if the Padres had traded for a well-known pitching prospect in the 25-year-old Hoffman. He was drafted into professional baseball as a middle infielder who, at one point in his career, was moved to second base over concerns that his arm wasn't strong enough for throws to first from shortstop.

So upon arriving in San Diego, the Hoffmans plotted a low-profile strategy over lunch.

"We didn't know what to make of the reaction in the community to the trade," said Trevor. "So we decided to come up with a fake profession for myself to head off a lot of questions."

The Hoffmans decided Trevor's profession would become a cookie maker.

"I can't remember why we decided on the 'cookie maker,'" said Tracy. "When you look back..."

Over 14 seasons with the Padres, Trevor Hoffman served up 40 dozen of his specialty—saves. On September 23, 2006, Hoffman passed Lee Smith to become the game's all-time leader in saves—the ultimate yardstick by which that last line of relief pitcher—the closer—is measured. Hoffman is inarguably the greatest closer to finish a game for the Padres. But he is far from the first great pitcher to hold that distinction.

During their history, the Padres have been represented by some of the great closers in baseball history—Rollie Fingers, Goose Gossage, Mark Davis, Randy Myers, and Rod Beck. The run started with Fingers, who had been one of the Padres' first major free agent signings on December 14, 1976. In four seasons with the Padres, Fingers, who was elected to the Hall of Fame in 1992, had 108 saves—still the second-highest total by a Padres closer—in 265 games.

As a Padre, Fingers led the National League in saves in both 1977 (35) and 1978 (37). His ERA as a Padre was 3.13. Fingers was traded to St. Louis in 1980 in a multi-player deal that brought catcher Terry Kennedy to the Padres.

Gary Lucas succeeded Fingers, leading to one of the more famous refrains in Padres history. In four seasons in the Padres bullpen, Lucas appeared in 230 games and had a sparkling 2.00 ERA in the strike-shortened 1981 season when he led the National League with 57 appearances. Lucas saved 49 games as a Padre. He also blew 20 saves—causing fans to chant, "Oh, no. Here comes Lucas," when the off-speed artist trotted in from the bullpen.

As the Padres started to gear up for what would become their first National League pennant campaign of 1984, general manager

TOP 10

Single-Season Saves

	Player	Year	Saves
1.	Trevor Hoffman	1998	53
2.	Trevor Hoffman	2006	46
3.	Mark Davis	1989	44
4.	Trevor Hoffman	2000	43†
	Trevor Hoffman	2001	43†
	Trevor Hoffman	2005	43†
7.	Trevor Hoffman	1996	42
8.	Trevor Hoffman	2004	41
9.	Trevor Hoffman	1999	40
10.	Trevor Hoffman	2002	38†
	Randy Myers	1992	38†

Jack McKeon knew his club desperately needed someone to get the final outs from the bullpen.

The Padres signed Richard Gossage as a free agent away from the Yankees, giving him more than $5 million over four seasons—one of the Padres' more expensive contracts at the time. Of course, Goose Gossage was more than a closer. He was an attitude—a living, breathing chip on the shoulder.

Gossage's stature and cold-hearted stare cast fear into opponents...as well as some teammates. As the Padres picked up steam in 1984, it was the fist-pumping Gossage who became the poster man. In the evolving world of the relief pitcher, Fingers and Gossage were old school—closers who went more than one inning. Both would enter the game as early as the seventh.

"We didn't just save games," said Gossage. "We'd work whenever there was a chance to win and we were ready. And we'd go until the job was done, one way or another."

The modern closer is much more of a specialist, who most often is called upon to get the final three outs of the game.

"You don't get that 27th out, you don't have success," Padres general manager Kevin Towers succinctly said of the modern closer.

PADRES SUPERLATIVES

Rolaids Firemen of the Year

	Player	No.	Years
1.	Rollie Fingers	3	1977, 1978, 1980
2.	Trevor Hoffman	2	1998, 2006
3.	Mark Davis	1	1989

During his two seasons with the Padres in 1988 and 1989, Mark Davis changed as a closer as the role of the closer changed. Davis was acquired from San Francisco in a six-player trade midway through the 1987 season. Along with Davis, the Padres got third baseman Chris Brown and pitcher Mark Grant. The Giants acquired third baseman Kevin Mitchell and pitchers Dave Dravecky and Craig Lefferts.

At the time, Lance McCullers, known as "Baby Goose," was sharing the closing duties in the Padres bullpen with Gossage. Acquired as the "player to be named later" in a 1983 trade with the Phillies, McCullers began his major league career as Gossage's understudy and, as a rookie, a foil for many of his pranks. On one notable trip to New York in the summer of 1985, McCullers fell asleep on the team bus on the postgame ride from Shea Stadium to the club's Manhattan hotel. The rest of the Padres ever-so-quietly exited the bus at the hotel, leaving a sleeping McCullers undisturbed across the rear seat. When McCullers awoke several hours later, he was startled to find himself in the back of an otherwise empty bus in the middle of an otherwise empty bus yard.

By 1987, McCullers was sharing the closing duties with Gossage. And McCullers actually led the Padres with 16 saves in 1987. He also blew 11 opportunities and had a 3.72 ERA.

Gossage, meantime, was clashing with Padres management over several issues, most notably a ban over beer in the clubhouse after games.

Enter Davis.

By the spring of 1988, the Padres believed the 23-year-old McCullers and Davis were the future of their bullpen. So they traded

Gossage to the Cubs just before the start of spring training. And although McCullers made strong gains in 1988 (2.49 ERA), Davis emerged as the Padres' primary closer and finished with 28 saves with a sparkling 2.01 ERA.

Just after the 1988 season ended, McCullers was traded to the Yankees for slugger Jack Clark. Davis responded by posting one of the greatest seasons in Padres history in 1989. The 28-year-old became the third Padre to win the National League Cy Young Award (the first two were starting pitchers Randy Jones in 1976 and Gaylord Perry in 1978).

Appearing in 70 games, Davis had 44 saves in 48 opportunities and had a 1.85 ERA. He had 92 strikeouts in 92⅔ innings. Rivals batted only .200 against Davis. Davis became only the seventh pitcher in major league history to record more than 40 saves in a season. He also became primarily a ninth-inning specialist—a hint of things to come.

Unfortunately for Davis and the Padres, his stay in San Diego was much shorter than expected. Eligible for free agency after the 1989 season, Davis hit a negotiations impasse with the Padres and opted to sign with Kansas City. For Davis, things never worked out as expected with the Royals.

In the meantime, the Padres began a search for that special "closer" to succeed Davis. The first stop was an old friend—Lefferts. "Lefty" was signed as a free agent before 1989 to take Davis's place and responded with 23 saves over each of the next two seasons. But he also blew 15 save opportunities over the 1990–1991 campaigns.

In December 1991, the Padres acquired Randy Myers in a trade from Cincinnati for outfielder Bip Roberts, and converted Lefferts into a starter. Myers responded with 38 saves, the second-highest total until that time in Padres history. But his 4.29 ERA was far above what the Padres were seeking.

By the NUMBERS **5**—Padres pitchers who have led the National League in saves. Rollie Fingers (1977 and 1978) and Trevor Hoffman (1998, 2006) twice apiece, and Mark Davis once in 1989 when he won the Cy Young Award.

Gene Harris was the Padres' primary closer in 1993, but his 3.03 ERA was higher than normal for the role.

But fate intervened in June in the form of the notorious fire sale. The "cookie maker" was ready to bake.

Hoffman was as disappointed to be in San Diego in the summer of 1993 as the Padres fans were disappointed in seeing him in a Padres uniform. Hoffman was the heir apparent to Bryan Harvey as the Marlins closer when he was traded to the Padres. At least he thought he was.

"When the Marlins took me in the expansion draft, they made it sound like I was going to be part of their future," said Hoffman. "At first, I didn't like Florida. But I pumped myself up. I was excited to be part of something building from the ground up. I was in it for the long haul. Two months."

Actually, 2½ months. But after 13½ seasons with the Padres, who's counting?

Trevor William Hoffman was born on October 13, 1967—the youngest of three sons of Ed and Mikki Hoffman. Hoffman's parents were products of World War II. Ed was a veteran of the battle for Iwo Jima. Mikki survived the bombing of London. They met in England when Ed was singing at the Paladium and Mikki was dancing in the chorus line.

Ed Hoffman was an established singer who performed with the likes of Frank Sinatra, Bing Crosby, and Bob Hope. But when his sons were young, he gave up life on the road to work for the post office by day and become the "Singing Usher" of Anaheim Stadium by night.

"Dad always loved to perform," says Trevor Hoffman. "He loved singing to the crowd. And on those nights when 'Eddie the Usher' sang the national anthem, the crowd really reacted. Those nights at Anaheim Stadium were a special part of my family's life."

Hoffman's parents were not only talented, they were athletic. Ed Hoffman was a man of stature—6'2" and 225 pounds. Mikki's father played professional soccer in England before World War II.

"And mom could dance," said Hoffman. "She's probably the best athlete in the family."

There was quite an age spread among the Hoffman boys that helped shape the youngest son. Greg Hoffman was 14 years older

TOP 10

Padres' Career Games-Pitched Leaders

	Pitcher	Games Pitched
1.	Trevor Hoffman	793
2.	Craig Lefferts	375
3.	Eric Show	309
4.	Rollie Fingers	265
5.	Randy Jones	264
6.	Scott Linebrink	262
7.	Dave Tomlin	239
8.	Mark Davis	230†
	Gary Lucas	230†
10.	Lance McCullers	229

than Trevor. Glenn Hoffman—who would play nine seasons in the major leagues as an infielder and join Trevor in San Diego in 2006 as the Padres' third base coach—was nine years Trevor's senior.

"They weren't as much playmates for me as mentors," said Hoffman. "I watched them, listened to them, and learned. Older brothers are great things.

"Greg grew up just knowing what was right, how you should act and what you should do. He taught me that the game and the team eclipsed individual achievement. He's a real in-your-face guy...he kept me on the straight and narrow.

"Glenn showed me by example. 'This is how you do it.' He was the guide while Greg was the drill instructor. It was best possible combination."

As a player, Trevor Hoffman followed Glenn's lead. He went to the University of Arizona as an infielder and was drafted by the Cincinnati Reds in the 11th round in 1989 as a shortstop.

But Trevor struggled as an infielder. In his third minor league season, the Reds converted Hoffman into a pitcher.

"I couldn't hit," says Hoffman. "Flat out, that's the bottom line. It's probably good that as a closer, I don't have to hit that often because I would be exposed. And I was struggling in other aspects as a shortstop."

But the Reds loved his arm and converted him to a pitcher. At one time, the Reds believed he might become a starter before deciding his 97-mile-per-hour fastball was more lethal in small doses.

"The fastball was my best pitch," said Hoffman.

But as soon as he started pitching, Hoffman began looking for more tools.

"I had been around just long enough to know that from a hitter's viewpoint, a pitcher who has only one pitch is going to be caught up to."

The pitch Hoffman worked on was the change-up, though it wasn't new to him.

"As an eight-year-old in my parent's backyard, I played around with the change-up when we were playing Wiffle ball," said Hoffman. "Everyone else was putting their fingers in the holes and spinning the ball and making it dance."

Thinking far outside the box, Hoffman wondered what would happen if you could get the ball to change speeds. Answer—nothing.

"A slow Wiffle ball is a hittable Wiffle ball," said Hoffman.

But the seed was planted. The movement used by most pitchers is up and down. Hoffman wondered what would happen if the

TOP 10

Padres' Career Saves Leaders

	Pitcher	Number
1.	Trevor Hoffman	480
2.	Rollie Fingers	108
3.	Goose Gossage	83
4.	Mark Davis	78
5.	Craig Lefferts	64
6.	Gary Lucas	49
7.	Randy Myers	38
8.	Lance McCullers	36
9.	Luis DeLeon	31
10.	Gene Harris	23

movement was horizontal rather than vertical. And if you could get vertical to go with horizontal...

Not long after Hoffman started pitching, he studied the change-up thrown by John Tudor. With the Reds, he learned his original change from Larry Barton. Then former teammate Donnie Elliott offered Hoffman ideas about perfecting the change by forcing the ball deeper into the palm of his hand to enhance the deception.

Not that he really needed the change when he arrived in San Diego. Hoffman threw hard. He blew hitters away. But not for very long.

Hoffman had just blossomed as a closer in his second year with the Padres when the season was abruptly stopped by a players' strike. It was while playing in the surf near his Del Mar home that Hoffman felt "something funny" in his arm. A short time later, he felt a "pop." The fastball was never the same.

Less than two years into his major league career, Trevor Hoffman reinvented himself a second time as a ballplayer.

"Most guys right there hit a wall," Padres general manager Kevin Towers said years later while discussing Hoffman's career. "Most of it is mental. You have lost your ticket. But maybe because Hoffy really hadn't had that much time invested in pitching, he changed himself.

"When you look at what Trevor has done compared to what has happened to other pitchers in the same situation, it's all the more amazing." More amazing yet when you consider that most closers don't rely on what is considered a "trick" pitch.

"You know it is coming," said Houston's Jeff Bagwell of Hoffman's change-up. "You plan for it. Fastball/change. You should have a 50–50 shot. You think you know it is coming...and you still can't hit it. It just never seems to get to home plate."

"Some guys fool you. Some guys overpower you. Hoffman embarrasses you," said former rival and 2006 teammate Mike Piazza. "You walk away wondering to yourself, 'What was that?'"

Hoffman's run with the Padres really took off in 1995 with the arrival of Bruce Bochy as Padres manager. All but 25 of his first 480 saves came after Bochy summoned him from the bullpen. Bochy knew how to use Hoffman. And it wasn't just Hoffman. Running the bullpen might have been Bochy's forte as a manager. And Hoffman knew Bochy.

"A great trust developed between us," said Hoffman. "I always knew Bruce had both my and the team's best interests at heart. And Bochy knew I was always prepared if I said I was ready."

Next to the change-up, preparation is Hoffman's strongest weapon. It has become a daily ritual, starting with his running program that commences four hours before game time—or some eight hours before Hoffman usually works. There is also his stretching program, including the use of elastic bands to stretch out his muscles. Then he waits—hopefully until the Padres have a lead going into the final inning. He'll rise in the bullpen, stretch, throw a handful of warm-up pitches, and head to the mound.

At PETCO Park, his trot toward the mound is accompanied by AC/DC's "Hells Bells"—his entrance anthem since July 25, 1998. The opening gong brings Padres fans to their feet much the same way Tony Gwynn's walk to the plate once did.

Hoffman's glory days began in 1996 during the Padres' run to their first National League West title since 1984. Hoffman had 42 saves—the first of his record eight 40-save seasons (he also holds the record for 30-save seasons with 11).

Two seasons later, Hoffman again led the Padres to the National League West title with a career-best 53-save season. The total ties the National League record, and he set a then–major league mark by converting 53-of-54 opportunities, including a record-tying 41 straight. Hoffman's ERA was a dazzling 1.48. Opponents hit only .165 against him. He finished second to Tom Glavine in the Cy Young Award voting and seventh in the Most Valuable Player voting in 1998. Thanks to Hoffman, the Padres went 62–4 in games he worked and they never lost a game he entered with the lead. His ERA in save situations was 0.59.

Hoffman's career was nearly derailed in 2003 due to surgery to shave an impingement away from the tip of his right scapula. He pitched only nine times that September and never in a save situation.

At the age of 38, Hoffman had the second-best season of his career in 2006, posting 46 saves en route to eclipsing Smith as the all-time leader in the statistic. His 2.14 ERA also equaled the second-lowest mark of his career. Hoffman's fastball seldom tops

88 miles-per-hour these days. But the separation between the fastball and change remains 10 miles-per-hour. And now he throws the occasional slider.

How long can Hoffman pitch? He is contracted through 2008. The magic number of 500 saves is on the horizon. Six hundred?

"It could all be over tomorrow," Hoffman said recently. "That's the lasting impression of 2003. Life can change tomorrow. Be prepared. Enjoy."

And that summer of 1993 seems so far in the past—both for Hoffman and the Padres.

"There was a lot of animosity about the organization," Hoffman recalls of his first days in San Diego.

"I remember Glenn telling me that it would work out...that San Diego would become a great place for me and my family. I knew it wasn't something I could change in a day. All I knew is that I could get the fans to respect the way I played the game.

"One pitch at a time, one out at a time, one game at a time."

It is the Hoffman way.

Towers and Bochy

Long after the media had departed and the last player had headed for home, Bruce Bochy and Kevin Towers often sat in the manager's office and shot the breeze. "We can talk for hours about anything," Bochy once said of his relationship with Towers. "But sooner or later it comes back to baseball." And the Padres.

The strangest thing about the start of the 2007 season will be the absence of Bruce Bochy as the Padres manager. With one year to go on his contract after the 2006 season, Bochy bid farewell to the Padres, ending a record 12-season run as manager. Bochy's decision to sign with the San Francisco Giants also ended the second-longest active run by a manager–general manger tandem in the major leagues.

Bruce Bochy became the Padres 15th manager on October 21, 1994. Kevin Towers became the Padres' seventh general manager on November 17, 1995. Only Atlanta's Bobby Cox and John Schuerholz had been together longer when the Bochy-Towers 11-season run ended.

"It's going to be strange not having Bruce here next year," Towers said after Bochy signed with the Giants. The previous year, it was Towers who interviewed with Arizona for the Diamondbacks' general manager vacancy. "Honestly, that was the first time I even thought about not working with Bruce again," said Towers. "It was not a happy time for me."

Although they had worked directly as partners with the Padres since 1995, their association with the team and each other went back much further.

Bruce Bochy joined the Padres on February 23, 1983, signing a minor league contract with San Diego after being released by the

Mets. He was promoted to the Padres on May 29, 1983, and spent most of the next 4½ seasons as the Padres back-up catcher.

Kevin Towers was the first-round draft choice of the Padres in 1982. A right-handed pitcher, Towers was a Texas League all-star in 1984 before a series of arm injuries stopped his promising career. Towers the pitcher made it as far as Triple A Las Vegas in 1988, where his catcher was Bruce Bochy.

"I knew my major league career was over," said Bochy. "I was in Las Vegas making the transition into coaching and managing."

"I didn't know my career was over yet," joked Towers. "But it became evident pretty quick."

Their backgrounds were quite different.

Born in France in 1955 to one of the U.S. Army's highest-ranking non-commissioned officers, Bruce Bochy led the vagabond life of an Army brat in his early years before playing most of his high school and junior college baseball in south Florida. Drafted by the Astros in 1975, Bochy first reached the majors with Houston in 1978.

At about the same time, Towers, who was born in 1962, was headed for Brigham Young University from Medford, Oregon. At BYU, Towers teamed with another future major leaguer, Wally Joyner, and became an all–Western Athletic Conference pick before signing with the Padres.

Towers's right arm still carries the scars of what happened to his pitching career. "What I went through comes into play any time I'm dealing with a pitching injury," admits Towers. "There's such a fine line."

TOP 5

Manager Wins

	Manager	Wins
1.	Bruce Bochy	951
2.	Dick Williams	337
3.	John McNamara	224
4.	Greg Riddoch	200
5.	Jack McKeon	193

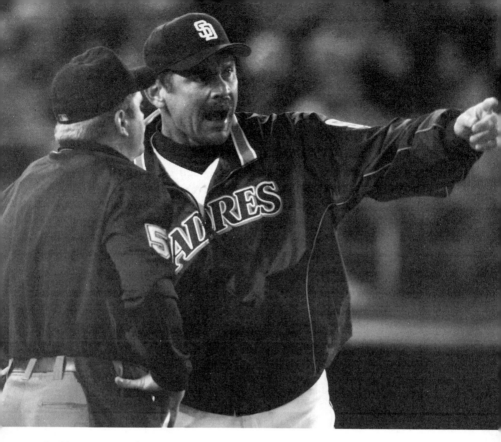

In 12 seasons under manager Bruce Bochy, the Padres won one National League championship (1998) and four National League West titles (1996, 1998, 2005, 2006). Before he stunned everyone by becoming the manager of the division-rival Giants for 2007, Bochy had spent 24 straight years in the Padres organization as a player, minor league manager, major league coach, and manager.

Towers and Bochy first worked together the season after their playing careers ended.

Towers had been hired by the Padres in 1989 as an area scout in Texas and Louisiana. As part of that assignment, he spent the summer working as the pitching coach of the Padres' short-season Class A rookie league team in Spokane, Washington.

Bochy launched his managing career with Spokane in 1989. The club won the Northwest League championship.

"It was more than fun," recalled Towers years later. "Bruce and I learned a lot about each other and the game...how we viewed the game—from strategy to handling players. As a partnership, we formed a pretty good evaluation team."

In 1990, Bochy moved on to manage the Padres' Class A Riverside team in the California League. Towers spent one more season in his dual role of regional scout and pitching coach with Spokane. Then their paths split.

Bochy would continue to climb the ladder in the Padres organization. When he did depart following the 2006 season, Bochy had spent 24 straight seasons as part of the Padres family—the last half as the Padres manager.

Towers left the Padres in 1991 to join the Pittsburgh Pirates 'scouting department—first as a regional cross-checker, then as a national cross-checker.

Just as the Padres were recognizing Bochy's ability to handle players and get the most out of the talent at hand, all of baseball was coming to recognize Towers's uncanny skills at evaluating talent.

"I love scouting," Towers said years after becoming the Padres' general manager. "I still love getting out to high school and college games and watching kids play the game and spotting players with the ability to make it.

"I think scouting is the heart of the game. The ability to assess talent as a scout is still the foundation you use as a general manager. The number-one job of a GM is evaluating talent on every level all the time."

Towers returned to the Padres as the director of scouting in 1993.

By that time, Bochy had managed four seasons in the Padres' minor league system and had returned to the major league team as third-base coach for then-manager Jim Riggleman. Bochy succeeded Riggleman as the Padres' manager following his second season as third-base coach.

On paper, Towers went from being under Bochy to being his boss when he was promoted to the general manager's seat 13 months after Bochy became the manager.

"But it was always a partnership," said Towers. "Over the years, I'd say Bruce and I spent almost as much time with one another as we did with our wives. Neither of us did many things that came as total surprises to the other."

TOP 15

Padres Managers' Winning Percentage

	Manager	Games	Wins	Losses	Pct.
1.	Bob Skinner	1	1	0	1.000
2.	Jack McKeon	357	193	164	.541
3.	Dick Williams	649	337	311	.520
4.	Greg Riddoch	394	200	194	.508
5.	Bruce Bochy	1,926	951	975	.494
6.	Roger Craig	323	152	171	.471
7.	Steve Boros	162	74	88	.457
8.	Jerry Coleman	162	73	89	.451
9.	Alvin Dark	113	48	65	.425
10.	John McNamara	534	224	310	.419
11.	Larry Bowa	208	81	127	.389
12.	Jim Riggleman	291	112	179	.385
13.	Don Zimmer	304	114	190	.375
14.	Frank Howard	110	41	69	.373
15.	Preston Gomez	496	180	316	.363

They watched baseball together. They ate together. They played cards and shared a beer or two over the years.

"The biggest thing is that Kevin and I respected what the other brought to the table," said Bochy. "I understood the limitations he was working with when it came to such things as budget and the ability to make moves. He knew the expectations were defined by limitations."

"If we give Bruce players he can win with, he will win," said Towers.

The problem was that the Padres, as a small-market team, couldn't always spend the money to produce a winner.

But Bochy and Towers had more than their share of success. Under their leadership, the Padres won their second National League pennant in 1998. And the Padres' four National League West titles—1996, 1998, 2005, and 2006—under Bochy and Towers since 1996 are unequalled by any of their division rivals.

As a general manager, Kevin Towers's forte is staying ahead of the curve on pitching and finding those key players to complete the puzzle—outfielder Rickey Henderson and first baseman Wally Joyner in 1996; pitcher Kevin Brown and catcher Carlos Hernandez in 1998; outfielder Dave Roberts and pitcher Woody Williams in 2005; outfielder Mike Cameron, catcher Mike Piazza, first baseman Adrian Gonzalez, and pitcher Chris Young in 2006.

As a manager, Bruce Bochy handles pitchers as well as anyone in the game and maintains the friendly respect of his players.

"You never see the type of discord in the Padres clubhouse under Bochy that you hear about in other places," said Tony Gwynn.

"I know he's called a player's manager," said Trevor Hoffman. "The players respect him. They know he understands them. At the same time, Bruce sets his expectations high. You don't want to let him down because you know he's on your side."

Kevin Towers would supply the players. Bruce Bochy would manage them. Bruce would let Kevin know what he needed. And Kevin would offer ideas to the manager.

"We've always had a partnership where ideas and suggestions are free-flowing," said Bochy. "At the same time, we pretty much knew what the other guy was thinking. Kevin knew as well as I did what we needed. And I knew what Kevin could do inside the framework of the organization."

The 1996 season was the first that Towers and Bochy worked together with the Padres, and the result was the first division title since 1984. Many view that 1996 season as the most exciting in Padres history—even over the pennant campaigns of 1984 and 1998.

"The 1996 season was such an uplifting experience," said Towers.

Bochy, who was the only man in uniform for all five of the Padres' postseason experiences, remembers it much the same way.

TRIVIA

Who was the Padres' only interim manager?

Answers to the trivia questions are on pages 219–220.

"I remember being in my office long after the Cardinals eliminated us," said Bochy. "There was some commotion in the clubhouse, so I went back out in the room. The players were putting their uniforms back on.

PADRES HISTORY

General Managers

	General Manager	Years
1.	Buzzie Bavasi	1969–1972
2.	Peter Bavasi	1973–1976
3.	Bob Fontaine	1977–1980
4.	Jack McKeon	1980–1990
5.	Joe McIlvaine	1993–1995
6	Kevin Towers	1996–

"I looked across the room and Wally Joyner said, 'The fans are still out there. No one has left the stands.' Joining the players and returning to the field that night is one of my favorite memories."

Bochy had been a player with the Padres National League champions of 1984 and got a pinch-hit single in his only World Series at-bat against Detroit. And he managed the Padres' next four division champions.

Following that 1996 season, Bochy became the only Padres manager to be named National League Manager of the Year. As a rookie manager in 1995, Bochy led a team that posted the most-improved record in National League.

Starting in 1996, the Padres rode a roller coaster. Injuries sidetracked the Padres in 1997. And following the 1998 pennant season, the team waited out a difficult holding pattern due to the delayed opening of PETCO Park.

"The seasons following 1998 were the most difficult," admitted Towers. "The number-one priority of John Moores was to clear away the legal challenges to PETCO Park and get the downtown ballpark built. If that project hadn't been completed, eventually there would not have been the San Diego Padres. I really believe that."

"There's only so much you can do in acquiring and keeping players when money is tight," said Bruce Bochy.

As in so many cases, the working relationship between Bruce Bochy and Kevin Towers strengthened during the franchise's darkest days. "I knew he was doing everything he could possibly do," said

Bochy. "Every time a name popped up on the waiver wire, Kevin would be asking me, 'What do you think?' Kevin's one of the best I've ever seen at spotting talent."

Case in point was Scott Linebrink, who developed into one of the game's leading setup relief pitchers after being claimed on waivers from Houston in the late spring of 2003.

Kevin Towers wasted no time in making his mark as a general manager. He made four moves that helped the Padres win the National League West title in 1996. A month after becoming general manager, Towers traded Bip Roberts to Kansas City for former BYU teammate Wally Joyner, knowing the first baseman would solidify the Padres' infield defense and offer a seasoned bat in the second half of the order. That same month, he signed outfielder Rickey Henderson and right-handed pitcher Bob Tewksbury as free agents. Then early in the season, Towers acquired shortstop Chris Gomez and catcher John Flaherty from Detroit for catcher Brad Ausmus and shortstop Andujar Cedeno.

The key to the 1998 pennant was the trade that obtained right-handed pitcher Kevin Brown from Florida for first-base prospect Derrek Lee and right-handed pitcher Rafael Medina.

But Towers had made other moves that were almost as important. Leadoff hitter and second baseman Quilvio Veras had been obtained in a November 1996 trade from Florida for pitcher Dustin Hermanson. Left fielder Greg Vaughn came from Milwaukee midway through the 1996 season in a three-for-one deal. Catcher

TOP 5

Games Managed

	Manager	Games
1.	Bruce Bochy	1,926
2.	Dick Williams	649
3.	John McNamara	534
4.	Preston Gomez	496
5.	Greg Riddoch	394

Carlos Hernandez had been a backup with the Dodgers before he joined the Padres as a free agent. Left-handed pitcher Sterling Hitchcock, who would become the MVP of the 1998 National League Championship Series, came from Seattle in a straight one-for-one trade for pitcher Scott Sanders in December 1996; and starting pitcher Mark Langston signed as a free agent in 1998.

Eight seasons later, Towers was still deftly at work.

Perhaps the key to the 2006 season were two off-season trades. Towers acquired center fielder Mike Cameron from the New York Mets for outfielder Xavier Nady. And a deal with Texas brought first baseman Adrian Gonzalez and right-handed pitcher Chris Young to San Diego for right-handed pitchers Adam Eaton and Akinori Otsuka. Plus, there was the early-season trade that brought in catcher Josh Bard and right-handed relief pitcher Cla Meredith. And

PADRES HISTORY

Managers

	Manager	Years
1.	Preston Gomez	1969–1972
2.	Don Zimmer	1972–1973
3.	John McNamara	1974–1977
4.	Bob Skinner	1977
5.	Alvin Dark	1977
6.	Roger Craig	1978–1979
7.	Jerry Coleman	1980
8.	Frank Howard	1981
9.	Dick Williams	1982–1985
10.	Steve Boros	1986
11.	Larry Bowa	1987–1988
12.	Jack McKeon	1988–1990
13.	Greg Riddoch	1990–1992
14.	Jim Riggleman	1992–1994
15.	Bruce Bochy	1995–2006
16.	Bud Black	2007–

he signed Hall of Fame–bound catcher Mike Piazza as a free agent for the bargain-basement sum of $1.25 million.

TRIVIA

What coach with the original Padres team of 1969 went onto become one of the more successful managers in Major League history?

Answers to the trivia questions are on pages 219–220.

"Kevin deserves some time to be recognized as one of the game's top executives," Bochy said during the 2006 season. "I don't think he's given enough credit for what he's done, whether it is getting Piazza for one season as a low-cost free agent or trading for a solidifying player like Mike Cameron."

With the start of the 2007 season, Towers will be beginning his 24th season in the Padres organization—the same amount of tenure as Bochy when he departed for San Francisco.

And like Bochy, Towers has the longest service time in Padres history at his position. Jack McKeon served as the Padres general manager for 10½ seasons, from 1980 to 1990. Only five active general managers have won more games than Towers with their present teams.

In the meantime, Bochy finished his run in San Diego with nearly three times as many wins (951) as the number-two man on the Padres win list—Dick Williams, who was Bochy's manager with the 1984 National League champions.

When Bochy left San Diego, only three other active managers had won more games with their current clubs—Atlanta's Bobby Cox (1,186), the New York Yankees' Joe Torre (1,079), and St. Louis's Tony LaRussa (977).

The burning question in San Diego was why exactly did Bochy leave the Padres with a year to go on his contract?

The events happened rapidly after the Padres were eliminated in the first round of the National League playoffs. The Cardinals' 3–1 blitz marked the third time in 12 seasons—and the second straight year—that St. Louis had ousted the Padres in the first round of the playoffs.

Immediately following the Padres' loss, CEO Sandy Alderson notified Bochy that an extension beyond 2007 wouldn't be

TRIVIA

How many of the Padres' 15 managers through 2006 have been replaced during the season?

Answers to the trivia questions are on pages 219–220.

forthcoming. Alderson also told Bochy, like he had told Towers the previous season, that the manager was welcome to talk to other teams if he wished.

Like Towers was by Arizona, Bochy was contacted by the San Francisco Giants. But while the Diamondbacks eventually didn't offer Towers their general manager position, the Giants did make Bochy a three-year offer. Uncertain of his future in San Diego with only one season remaining on his contract, Bochy decided to accept a three-year contract with San Francisco.

One of the greatest runs in Padres history was over.

"It was sad to move on," said Bochy. "I'd be lying if I said I was anxious to leave. But sometimes you just have to do what looks to be better for you and your family. San Francisco was the right decision at this time."

In addition to being the National League Manager of the Year in 1996, Bruce Bochy managed the National League team in the 1999 All-Star Game. Bochy was also a coach on the National League All-Star team in 1997 and 2001.

Bochy became the Padres' winningest manager on April 10, 1999, in an 11–1 victory over San Francisco.

1996

We'll never know the entire story. Sadly, Ken Caminiti took it to his grave.

On October 10, 2004, Caminiti died of a drug overdose in New York City. Two years earlier, the third baseman admitted he had used steroids during the 1996 season.

His admission placed an asterisk—if not a question mark—next to perhaps the greatest individual and team performances in Padres history.

"I always thought the 1996 season was magical," said Tim Flannery, one of the most popular Padres ever. Flannery had returned to uniform that season as the third-base coach for second-year Padres manager Bruce Bochy.

"Watching that season from top to bottom...watching Tony [Gwynn], Cammy, and Steve Finley...being part of that final weekend in Los Angeles, it was a great ride," said Flannery. "To really understand 1996, you had to look back over the previous couple of seasons."

Not that far removed from the fire sale of 1993 and the arrival of owner John Moores in 1994, the Padres still looked to be in the rebuilding mode in 1996 when they caught fire behind Caminiti late in the season. Then they went to Los Angeles for the final weekend of the season and beat the Dodgers three times in as many nail-biters to claim their first division title since 1984.

Alas, the balloon burst. The Cardinals eliminated the Padres in the first round of the playoffs—in three close games.

But when it was over, it wasn't over. Perhaps sensing the enormity of the Padres' feat, considering where they had been, Padres

TRIVIA

What is the Padres record for runs scored in a single game?

Answers to the trivia questions are on pages 219–220.

partisans remained in the stands of Jack Murphy Stadium long after the final out. Somewhat shocked, the players returned to the field to take an encore bow.

"What would they have done had we won?" wondered pitcher Fernando Valenzuela. "This was crazy," continued the icon who had created Fernandomania in his youth as a Dodger.

"It sent chills down my spine," said shortstop Chris Gomez of the reaction of the Padres fans. "When I first went back out there, it was so loud that it was a little bit intimidating."

Certainly, it was a season to celebrate.

And while future revelations would tarnish some of the glory of 1996, the season still stands as one of the greatest memories for most Padres fans—starting with the home season opener.

On April 8, 1996, the Padres decided to open the season with a tribute to the heritage of professional baseball—and the Padres name—in San Diego. It was the 60th anniversary of the first season of the Pacific Coast League Padres. With Tony Gwynn offering a steadying hand, San Diego native son and Hall of Famer Ted Williams threw out the ceremonial first pitch. After all, Williams had come straight out of Hoover High to play for those 1936 Padres.

As the capacity crowd looked around Jack Murphy Stadium, they noticed a number of improvements—most notably the new out-of-town scoreboard that covered the 17-foot wall down the right-field foul line.

And returning for the first time since the 1984 pennant season was the "Swinging Friar" logo. The Friar mascot was introduced in 1997 and has been part of the Padres family since. "Keep the Faith," became the mantra.

"You got the feeling that day that baseball was being relaunched in San Diego," remembered Flannery. "It was such a fresh feeling. And at the same time, they connected with the past."

It didn't take Ken Caminiti that long to make a play that would put the Padres in the national spotlight and serve as a signature for the rest of the season.

On April 22, Florida's Greg Colbrunn hit a drive over third that appeared destined to bounce around in the left field corner as a double. But Caminiti dove to his right and made a diving stop. Since he was seated along the foul line, it appeared Caminiti had held Colbrunn to single. But Caminiti threw a strike from the sitting position that beat Colbrunn to first.

"Not only was it an amazing stop, the throw had a lot on it," said first baseman Wally Joyner. "Either part of that play was incredible. Put it together and it was one of the greatest plays I've ever seen."

But it was far from the only great play Caminiti made in the course of the season. And it was not the only time he threw out a runner from the seat of his pants.

"We'd go out there thinking, 'What [is] Cammy going to do tonight?'" said Finley.

And then there was Caminiti's bat.

Over the course of the 1996 season, the switch-hitting third baseman hit .326 with 40 homers and 130 RBIs—both Padres records at the time. The RBI mark still stands.

When the season was over, Ken Caminiti became the first Padre honored as the National League's Most Valuable Player. The vote was more like a coronation. The balloting of the Baseball Writers' Association of America was unanimous in support of Caminiti.

"Offense, defense, clutch hitting, motivation, that was the greatest all-around season I've ever seen from a player," said Padres manager Bruce Bochy. "It was like every day, he did something else."

Caminiti officially became a San Diego icon in mid-August when the Padres and Mets flew to Monterrey, Mexico, to play Major League Baseball's historic first regular season series on foreign soil.

By the NUMBERS

7—Times in 1996 that the Padres topped 50,000 in attendance.

11—Runs scored by the Padres in the sixth inning of a 12–5 1997 Opening Day win over the Mets. The total is the most scored in an inning by a team on Opening Day in the 20th century.

60,230—Fans on hand as the Padres set an attendance record in the expanded Qualcomm Stadium on August 29, 1997.

Caminiti fell extremely ill on the morning of August 18. "I've never seen a ballplayer look in worse shape," said Bochy. "I was thinking we were going to have to get him to a hospital emergency room."

Caminiti was almost delirious as Padres trainers and doctors stretched him out on a table in the training room and pumped fluids into his dehydrated system through an IV in his arm.

"When I asked him how he was feeling, I was really asking if he was going to need more medical attention," said Bochy. "But Cammy says, 'I think I'll be ready.' I told him there was no way he was playing. And Cammy said, 'Don't give up on me.'"

Just before the game was scheduled to start, Caminiti unhooked himself from the IV, downed a couple of now-famous Snickers candy bars, and made his way to the field. He opened at third base and in his customary cleanup spot in the order.

Caminiti hit a solo homer in his first at-bat. Then he hit a three-run homer. And he made two highlight-film stops in the field before he finally had to remove himself from the game.

Talking his way into the lineup became common practice for Caminiti in 1996. Early in the season, Caminiti suffered a painful shoulder injury. Although he had admittedly used drugs in the past, Caminiti said it was the pain of the shoulder injury that turned him to steroids in 1996.

Almost daily during the season, Caminti battled the pain of the shoulder injury as he prepared for that night's game. Sometimes he was unable to swing the bat in batting practice.

Almost every time Bruce Bochy tried to give Caminiti a day off, the third baseman would appear at the manager's door pleading to be put back in the lineup. Bochy knew Caminiti was fibbing about his condition. "He'd limp in here wrapped like a mummy with his arm a bright red thanks to the ton of ice used in treatment," said Bochy. "He'd lie every day about his condition."

Eventually, Bochy grew concerned about Caminiti's pitch.

"I'm not going to play you tonight because I know you're lying to me about your condition," Bochy told Caminiti one evening. "Play me tonight and I promise I'll lie to you less from now on," said Caminiti.

"Cammy had this unusual logic," Steve Finley said years later. "He wanted to play every day because he believed he didn't know how

Ken Caminiti has become one of the more controversial figures in Padres history. The third baseman was the unanimous National League MVP pick in 1996 for hitting .326 with 40 homers and 130 RBIs, in addition to playing spectacularly in the field. Caminiti, who hit 121 homers in four seasons with the Padres, later admitted he used steroids during his career, including the time he spent in San Diego. Caminiti died due to tragic circumstances in 2004 at the age of 41.

much longer he would be able to play. I don't know why he thought that way.

"But he knew he was going so good in 1996 that he didn't want to miss a single day."

"He was absolutely amazing," said Padres pitcher Andy Ashby. "And he got stronger the deeper we got into the season."

Ken Caminiti had 14 homers and 38 RBIs in August. He had nine homers and 23 RBIs in September.

Despite his heroics, the Padres still trailed the Dodgers by two games in the National League West going into the final three games of the season September 27 through 29 at Dodger Stadium. Fresh in the minds of many Padres was the celebration the Dodgers threw at Jack Murphy Stadium the previous September when Los Angeles clinched the National League West title.

"We wanted it bad," recalled Tony Gwynn of the final weekend. "With one win, we'd probably clinch a playoff berth as the wild-card. With two wins, we were definitely in the playoffs. With three wins, we'd be West champions. So everyone else in the city is thinking, make the playoffs. But we wanted the sweep. What are the chances?"

It turned out to be 100 percent. On Friday night, Caminiti's tenth-inning double snapped a 2–2 tie and led the Padres to a 5–2 win—clinching the Padres' tie for the wild-card berth.

On Saturday, Tony Gwynn was the hero with a two-run, eighth-inning single that broke another 2–2 tie. The 4–2 win clinched the Padres a playoff berth—marking only the second time in the club's 28-year history that they reached the postseason.

On Sunday, for the first time since 1908, a National League title was going to be settled on the final day of the season in a head-to-head matchup between the two involved teams. And it ended in one of the more memorable moments of Tony Gwynn's career.

Thanks to the off-speed mastery of Bob Tewksbury, the Padres were in a scoreless tie going into the eleventh. Steve Finley and Ken

DID YOU KNOW . . . That Bruce Bochy is the only Padre ever to be named Manager of the Year? He won the award in 1996 when the Padres won the National League West title.

Caminiti led off the Padres' side of the inning with singles. Chris Gwynn, Tony's younger brother, was sent up as a pinch-hitter. A former Dodger, Chris Gwynn had struggled throughout his only season as a Padre. He was hitting .169 as he approached the plate.

"They should have made a movie of what followed," laughs Tony Gwynn.

TRIVIA

Who was the first switch-hitter in major league history to homer from both sides of the plate in the same game three times in a season?

Answers to the trivia questions are on pages 219–220.

His younger brother laced a ball deep into the unprotected gap in right center. Finley and Caminiti both scored. The Padres were up 2–0.

"We're going wild and celebrating and then we realized we had another half inning to play," said Finley. No problem. Trevor Hoffman was in the bullpen. He picked up his third save in as many days.

The Padres were champions of the National League West.

Certainly, Caminiti was the man of the year. But he was far from the only player who came through for the Padres.

Hoffman had 42 saves and was named the National League Fireman of the Year. Despite playing the season with Achilles tendon problems, Tony Gwynn hit .353 to win his seventh National League batting championship.

Rickey Henderson, who was signed as a free agent to fill the Padres' void in the leadoff slot, had a .410 on-base percentage despite hitting only .241. Henderson drew 125 walks, stole 37 bases, and scored 110 runs.

But that was only the second-highest total among the Padres. Center fielder Steve Finley also had a banner season. He hit .298 with 45 doubles, 9 triples, and 30 homers—a total of 84 extra-base hits—and finished with a club-record 126 runs scored and 95 RBIs.

During the season, Padres general manager Kevin Towers made two important trades. The Padres acquired catcher John Flaherty and shortstop Chris Gomez from Detroit for catcher Brad Ausmus and shortstop Andujar Cedeno during a 4–19 "June Swoon." Gomez was the key. The Padres sought him to stabilize the infield defense. And he did. But Flaherty hit an unexpected .303 for the Padres.

Included in his season was a 27-game hitting streak that is still the second-longest in Padres history.

Then the Padres acquired left fielder Greg Vaughn from Milwaukee at the trading deadline, creating something of a problem, since Rickey Henderson was playing left. The pair entered a platoon where it took all the grace and guile possessed by manager Bruce Bochy to make it work. Although Vaughn hit only .206 for the Padres, he had several clutch hits down the stretch.

Come-from-behind victories are what propelled the Padres to the top. They came from behind in 32 of their 91 wins and won 22 games in their final at-bat. Seven of the 12 last-at-bat victories came during the Padres' final 12 wins of the season, including two in Los Angeles.

The three-game, season-ending sweep in Los Angeles should have provided the Padres plenty of momentum going into the play-offs. But the Cardinals made short work of San Diego. However, even the opening 3–1 and 5–4 losses in St. Louis didn't dim the hopes of the Padres faithful, who remembered the remarkable comeback scored by the 1984 team against the Cubs in a best-of-five playoff series.

The opener of the series was over almost before it began, with Gary Gaetti hitting a three-run homer off 15-win Padres starter Joey Hamilton in the first. In the second game, the Cardinals pushed across the decisive run in the eighth without the benefit of a hit.

The third game in San Diego attracted 53,899 to Jack Murphy Stadium. Surely, lightning would strike a second time in 12 years. It didn't.

Ken Caminiti tied the game at 5–5 with his third homer of the series in the bottom of the eighth. But Brian Jordan, who had driven in the winning run in the second game with a liner that ticked off Trevor Hoffman's glove, hit a tie-breaking, two-run, tape-measure homer in the ninth.

The 1997 season became a headache for the Padres in more ways than one.

Construction was underway that would expand the capacity at the stadium—which was renamed Qualcomm Stadium for the sponsor of the improvements—to 71,500 for football and 66,307 for baseball.

DID YOU KNOW . . . That the Padres went outside the continental 48 in both 1996 and 1997? In 1996, they hosted the New York Mets for three regular-season games in Monterrey, Mexico. The following year, the Padres hosted St. Louis for three regular-season games in Hawaii.

The Padres were already campaigning for a baseball-only ballpark. The stadium expansion only stepped up the schedule. And when the NFL Chargers were granted further revenue concessions from the city of San Diego, the Padres declared their future in Mission Valley was untenable.

The Padres did benefit from a second JumboTron video board installed as part of the stadium's expansion.

Offensively, the Padres, led by Gwynn, had their greatest season in 1997.

As a team, they batted .271 and set the franchise record with 795 runs scored and 1,519 hits. Steve Finley hit 28 homers. Ken Caminiti hit 26. Wally Joyner batted a career-high .327.

But the all-around hitting leader was Gwynn, who batted .372 with a club-record 49 doubles, 17 homers, and a career-high 119 RBIs. Gwynn won his eighth batting championship, tying Honus Wagner's National League record.

The pitching highlight of the season came on September 5 when right-hander Andy Ashby took a no-hitter into the ninth inning against Atlanta. But Kenny Lofton led off the last inning with a single—again denying the Padres their first no-hitter.

The Padres struggled in 1997 to put together a rotation. Nine different pitchers started games, and all but one of those started in at least eight games. The Padres' staff ERA soared from 3.73 of the 1996 division champs to 4.99, which explains their 15-game fall to 76–86.

On June 23, Trevor Hoffman became the club's all-time saves leader.

1998

As 1998 approached, the Padres had only two needs: a top-of-the-rotation pitcher and a championship.

The 1998 season was looming as the most important in franchise history. What happened on the field was likely going to influence an off-the-field matter that could simply determine the future of the franchise.

Scheduled just beyond the end of the season was a general election. On the ballot was a referendum and bond issue regarding the proposed baseball-only ballpark planned for downtown San Diego. Padres owner John Moores was very clear where he stood on the issue.

No new ballpark. No Padres.

"Major league baseball cannot survive in San Diego without the new ballpark," said Moores.

"We all knew the stakes," said starting pitcher Sterling Hitchcock. "If we didn't win…"

Hitchcock was one of three dependable starters the Padres had for the middle of the rotation. What they didn't have was that number one at the top; the veteran pitcher who would make everyone under him better; the ace.

Aces don't come cheap…unless a team is trying to dump salary.

Enter the Florida Marlins. Immediately after winning the 1997 World Series, Florida owner Wayne Huizenga embarked on a scorched-Marlin fire sale that made the Padres 1993 dismantling look like a camp fire.

And on the market was Kevin Brown, a tough-minded, no-nonsense right-hander. There were two reasons why the Marlins wanted to trade Brown. First, he was expensive. Second, he was going to become a free agent at the conclusion of the 1998 season.

"We knew acquiring Kevin Brown could be a one-season rental," said Padres general manager Kevin Towers. "But he was the missing piece. Kevin Brown was going to make us a much better baseball team."

Maybe a good enough team to win the National League pennant and, perhaps, the World Series. And how many votes come election time would a pennant or a world championship be worth?

The Marlins weren't going to give Kevin Brown away. To acquire the pitcher who might save a franchise, the Padres had to part with two of their brighter prospects—first baseman Derrek Lee (who would become a National League All-Star) and right-handed pitcher Rafael Medina (who would not). Towers completed the deal on December 15, 1997.

"If there is a player out there who can make you a contender, you go for him," said Kevin Towers. "You are not going to get that many chances to win."

The Padres definitely had a chance to win in 1998. Brown just upped the ante.

All that was left for Towers was to put some finishing touches on the product. One of his best moves was to persuade Dave Stewart to put his front-office aspirations on hold for a season and return to uniform as the Padres pitching coach. Stewart had served Towers as an assistant the previous season. And Towers acquired career-long Dodgers backup Carlos Hernandez to be the Padres front-line catcher.

The Opening Day roster was one of the most balanced in Padres history.

"I really liked our order," said Padres manager Bruce Bochy, who made few changes during the season.

Second baseman Quilvio Veras led off. He was followed by center fielder Steve Finley, right fielder Tony Gwynn, and Ken Caminiti, although the third baseman's lengthening list of injuries was cutting into his effectiveness.

No problem. Hitting behind Caminiti was Greg Vaughn, who would put up the greatest single-season power number in Padres

Tony Gwynn had the "biggest hit" of his career in the first game of the 1998 World Series against the Yankees. He drove a David Wells pitch off the upper deck façade in right to give the Padres a 4–2 lead. Alas, the lead was short-lived as the Yankees swept the Padres. Plagued by painful heel problems during the regular season, Gwynn's 16 homers was still the second-highest total of his career.

history—50 homers. Rounding out the lineup was first baseman Wally Joyner, catcher Carlos Hernandez, and shortstop Chris Gomez. Behind Kevin Brown in the rotation were Andy Ashby, Joey Hamilton, Sterling Hitchcock, and Mark Langston, who Kevin Towers signed as a free agent. The bullpen was anchored by Trevor Hoffman with Donne Wall and Dan Miceli as the main setup men.

The impact of Dave Stewart as pitching coach cannot be understated. As a pitcher, Stewart was a competitor of the Brown mode. "He showed us all how to be tougher and expect more from ourselves," said Andy Ashby. "He didn't want us to be happy about coming out of a game for a reliever. He and Brown had much the same views on pitching. Give me the ball and stand back.

"Dave liked you to have an attitude."

Clearly, the Padres' biggest improvement in 1998 over the disappointing 1997 season was pitching. The 1997 staff ERA was a franchise-worst 4.99. The staff ERA in 1998 plunged to 3.63. The starting pitchers ranked third in the major leagues with a 3.70 ERA. And the bullpen had a 3.46 ERA and led the major leagues with 31 wins and 59 saves.

The pitchers weren't always happy with Stewart. Hitchcock was a career-long starter. But he opened the season in the bullpen. Clearly unhappy at the start of the season, Hitchcock finished the 1998 season by being named the Most Valuable Player of the National League Championship Series.

If the stars weren't in perfect enough alignment, on the Opening Day of the season the Padres unveiled a banner honoring former owner Ray Kroc. The banner carried the R.A.K. initials that the National League champion 1984 Padres wore on their uniforms.

Slowed by early-season injuries to such key players as Ken Caminiti, Tony Gwynn, and Quilvio Veras, the Padres started slowly, although they managed to keep a slight lead in the National League West. Then the Padres exploded in midseason, going on a 54–28 run from June through August that included an 11-game winning streak.

"I don't think we've ever played better for an extended period of time," said Bochy. "We had a lot of guys who contributed...not just in one game but night after night. We were dangerous any time a number of guys came up."

Greg Vaughn was not the only Padre having a career season. Andy Ashby flourished as the number two to Kevin Brown, going 17–9 with a 3.34 ERA in a supporting role to Brown. And, after spending years as a Dodgers reserve, Carlos Hernandez hit .262 with nine homers and 52 RBIs as the Padres catcher.

Trevor Hoffman had a record-breaking season, during which one of the Padres' enduring traditions began. On July 25, as Hoffman came out of the Qualcomm Stadium bullpen seeking his 41st straight successful save conversion—which at the time would tie the major league record for consecutive saves—the sounds of AC/DC's "Hells Bells" debuted as the closer's anthem. Hoffman struck out Moises Alou to finish a 6–5 victory over Houston. The record belonged to Hoffman. So did the accompanying music.

Hoffman finished the season by tying the National League record with 53 saves in 54 attempts. That gave him a then–major league record .981 save percentage. Working 73 innings in 66 outings, Hoffman also had a 1.48 ERA. Rival batters got only 41 hits off Hoffman.

Sadly, Hoffman finished second to Atlanta's Tom Glavine in the voting for the National League Cy Young Award. Kevin Brown would finish third with a 18–7 record and a 2.38 ERA. He threw three shutouts and seven complete games in his 35 starts. Ashby was a far better pitcher working in the number two slot behind Brown than he had been in 1997.

The regular season flew by.

The Padres led the National League West 175 of 181 days. They won 98 games and went 54–27 at home—both marks being franchise records. The wins were six more than recorded by the 1984 Padres. And the 54 wins topped the franchise record of 50 set in 1978.

The Padres' bench played a huge role throughout the 1998 campaign. Center fielder Steve Finley and left fielder Greg Vaughn were the only Padres to play more than 145 games.

Back problems plagued Ken Caminiti. Tony Gwynn hit over .300 for the 16th straight season but spent time on the disabled list with problems to his left Achilles tendon. Second baseman Quilvio Veras had shoulder problems.

"Offensively, Vaughnie saved us," said Wally Joyner, whose 80 RBIs was third on the Padres behind Vaughn's 119 and Caminiti's 82.

PADRES SUPERLATIVES

Padres' Single-Season RBI Leaders by Position

Pos.	Player	Year	RBIs
1B	Ryan Klesko	2001	113
2B	Mark Loretta	2004	76
SS	Khalil Greene	2005	70
3B	Ken Caminiti	1996	130
OF	Tony Gwynn	1997	119
OF	Greg Vaughn	1998	119
OF	Dave Winfield	1979	118
C	Terry Kennedy	1983	98
P	Tim Lollar	1984	15

"We had guys in and out of the lineup and other guys who weren't having their best year. But Greg not only had a career season, much of it was done in the clutch."

The 1998 season will long be known as the Year of the Homer. It was the epic home-run race between Mark McGwire of St. Louis and Sammy Sosa of the Chicago Cubs that fueled renewed interest in America's pastime. McGwire finished with 70 homers to shatter Roger Maris's single-season record of 61. Sosa finished with 66.

Vaughn became the 27th player to hit 50 or more homers in a season. And he did it in somewhat dramatic fashion. A streak hitter, Vaughn hit his 49th homer on September 14. He didn't get number 50 until his final at-bat of the season after going homerless in nearly 40 at-bats. "That's just me," said Vaughn. "I've always been like that, things come in bunches and don't come in bunches."

Vaughn's 1998 season provided a poignant last-laugh for the Padres.

After being acquired from Milwaukee late in the 1996 season, Vaughn had struggled as a Padre. He hit only .206 in 141 at-bats with the Padres in 1996 and shared time in left with Rickey Henderson—a platoon that left neither player very happy.

Vaughn was struggling again in the summer of 1997 when Padres general manager Kevin Towers negotiated a trade that would send

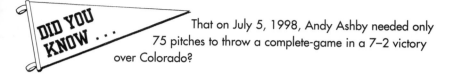

That on July 5, 1998, Andy Ashby needed only 75 pitches to throw a complete-game in a 7–2 victory over Colorado?

Vaughn to the Yankees for pitcher Kenny Rogers. There were immediate reports out of New York that Yankees boss George Steinbrenner wasn't happy with the trade. A physical was requested of Vaughn.

Although Vaughn had passed every physical he had ever taken as a Brewer and a Padre, he failed the Yankees physical. The Yankees voided the trade. Neither the Padres nor Vaughn, who had been labeled damaged goods, were happy.

"Sometimes, the best trades are the ones that fall through," said Towers in 1997 while trying to put the best possible spin on the voided trade. How true it was. The GM's comments 14 months later: "I don't know where we would have been had that trade with Vaughn to the Yankees gone through."

And some of the worst deals are the ones that get done.

The Padres began plotting strategy for the 1998 playoffs long before they clinched the National League West title. In late July, Towers became convinced the Braves were looking for a closer. Towers arrived at the opinion that the Braves had targeted left-hander Randy Myers, who was being shopped by the Toronto Blue Jays, for the job.

Myers and the Padres had a history. In 1992 Myers had 38 saves as the Padres closer after being acquired from Cincinnati for Bip Roberts. At the end of the 1992 season, Myers walked away from the Padres as a free agent, and the next year set the National League record with 53 saves for the Chicago Cubs.

As the end of the 1998 season approached, Myers was nearing his 36th birthday. With the Blue Jays, he had a 3–4 record with 28 saves, although his 4.46 ERA was high for a closer.

Clearly, the Padres' motivation in pursuing Myers was blocking him from going to Atlanta. And when the Blue Jays made him available on waivers in early August, the Padres—with a slightly poorer record—were in position to put in a claim that would be ahead of Atlanta's.

Unfortunately for the Padres, the Blue Jays accepted San Diego's offer of minor league catcher Brian Loyd. More critical to Toronto was dumping Myers's salary. Myers was still owed $1 million in 1998 plus another $13.6 million over 1999–2000.

Myers pitched 21 games for the Padres down the stretch of the 1998 season with a 6.28 ERA. But he never pitched another inning after 1998. The Padres were unsuccessful in their efforts to trade Myers away in the winter of 1998–1999. And during the following spring, Randy Myers developed arm problems that ended his career with the Padres holding the bag.

As it turned out, the Braves might not have been seeking Myers in those final days of the 1998 season.

The Padres clinched their third National League West championship in grand fashion on September 12. Trailing their arch-rival Dodgers 7–0 in the fifth inning before a sellout crowd of 60,823, the Padres rallied to defeat the Dodgers 8–7. The comeback started with a Wally Joyner homer and a two-run double by Chris Gomez in the fifth. An inning later, the Padres batted around while scoring five runs. Greg Vaughn started the rally with a single and capped it by singling home the winning run. In between, Dodgers pitchers walked six Padres to the ever-increasing delight of the packed house.

An hour after the Padres clinched, fans were still celebrating in the stands.

Although the Padres won the National League West by 9½ games and posted their best record ever, the two other National League division champions both had more than 100 wins. The Padres would not have the benefit of the home-field advantage.

Their opening-round opponent would be Houston from the National League Central. Not only had the Astros won 102 games during the regular season, they had been the league's hottest team down the stretch thanks to 6′10″ Randy Johnson, who was 10–1 with a 1.28 ERA after joining Houston.

The series opener at the Astrodome matched Johnson with Kevin Brown. The game was scoreless into the top of the sixth when Tony Gwynn doubled and scored on a sacrifice fly by Jim Leyritz. Greg Vaughn added a solo homer in the eighth. Brown, meanwhile, struck out a Division Series–record 16 while allowing only two hits over eight scoreless innings. The Astros would score an unearned run in the ninth before Hoffman closed out the win.

"Brownie lifted us to the next level," said Bochy. "He went up against their ace and never wavered. That type of performance gives any team quite a lift."

The Padres almost claimed the second game at Houston. Trailing 4–2 in the ninth, San Diego tied the score on a two-run homer by Jim Leyritz off Billy Wagner...the drive down the right-field line refusing to hook foul. The Astros won the game in the bottom of the inning on a single by Bill Spiers. Still, the Padres had gained an improbable split in Houston.

Now they were headed home to Qualcomm Stadium, which had become the Padres 10th man during playoff runs.

As had become tradition, more than 5,000 fans were awaiting the arrival of the Padres as their busses returned to Qualcomm Stadium around midnight after their second-game loss in Houston.

"Is it always like this in the playoffs?" Mark Sweeney asked Tony Gwynn as the players headed for their cars. "Always," replied Gwynn, laughing because "always" in terms of Padres playoff history had been 1984 and 1996.

Truth is, Qualcomm Stadium could be a house of horrors for any visiting team come playoff time. It was big. It was loud. And there always seemed to be a sea of white towels or shorts being twirled above heads.

"Qualcomm Stadium for a visiting team in the playoffs was a headache," Jeff Bagwell noted.

A sellout crowd of 65,235 packed The Q for the third game as Kevin Brown, on a gamble by manager Bruce Bochy, took the mound for the Padres on three days' rest. Brown was sensational. He allowed the Astros only one run on three hits over 6⅔ innings. In the meantime, Jim Leyritz was turning himself into the Padres version of Mr. October, his tie-breaking solo homer giving the Padres a 2–1 victory.

Still, Game 4 appeared iffy for the Padres. Randy Johnson would be working on his normal rest against Padres left-hander Sterling Hitchcock—who finished the season with a 9–7 record and 3.93 ERA with 12 of his 39 appearances being in the unsettling early-season role as a reliever.

TOP 10

Padres' Single-Season Home Run Leaders

	Player	Year	Home Runs
1.	Greg Vaughn	1998	50
2.	Phil Nevin	2001	41
3.	Ken Caminiti	1996	40
4.	Nate Colbert	1970	38t
	Nate Colbert	1972	38t
6.	Fred McGriff	1992	35
7.	Dave Winfield	1979	34t
	Phil Plantier	1993	34t
9.	Gary Sheffield	1992	33
10.	Fred McGriff	1991	31t
	Phil Nevin	2000	31t

Johnson was again on his game. But Hitchcock out-pitched the Astros ace, allowing Houston one run on three hits. In six innings, Hitchcock had 11 strikeouts and departed with a 2–1 lead thanks to a another solo homer by Jim Leyritz. The Padres exploded in the bottom of the eighth as a two-run triple by John Vander Wal and a two-run homer by Wally Joyner shot the Padres to a series-clinching 6–1 victory that produced another wild celebration from the 64,898 on hand.

The National League Championship Series would match the Padres and Braves. Atlanta had won 106 games during the regular season behind pitching greats Greg Maddux, Tom Glavine, and John Smoltz.

Because Kevin Brown had worked two games against Houston in the first round, Andy Ashby got the call to start the series opener for the Padres at Turner Field in Atlanta. Although a heavy rain delayed the start by more than two hours, Ashby was on top of his game, allowing the Braves one run on five hits over seven innings. But the Padres needed a tenth-inning homer from 1996 hero Ken Caminiti to pull out a 3–2 victory.

Game 2 in Atlanta would fall to a rested Brown, who responded with a complete-game, three-hit shutout with 11 strikeouts. Among his three hits, Quilvio Veras had the game-winning single in the Padres' 3–0 lead.

The Padres had a 2–0 lead in the series as they headed home to Qualcomm Stadium with a chance to win the pennant at home.

The third game in the series matched Hitchcock against four-time Cy Young Award–winner Greg Maddux. And Hitchcock prevailed, with the help of four relievers—anchored by Trevor Hoffman. The Padres 4–1 win gave them a 3–0 edge. They were within a game of a sweep.

But the Braves would not go quietly. Not only did they win the next two games, they threw a huge scare into the Padres as they sent the series back to Atlanta.

A grand slam by Andres Galarraga capped a six-run seventh as the Braves rallied to win the fourth game by an 8–3 count and forced the Padres faithful to put away the brooms they had snuck into Qualcomm Stadium. Still, the Padres were up 3–1 in the series and apparently had the Braves put away the following night: Kevin Brown entered the game in a rare relief role with the Padres ahead 4–2 on a pair of two-run homers by Ken Caminiti and John Vander Wal in the eighth. But Michael Tucker capped a five-run rally with a three-run homer off Brown in a 7–6 Braves victory. "I probably left Brown in a hitter too long," said Padres manager Bruce Bochy.

The Padres had not only lost the game—they had seemingly lost the momentum, and possibly Kevin Brown for the remainder of the NLCS—as the series headed back to Atlanta. But on the long flight that night to Georgia, the Padres were actually in a light mood.

"We're up 3–2, not down 3–2," Trevor Hoffman told his teammates. "All we need is one good game."

Enter Sterling Hitchcock. Paired against Tom Glavine in Game 6, the left-handed Hitchcock tossed five innings of two-hit shutout ball while striking out eight Braves. But the game was still a scoreless tie

By the NUMBERS

7–0—Padres record on their first homestand of the 1998 season.

going into the top of the sixth when the Padres struck for five runs in the top of the sixth.

Greg Vaughn and Ken Caminiti opened the inning with singles, and Leyritz gave the Padres their first run with a ground out. Wally Joyner made it 2–0 with an RBI single. With the Padres ahead and two on, the Braves walked Chris Gomez to force Bruce Bochy to make a decision: let his hottest pitcher hit or remove Hitchcock for a pinch-hitter. Bochy sent Hitchcock up to hit. The light-hitting Hitchcock hit a flare toward Danny Bautista in left. The Braves out-fielder blew the catch and two more runs scored to make it 4–0. Quilvio Veras singled home the fifth run.

Up by five runs, Bochy decided to take Hitchcock out after the first two Braves reached base in the sixth and turn the game over to his bullpen. Relievers Brian Boehringer, Mark Langston, Joey Hamilton, and Trevor Hoffman closed out Atlanta's season with four innings of no-hit ball.

Sterling Hitchcock was named the Most Valuable Player of the National League Championship Series for winning two games against Atlanta with a 0.90 ERA after beating the Astros in the Division Series. In four starts that postseason, Hitchcock was 3–0 with a 1.23 ERA. He allowed 15 hits in 22 innings.

But the MVP award could just as easily have gone to Leyritz, who was 6-for-22 with four homers and nine RBIs in the National League playoffs.

Playing without the home-field advantage, the Padres had gone 7–3 against the Astros and Braves. Their pitchers had a collective 2.39 ERA.

On to the World Series. On to New York and a showdown with the American League champion Yankees. Can the World Series be decided on a single pitch? The Padres believe the 1998 fall classic was.

But before we get to the actual World Series, take a short side trip with Tony Gwynn.

"It had always been my dream to play in a World Series at Yankee Stadium," said Gwynn. "To visit the monuments in center field, hear the voice of Bob Sheppard announce my name in the lineup, to ride the subway to Yankee Stadium."

Gwynn did all that...and more.

TOP 10

Padres' Single-Season Wins by a Relief Pitcher

	Player	Year	Record
1.	Butch Metzger	1976	11–4
2.	Rollie Fingers	1980	11–9
3.	Dan Miceli	1998	10–5
4.	Goose Gossage	1984	10–6
5.	Larry Hardy	1974	9–3
6.	Luis DeLeon	1982	9–5t
	Trevor Hoffman	1996	9–5t
8.	Lance McCullers	1986	9–6
9.	Craig Lefferts	1986	9–8
10.	Rollie Fingers	1979	9–9

He got the Padres off to a fast start against one of the greatest Yankees teams ever assembled. The Yankees had tied an American League record with 114 wins during the regular season.

The Yankees jumped out to a 2–0 lead in the first game. Greg Vaughn then tied the game with a two-run homer in the third. And two innings later, the Padres took a 5–2 lead on back-to-back homers by Gwynn and Vaughn.

Gwynn said his home run—off San Diego native and future Padre David Wells—was one of the "more dramatic moments of my career." His blast hit off the upper-deck façade at Yankee Stadium.

The opener had matched Wells against Kevin Brown, and the Padres ace seemed to pick up momentum after giving up two runs in the second. But in the fifth and sixth, Brown began to feel the effects of a flu bug that was working its way through the Padres clubhouse.

In the bottom of the seventh, the Yankees quickly tied the score at 5–5 on Chuck Knoblauch's three-run homer off reliever Donne Wall.

After Wall gave up another hit, Bochy called Mark Langston out of the bullpen. Langston retired two Yankees but walked two as well. The bases were loaded.

That brought up the left-handed hitting first baseman Tino Martinez. Langston went to a 2-and-2 count. He then appeared to throw a pitch right down the middle to Martinez, who took the pitch. Home-plate umpire Richie Garcia appeared ready to raise his hand for strike three when he called it ball three.

On the next pitch, Martinez hit a grand slam that carried the Yankees to a 9–6 win in the first game.

"It was a bad call, that was strike three," said Padres pitching coach Dave Stewart. Years later, Bochy said he still believed Langston's 2-and-2 pitch cut the heart of the plate for the third strike that would have gotten the Padres out of the inning tied at 5–5.

If Martinez's homer wasn't an omen, certainly the catch made by Yankees right fielder Paul O'Neill in the first inning of the second game was. With two on and two out, O'Neill robbed the Padres of a three-run lead with a circus catch of a Wally Joyner drive at the wall. "That was a crusher," said Joyner. "I thought that ball was in the seats."

The Yankees responded by exploding for nine runs on 14 hits in the first five innings against Padres starter Andy Ashby and reliever Brian Boehringer. An error by Ken Caminiti at third led to the Yankees three runs in the first.

The World Series then shifted to San Diego. Qualcomm Stadium would become the first facility to host a Super Bowl and a World Series in the same calendar year.

And once again, the Padres would respond. The turnout for Game 3 was 64,667. That was topped by the all-time record San Diego crowd of 65,427 that witnessed the fourth—and sadly last—game of the World Series. The Padres had drawn 2,555,874 fans during the regular season and another 447,036 for seven postseason games—a total of 3,002,910 for the entire season.

In the third game, Hitchcock continued his postseason magic. He blanked the Yankees through six innings. And in the bottom of the sixth, the Padres struck for three runs against Yankees starter David Cone. A solo homer by Yankees third baseman Scott Brosius and an error by Ken Caminiti led to two Yankees runs in the top of the seventh.

Still, the Padres were holding onto a 3–2 lead going into the top of the eighth. Randy Myers issued a leadoff walk to Paul O'Neill. With one out, Trevor Hoffman walked Tino Martinez. Then Brosius hit his second homer of the game—a three-run shot that led to his being named the Most Valuable Player of the World Series.

Game 4 was all Yankees thanks to Andy Pettitte, who blanked the Padres on five hits for 7⅓ innings. Meanwhile, Kevin Brown held the Yankees in check for five innings before the American League champs took a 1–0 lead in the sixth on an RBI grounder by Bernie Williams. The Yankees then pushed across two more runs in the eighth. The Padres had one last chance. They loaded the bases in the bottom of the eighth. The hitter was Jim Leyritz, the batting hero of the National League playoffs. But Yankees closer Mariano Rivera got Leyritz—who was 0-for-10 in the World Series—to line out to center.

For the second time in as many World Series appearances, the Padres had been beaten handily—both times by one of the most formidable teams in American League history, the 1984 Tigers and the 1998 Yankees.

The season was over. But it wasn't.

First, Qualcomm Stadium remained packed long after the final out. By this time, the Padres fully expected the reaction. They remained dressed. Players returned to the field for two and three curtain calls. The Yankees did not expect it. As the celebration continued, several of the Yankees could be seen returning to the visitors' dugout from their victory celebration to witness the "losing celebration."

"Think something like this would happen in Yankee Stadium if we had been swept?" said Brosius. "Not in a thousand years. This is unbelievable."

And there was the matter of a postseason parade...and that vote on the new downtown ballpark.

The Padres had played in Mission Valley. But their first-ever postseason parade wound through the downtown streets—close to the site for their proposed new ballpark. Two weeks later, 60 percent of the San Diego electorate voted to finance a new downtown home for the Padres.

The Padres had won the only thing bigger than a World Series.

Dry Spell

The Padres knew there was going to be a bump in the road following the 1998 World Series.

With the passage of the ballot measure to build their new downtown ballpark, the Padres' attention was split between the team playing in Mission Valley and what was going on downtown.

Money figured to be a little tight. At Qualcomm Stadium, the Chargers now controlled a lot of the outside revenue created by advertising and sales inside the stadium. But the Padres figured the drought would be short. They expected to be moving into their new home by the start of the 2002 seaon.

Then the other shoe fell.

Almost as soon as the ballpark ballot measure was passed by a 60 percent vote, a group of obstructionists, led by former San Diego City Councilman Bruce Henderson and taxpayer advocate Richard Rider, began filing a series of lawsuits aimed at blocking construction of the downtown ballpark. A total of 17 lawsuits would be filed. A total of 17 lawsuits would eventually de dismissed. But each had to wind its way through the legal system.

The cost to the Padres—in both legal fees and lost construction time—was near catastrophic. A year into the building process, construction on the partially constructed ballpark was shut down. Little work would be done for a full year. Concerns grew that the exposed metal in the ground might need to be replaced if the project was delayed much longer. Removal of the already completed work to start over was not an option, said Padres owner John Moores. Finally, he served notice. If construction didn't soon resume, the Padres were headed elsewhere.

By the NUMBERS

10—Grand slams hit by the Padres in 2001, including four by Phil Nevin. The Padres led the major leagues in grand-slam homers.

14—Straight wins from June 18 to July 2, 1999, a Padres team record.

24—Most hits in a game by the Padres, twice, against San Francisco on April 19, 1982, and against Atlanta on August 12, 2003.

Fortunately, the courts were also growing tired of the lawsuits. The legal system put a stop to the legal shenanigans and gave the green light for construction to resume. But the damage was immense. The Padres wouldn't be able to move into their new downtown home until the start of the 2004 season.

Over the five seasons from 1999 through 2003, budgets would be slashed and players would come and go. In fact, a lot would go in the weeks immediately following the 1998 World Series. Right-handed pitcher Kevin Brown, third baseman Ken Caminiti, and center fielder Steve Finley all departed the Padres following the 1998 season as free agents. The Padres didn't put up much of a fight to re-sign the two players who had come from Houston in the 1995 trade that laid the foundation for the 1996 and 1998 title seasons. Finley got a $2 million raise to sign with Arizona, and Caminiti returned to Houston for $1 million more than the Padres had paid him in 1998.

But Padres owner John Moores personally made the biggest offer in team history in an attempt to retain Kevin Brown. Moores committed more than $65 million in a five-year package—only to fall $40 million short of the Dodgers' offer.

"I am astounded the Dodgers would pay that much," said a stunned Moores. "We went much farther than we ever have before because of what Kevin did for this franchise last year and what he would mean in the future. But I never had any intention of going where the Dodgers did. I wonder who they were bidding against at the end."

By the start of the 1999 season, half the regulars from the 1998 National League champions would be gone. Left fielder Greg Vaughn and utilityman Mark Sweeney were traded to Cincinnati just before the start of spring training for left fielder Reggie Sanders and infielder-outfielder Damian Jackson. Catcher Carlos Hernandez suffered a ruptured left Achilles tendon with two weeks to go in spring training and missed the entire season on the disabled list. And Brown wasn't the only pitcher missing from the rotation. Joey Hamilton was traded to Toronto for Woody Williams.

The season was one of continual change. Forty-one players represented the Padres during the season and 18 made their Padres debuts. Six of those made their major league debuts. And two players the Padres counted on to replace the departed Finley and Caminiti failed, forcing the club to make more changes.

The Padres considered Ruben Rivera one of the top prospects to come along in years. They had acquired the Panamanian in a 1997 trade that transferred the rights of Japanese pitcher Hideki Irabu to the Yankees. The pending arrival of Rivera was one of the reasons why the Padres didn't attempt to retain Finley. They believed the 25-year-old would be their center fielder for years—he could run, hit, hit for power, and field. But he hit only .195 in 1999. And while he did have 23 homers, he finished with 48 RBIs.

At third base, the heir apparent was George Arias, who was coming off a banner season with the Padres Triple A affiliate. But as Arias got off to a slow start, the Padres turned to a player acquired in one of those trades that general manager Kevin Towers is famous for.

The California Angels were looking for a utility infielder as spring training neared an end. The Padres had a good candidate in Andy Sheets. What would the Padres want in return? How about Phil Nevin?

To that point, the 28-year-old Nevin had been a career-long underachiever. The first player taken in the 1992 draft by Houston after being named the Collegiate Player of the Year at Cal State–Fullerton, Nevin had stumbled as a professional player. He had been passed from Houston to Detroit to Anaheim. The

TRIVIA

Who is the only Padres pitcher to strike out the side on nine pitches?

Answers to the trivia questions are on pages 219–220.

1998 season marked his first full season in the major leagues, and although he appeared in only 75 games as a backup catcher, he led the American League with 20 passed balls. He had also hit only .228.

During five straight losing seasons to end the Padres' run at Qualcomm Stadium in Mission Valley, Phil Nevin provided much of the excitement. He led the Padres three times in homers and four times in RBIs. Nevin's total of 156 homers is second to Nate Colbert (163) on the Padres' all-time career chart.

Nevin joined the Padres as a reserve. And through the end of June, he was hitting only .231 in 121 at-bats with eight homers and 22 RBIs. That's when Padres manager Bruce Bochy decided—partially out of dire necessity—to give Nevin a shot at a bigger role. And by the first day of August, Nevin had become the Padres every day third baseman. He responded, finishing with a .269 average, 24 homers, 85 RBIs in just 383 at-bats, and was named the Most Valuable Player of an otherwise forgettable Padres season.

Indeed, the highlight of 1999 came on August 6 when Tony Gwynn got the 3,000[th] hit of his storied career—a first-inning single to right-center at Montreal's Olympic Stadium. The deliverer of the historic hit was the Expos' Dan Smith, who was facing Gwynn for the first time. Upon becoming the 22nd player to reach the 3,000-hit plateau—and only the seventh to have achieved the mark while spending his entire career with just one team—Gwynn's reaction was more of relief than jubilation.

"It's been a long journey," said Gwynn.

And it would get longer.

Gwynn twice went on the disabled list in 1999. In fact, 15 Padres endured 16 trips to the disabled list during the season. Ruben Rivera was the lone Opening Day starter not to spend at least two weeks on the disabled list. The club's 74–88 record marked a 24-game plunge from their record 98-win season of 1998.

If the Padres had a strength in 1999, it was their legs. San Diego stole 174 bases to lead both the National League and the major leagues. For the first time in franchise history, four Padres topped the 30-steal mark—Reggie Sanders (36), Damian Jackson (34), Eric Owens (33), and Quilvio Veras (30). Owens stole home on May 21 to pace the Padres 5–4 victory over Cincinnati, marking the first time since 1984 (Alan Wiggins) that a Padre had made a straight steal of home.

Stolen bases also played a role in the most improbable part of the long 1999 campaign. From June 18 to July 2, the Padres went on a franchise-record 14-game winning streak. Ten of the wins came at Qualcomm Stadium, including an 8–7 victory over Colorado on June 28 during which the Padres stole five bases as a team. Damian Jackson stole five bases alone to tie a club record established by Wiggins in 1984 and tied by Tony Gwynn in 1986.

"That team could create runs," Padres manager Bruce Bochy said years later. "We drew a lot of walks (631) and turned a lot of those into doubles with our speed."

TRIVIA

Which two records did Rickey Henderson break as a Padre in 2001?

Answers to the trivia questions are on pages 219–220.

The 1999 Padres remained hard to beat at home—46–35. But they were a miserable 28–53 on the road.

As disappointing as the 1999 season was, however, it was only the start of a franchise-wide malaise. The Padres wouldn't play .500 again until they reached their new home in 2004. And by the start of the 2000 season, only three Padres in the Opening Day lineup were members of the 1998 National League champions—Tony Gwynn, catcher Carlos Hernandez (who had returned after missing all of the 1999 season with a ruptured left Achilles tendon), and left-handed pitcher Sterling Hitchcock.

The Padres had made several major trades during the 1999–2000 off-season. San Diego and Atlanta exchanged the right sides of the infields, the Padres getting first baseman Ryan Klesko and second baseman Bret Boone for first baseman Wally Joyner and second baseman Quilvio Veras plus outfielder Reggie Sanders, who had hit .285 with 26 homers and 72 RBIs for the 1999 Padres. Left fielder Al Martin was acquired from the Pirates for pinch-hitter John Vander Wal. And right-handed pitchers Carlton Loewer, Adam Eaton, and Steve Montgomery were acquired from Philadelphia for right-handed pitcher Andy Ashby. Towers believed the latter trade would play an important role in the Padres' future. Loewer and Montgomery figured to be immediate members of the Padres staff, while Towers projected the 22-year-old Eaton to join the Padres by season's end.

And although Towers's prophecy on Eaton proved correct, the trade became a bust. Loewer shattered his right leg shortly after the trade while falling out of a tree in a hunting accident. Not only was he lost for the full 2000 season, his career was essentially over. And Montgomery was quickly shelved with arm problems.

Before the 2000 season was over, the record turnover of the 1999 campaign would be remembered as the good ol' days of continuity. A then-record 56 players appeared in Padres uniforms in 2000, including a National League–record 29 pitchers. The list included 17 rookies, 11 of whom had never before played in a major league game.

"You just can't do much with that kind of turnover," admitted Towers. "It seemed like for a while there, we were introducing a new player in the clubhouse every day."

The turnover did lend opportunity to a number of younger Padres—pitchers Adam Eaton, Kevin Walker, and Brian Tollberg; out-fielders Mike Darr and Xavier Nady; and catchers Ben Davis and Wiki Gonzalez. And a year after his rookie season, right-hander Matt Clement would lead the Padres in wins (13) and starts (34) in 2000. But he would be one of a dozen pitchers who started games for the Padres.

Offensively, the 2000 season marked a changing of the guard for the Padres.

Tony Gwynn had played only 36 games before his season officially ended on June 23 with surgery to his left knee. Clearly, Gwynn was on the sundown side of a brilliant career.

The offensive baton was passed to one of the best 1-2 combinations in Padres history—Ryan Klesko and Phil Nevin. Together, the pair hit 57 homers with 199 RBIs in 2000. They appeared to be the perfect compliment at the 3 and 4 spots in the order. The left-handed–hitting Klesko hit .283 with 26 homers, 92 RBIs, 23 steals, 91 walks, and a .393 on-base percentage. The right-handed slugger Nevin hit .303 with 31 homers and 107 RBIs.

But that was pretty much it. The next highest Padres in homers were Bret Boone and Ruben Rivera with 19 and 17, respectively. But Rivera hit only .208. The hustle of Eric Owens made him a fan favorite, and he hit .293 with 29 steals in Gwynn's absence. But only Woody Williams joined Clement with 10 or more wins. By this time, Trevor Hoffman had succeeded Gwynn as the most consistent producer in the Padres family. Hoffman had 43 saves, then the second-highest total in his career.

The 2001 season would be a turning point in Padres history. It would be Gwynn's 20th and last year. And although he closed out his career with a 19th consecutive .300 season, injuries had finally finished him off as an effective player. Sadly, after so many seasons of battling problems in his left leg, it was his good right leg that failed him. Gwynn would get only 102 at-bats.

The Padres reserved the final day of the season to pay tribute to Mr. Padre. But Gwynn wound up sharing the headlines with another future Hall of Famer. On the final day of the season, Rickey Henderson, who returned to the Padres as a free agent in 2001, hit a first-inning double off Colorado's John Thomson to join Gwynn in the elite 3,000-hit club. Earlier in the season, Henderson had set two major league records as a Padre—surpassing Babe Ruth as the all-time leader in walks on April 25 (with his 2,063rd free pass) and topping Ty Cobb as the all-time leader in runs scored with number 2,246 on October 4. Henderson reached the latter milestone with a fourth-inning homer off the Dodgers' Luke Prokopec. As he approached home plate, Henderson broke from his trot and slid into the plate.

"Rickey scored most of his runs on his fanny," joked Henderson. "That's how I should get the record. That's how people will remember Rickey."

As if anyone could ever forget Rickey Henderson.

Again, there was considerable change. Bret Boone left as a free agent and was replaced at second by Damian Jackson. Free agent signees Bobby Jones and Kevin Jarvis were the workhorses of a rotation filled with such prospects as Adam Eaton, Brian Lawrence, and Brian Tollberg. And on the eve of the season opener, the Padres acquired center fielder Mark Kotsay from Florida to replace the disappointing Ruben Rivera. The cost was Eric Owens.

The most controversial move of the season came just after the trading deadline, when the Padres sent right-handed pitcher Woody Williams to St. Louis for outfielder Ray Lankford in a waiver deal. Williams helped the Cardinals to the pennant, while Lankford produced few dividends for the Padres.

The 2001 season would feature some exceptional marks on both ends of the spectrum.

The Padres, who had not been no-hit since 1991 and hadn't suffered a home no-hitter since Dock Ellis's career "high" of 1970, were no-hit twice at Qualcomm Stadium by Florida's A. J. Burnett (May 12) and Bud Smith of St. Louis (September 3).

Padres hitters would set franchise records—that still stand—for both strikeouts (1,273) as well as walks (678). Led by Phil Nevin's four, the Padres would set a club record with 10 grand slams. And their 789 runs scored would come within six of the franchise record. But the Padres would also be shut out 16 times, including the two no-hitters.

That in 2000, the Padres tied a major league record by using 56 players, including a National League record 29 pitchers? During the 76–86 season, the Padres had 23 players on the disabled list, missing a total of 1,408 games.

"We blew red hot and cold all season," said Phil Nevin of the club that finished 79–83.

Offensively, the 2001 season was a repeat of 2000 with Nevin and Ryan Klesko carrying the load—this time combining for 71 homers and 239 RBIs (the highest combined total ever for a pair of Padres). It was only the second time a pair of Padres had hit 30 or more homers in the same season.

Clearly, the Padres believed that in Klesko and Nevin they had a 3-4 combination to build around for the future. As the 2001 season ended, both would be 31 and in the prime of their careers entering the 2002 season. And over the 2000–2001 seasons, the pair had combined to hit 132 doubles and 128 homers with 438 RBIs.

The Padres moved quickly to tie both to long-term contracts. But there were several problems. Neither was particularly strong defensively at their assigned positions. Klesko was a marginal left fielder who had been moved to first. Nevin's best position was probably first, but he was playing third. But starting with 2002, due mainly to injuries, the pair never reached the heights of 2000–2001.

Overall, the 2002 season was among the most forgettable in Padres history. Remember, 2002 was to have been the year that the Padres moved into their new downtown home. Instead, construction was just resuming as the last of the 17 legal challenges was being cleared and a judge finally told the plaintiffs that enough was enough.

On the eve of spring training, popular outfielder Mike Darr, who had hit .277 in 2001, died in a single-car accident near the Padres training site in Peoria, Arizona. Like they had in 1984 following the death of owner Ray Kroc, the Padres wore a black patch with the 25-year-old Darr's No. 26 on their jersey throughout the season.

The revolving door that had become the Padres' roster spun into dangerous overdrive in 2002. The Padres upped their own records for participation as they used a total of 59 players (the National League mark), including a major league record 37 pitchers. Twenty-three of those pitchers won at least one game (another major league record).

Twenty Padres made a total of 27 trips to the disabled list—costing the Padres the equivalent of 1,406 games.

Among the players making their debuts in 2002 was a 21-year-old right-handed pitcher named Jake Peavy, whose first major league start came on June 22 against the New York Yankees before the largest crowd (60,021) of the 2002 season. Peavy allowed only one run on three hits over six innings before a national television audience, but suffered a 1–0 loss.

The Padres' record in 2002 plunged to 66–96. They won only 25 games on the road—only one more than the record-low in franchise history.

Ryan Klesko paced the offense with a .300 average, 29 homers, and 95 RBIs. But the other half of the Padres' dynamic duo, Phil Nevin, battled his way through an injury-plagued season. He twice wound up on the disabled list. First he suffered a strained left elbow while diving for a grounder at third in April. Shortly after returning to action, he broke the humerus bone in his left arm while diving for another ball. The Padres would go 17–33 without Nevin. And when the three-time Padres Most Valuable Player returned in July, he struggled. Nevin would finish with a .285 average, 12 homers, and 57 RBIs. The team would never get another complete season out of the Klesko-Nevin tandem.

TRIVIA

Which Padre got the 3,000th hit of his career at home?

Answers to the trivia questions are on pages 219–220.

The 2003 campaign would be the Padres' last in Qualcomm Stadium. Sadly, they couldn't go out on a winning note, finishing last in the National League West for a second straight season with a 64–98 mark that represented the club's worst performance since the fire sale season of 1993.

It didn't help that both Phil Nevin and Ryan Klesko missed large parts of the season on the disabled list. The Padres went to spring training with the thought of moving Nevin to left field to protect his tender left arm. Klesko would move from left field to first base. But on March 7, Nevin dislocated his left shoulder diving for a ball in the outfield during an exhibition game in Tucson. Four days later, Nevin underwent surgery that would sideline him until after the All-Star break. He would play just 59 games with 13 homers and 46 RBIs.

Meanwhile, Klesko was limited to 121 games due to back and shoulder problems. After hitting 19 homers in the first half of the season, Klesko hit just two after the break before cutting his season on September 5 to have surgery to the AC joint of his right shoulder.

But the key injury of 2003 was to closer Trevor Hoffman. Two weeks into spring training, Hoffman underwent surgery to have the tip of his right scapula trimmed to remove an impediment. The surgery would sideline Hoffman until September, and he never appeared in a save situation during the 2003 season.

Of course, there weren't a lot of save situations. But it wasn't until the Padres signed veteran Rod Beck on June 2 that the Padres found a reliable closer. Beck would finish with a 3–2 record, 20 saves, and a 1.78 ERA.

The Padres were already making plans for the opening of their new home. On August 26, the Padres acquired outfielder and San Diego County native Brian Giles from Pittsburgh for outfield prospect Jason Bay and left-handed pitcher Oliver Perez. Right-handed pitcher Clay Hensley was obtained from the Giants for relief pitcher Matt Herges. Catcher Ramon Hernandez and outfielder Terrence Long came from Oakland in exchange for outfielder Mark Kotsay.

And after signing Mark Loretta as a free agent going into the 2003 season, the Padres extended his contract two years as the veteran second baseman responded with a career-best season—a .314 average with 13 homers and 72 RBIs.

During the Padres "Say Goodbye to the Q" final homestand, they announced their all-time team as selected by the fans.

Naturally, Tony Gwynn received the most votes and was joined in the outfield by Dave Winfield and Steve Finley. The infield consisted of Steve Garvey (first), Roberto Alomar (second), Ozzie Smith (short), and Ken Caminiti (third). Benito Santiago was the catcher. Randy Jones was named the starting pitcher, with Trevor Hoffman the closer. Bruce Bochy was the manager.

The Padres bid farewell to Qualcomm Stadium on September 28, 2003. Ready or not, they were headed downtown.

QUALCOMM ALL-TIME LEADERS

Games Played

Padres		Opponents	
Player	**Games**	**Player**	**Games**
1. Tony Gwynn	1,220	1. Dave Concepcion	136
2. Garry Templeton	651	2. Pete Rose	129
3. Dave Winfield	555	3. Jose Cruz	120

Batting Average (minimum 50 at-bats)

Padres		Opponents	
Player	**Avg.**	**Player**	**Avg.**
1. Gary Sheffield	.360	1. Jay Johnstone	.429
2. Jay Johnstone	.348	2. Wayne Krenchicki	.420
3. Tony Gwynn	.343	3. Mark McGwire	.404

At-Bats

Padres		Opponents	
Player	**At-Bats**	**Player**	**At-Bats**
1. Tony Gwynn	4,534	1. Pete Rose	514
2. Garry Templeton	2,249	2. Dave Concepcion	486
3. Dave Winfield	1,944	3. Dale Murphy	435

Hits

Padres		Opponents	
Player	**Hits**	**Player**	**Hits**
1. Tony Gwynn	1,555	1. Pete Rose	149
2. Garry Templeton	540	2. Barry Bonds	129
3. Dave Winfield	526	3. Jose Cruz	127

QUALCOMM ALL-TIME LEADERS

Runs Scored

Padres		Opponents	
Player	**Runs**	**Player**	**Runs**
1. Tony Gwynn	698	1. Barry Bonds	101
2. Dave Winfield	274	2. Joe Morgan	72
3. Gene Richards	224	3. Pete Rose	70

Doubles

Padres		Opponents	
Player	**No.**	**Player**	**No.**
1. Tony Gwynn	262	1. Pete Rose	25
2. Garry Templeton	92	2. Tony Perez	24
3. Dave Winfield	90	3. Steve Garvey	23

Triples

Padres		Opponents	
Player	**No.**	**Player**	**No.**
1. Tony Gwynn	49	1. Willie Davis	8
2. Gene Richards	28	2. Joe Morgan	7
3. Garry Templeton	19		

Home Runs

Padres		Opponents	
Player	**No.**	**Player**	**No.**
1. Nate Colbert	72	1. Barry Bonds	40
2. Dave Winfield	71	2. Dale Murphy	24t
3. Tony Gwynn	66	Johnny Bench	24t

QUALCOMM ALL-TIME LEADERS

RBIs

Padres

Player	RBIs
1. Tony Gwynn	542
2. Dave Winfield	297
3. Terry Kennedy	225

Opponents

Player	RBIs
1. Barry Bonds	96
2. Dale Murphy	72
3. Andre Dawson	69

Steals

Padres

Player	Steals
1. Tony Gwynn	147
2. Gene Richards	120
3. Alan Wiggins	93

Opponents

Player	Steals
1. Cesar Cedeno	35
2. Joe Morgan	27
3. Davey Lopes	25t
Lou Brock	25t

Pitching—Wins

Padres

Player	No.
1. Randy Jones	54
2. Eric Show	52
3. Ed Whitson	39

Opponents

Player	No.
1. Tom Seaver	18
2. Joe Niekro	15
3. Don Sutton	14

Pitching—Saves

Padres

Player	No.
1. Trevor Hoffman	181
2. Rollie Fingers	52
3. Rich Gossage	44

Opponents

Player	No.
1. John Franco	18
2. Gene Garber	18
3. Bruce Sutter	15

QUALCOMM ALL-TIME LEADERS

Pitching–Losses

Padres		Opponents	
Player	**No.**	**Player**	**No.**
1. Clay Kirby	45	1. Phil Niekro	13
2. Randy Jones	42	2. Don Sutton	11
3. Eric Show	39	3. Greg Maddux	10t
		Bob Knepper	10t

ERA (minimum 25 innings pitched)

Padres		Opponents	
Player	**Avg.**	**Player**	**Avg.**
1. Donne Wall	1.17	1. Mel Rojas	0.69
2. John Urrea	1.73	2. Denny Neagle	0.96
3. Mike Matthews	1.78	3. Bill Hands	0.96

Games Pitched

Padres		Opponents	
Player	**No.**	**Player**	**No.**
1. Trevor Hoffman	324	1. John Franco	44
2. Craig Lefferts	189	2. Gene Garber	43
3. Eric Show	152	3. Gary Lavelle	39

Innings Pitched

Padres		Opponents	
Player	**No.**	**Player**	**No.**
1. Randy Jones	953	1. Phil Niekro	232
2. Eric Show	820	2. Don Sutton	217⅓
3. Ed Whitson	712⅓	3. Tom Seaver	205⅔

QUALCOMM ALL-TIME LEADERS

Strikeouts

Padres

Player	No.
1. Andy Benes	557
2. Eric Show	540
3. Clay Kirby	451

Opponents

Player	No.
1. Tom Seaver	159
2. Don Sutton	148
3. Phil Niekro	145

PETCO Park

Shortly after taking his first cuts at the Padres new downtown ball-park, Barry Bonds was asked if the designers of PETCO Park had made it Bonds-proof.

"No," said the Giants slugger. "They made it baseball-proof."

Beauty, it is said, is in the eyes of the beholder.

And most of the people who view PETCO Park see it as the diamond it was designed to be—the glistening cornerstone of both the Padres' future and the eastern extension of San Diego's down-town redevelopment program.

Pitchers also have no problem spotting the beauty of PETCO Park.

Hitters?

"It's pretty clear they didn't design this ballpark with the team we have now in mind," Ryan Klesko said after taking his first left-handed swings at PETCO Park in the late winter of 2004. None of the balls Klesko and Brian Giles launched toward right center reached the distant 411-foot fence. Drive as they might, every shot fell short.

Even before the Padres had played an official game in their new home, the mystique of PETCO Park was in place. The beauty was also a beast, particularly if you were a left-handed power hitter...or a right-handed hitter who drove the ball to right-center, like the Padres' Phil Nevin.

The remote distance to the fence in right-center wasn't the only factor conspiring against hitters. As the experts worked to set the outfield dimensions at PETCO Park—which is named for the San Diego–based pet supplies distributor—they noticed the breeze blew from the left-field corner to the right-field corner. What they didn't

PETCO Park

Left-Field Foul Line: 334 feet

Left: 367 feet

Left-Center Power Alley: 402 feet

Center: 396 feet

Right-Center Power Alley: 402 feet

Right: 387 feet

Right-Field Foul Line: 322 feet

Lighting: Eight standards carrying 720 fixtures with the equivalent of 58 million candles

Main Scoreboard: 34' high by 80' wide (with a 30' x 53' video board)

Seats: 42,445 (15,225 on field level between foul poles).

recognize was that the sometimes-stiff wind was a sea breeze that usually faded out at dusk.

Plus, there is an atmospheric condition that affects PETCO Park, particularly in the spring and early summer when the prevailing evening marine layer is laden with moisture.

"The ball just doesn't carry at PETCO Park until it gets drier with summer," says Brian Giles. "Plus, there have been nights when I'm standing in right field and I can feel the wind blowing down the back of my shirt. Down. I'm not kidding."

You don't have to tell Geoff Blum. On June 1, 2005, Blum launched what surely appeared to be a game-winning, grand-slam homer toward the seats in right. "That ball was out of here," said Blum. "And it came straight down. Honest. I've never hit a ball harder." Blum wasn't alone in that assessment.

"Some balls that would be out of any other park are routine outs here," says Ryan Klesko.

To which pitchers say, "Hooray!"

"There are so many hitter's parks in the major leagues these days, why shouldn't there be one pitcher's park?" said former Padres pitcher Woody Williams. "Besides, you can hit the ball out of here. A lot of players have."

Truth is, PETCO Park worked out to be exactly what Padres owner John Moores and the ballpark's designers wanted it to be—a beautiful and unique place packed with idiosyncrasies.

What other ballpark was designed with the corner of a historic building forming the left-field foul line? What other ballpark has a park beyond the center-field fence?

Dick Freeman wasn't with the Padres when PETCO Park was designed. But after he returned in October of 2002 to oversee the completion of the ballpark's construction, the Padres president marveled at how elements of PETCO Park came together.

"At every turn as you walk through this facility, there is something else that awes you, whether it is the Western Metal Supply Company building, the Park at the Park, the views of the city and San Diego Bay, or the field itself," said Freeman. "This ballpark captures the essence of San Diego."

PETCO Park occupies 17.3 acres on the southeastern end of downtown San Diego—an extension of the city's popular Gaslamp dining and entertaining district. From its near-bayfront setting to the "Padre gold" earthtones of the exterior buildings, PETCO Park fits into San Diego.

Although creating a baseball-only ballpark was part of John Moores's dream when he bought the Padres in 1994, the idea didn't gain momemtum until two years later, when the third and final expansion of Qualcomm Stadium made the 70,000-seat facility an unwieldy host for baseball.

"I remember when you could see the mountains out beyond right field," remembered Tony Gwynn. "San Diego Stadium had a

16—Rainouts in Padres history, including one in three seasons at PETCO Park.

That the official address of PETCO Park is 19 Tony Gwynn Drive?

cozy feel. When they completely enclosed the stadium with the third deck, the new Qualcomm Stadium lost a lot of the ambience that baseball needs."

Not only was Qualcomm Stadium growing bigger, it was growing older. Across the land, new ballparks with an old warmth—starting with Jacobs Field in Cleveland and Camden Yards in Baltimore— were changing baseball. Moores and Padres president Larry Lucchino wanted that feel for San Diego. And palm trees in the out-field weren't going to do it.

"This franchise needs a new ballpark to survive and thrive," said Lucchino, who was Moores's more-than-capable front-man on the ballpark project.

By the end of the 1997 season, a mayor's task force agreed with the Padres' argument that a "new, baseball-oriented ballpark was essential to the long-term success of the Padres in San Diego."

Late in 1997, the Padres assembled an architectural team led by HOK Sports + Venue + Event and design architect Antoine Predock. The Padres, the city of San Diego, and the design team soon targeted a redevelopment area in the city's East Village as the site for a project that became known as "A Ballpark for San Diego."

In August 1998, as the Padres were headed toward their third National League West title (and second in three seasons), the San Diego City Council voted to place the ballpark measure on the November ballot. Almost immediately, former San Diego city councilman and ballpark opponent Bruce Henderson filed suit to invalidate the ballpark ballot measure and block the vote. On September 4, the San Diego Superior Court ruled Proposition C was valid and could go on the November 3 general election ballot.

The vote was on. So were the Padres. They would win their second National League pennant in October. And not even a four-game sweep by the Yankees in the World Series could dull the electorate's enthusiasm for the proposed ballpark. The ballpark ballot measure passed with 59.64 percent support.

On February 15, 1999, the Padres unveiled a model of the new ballpark. On February 10, 2000, demolition at the site began. Two days later, San Diego native and Hall of Famer Ted Williams was on hand as the Padres planted a demonstration right-field foul pole. Excavation of the site began on May 22, 2000, and the first piles were driven at the site on June 19.

But a volley of suits filed by Henderson and his supporters took their toll. Because of pending litigation—and an investigation into assistance Moores made on the behalf of cancer-stricken San Diego City

Although it opened two years behind schedule, in 2004, due to a series of legal challenges, PETCO Park immediately became a downtown landmark in San Diego and a focal point for continued area redevelopment. Two of the park's unique features—the Western Metal Supply Co. building standing at the left-field foul line and the Park at the Park to the right of the batter's eye in right center—set the Padres' home apart from any other ballpark.

DID YOU KNOW ... That the first Padre to steal a base at PETCO Park was pitcher Adam Eaton on April 13, 2004?

Councilwoman Valerie Stallings—construction at the ballpark site was suspended on October 2, 2000, with the project 15 percent complete.

Gone was the dream of opening the new ballpark in 2002. Gone also was Tony Gwynn's dream of finishing his career in the new ballpark. Gwynn retired at the end of the 2001 season. "If the ballpark was opening in 2002 as originally planned, I was going to be there," said Gwynn. "No way I could make it to 2004."

The legal challenges to the ballpark project came to a head on December 6, 2001, when opponents filed a suit seeking to have the courts void the 1998 vote that approved the ballpark and order a new vote. The 16th suit filed in opposition to the ballpark was an all-or-nothing challenge. And the San Diego Superior Court's dismissal of the suit on January 30, 2002, doubled as a go-ahead for the project.

Construction at the ballpark site resumed on February 18, 2002—six weeks before the originally scheduled opening date— three days after the ballpark bonds were sold.

Work advanced rapidly. Padres owner John Moores and San Diego Mayor Dick Murphy put a ceremonial bag at second on December 18, 2002, when construction reached the half-way point. The final piece of structural steel was put in place on February 14, 2003. The first seat was installed on May 5, 2003. The first lockers in the Padres clubhouse were installed on June 25, 2003. On August 4, construction was 75 percent complete.

The Padres officially moved into their new home on January 4, 2004, although construction wouldn't officially be completed until mid-February.

PETCO Park was worth the wait.

"My, this is amazing," a longtime Padres fan said on April 8, 2004, as the Padres officially christened their downtown home with a 4–3, 10-inning victory over San Francisco.

"It glistens," said another fan, as the afternoon sun hit on the "Padre gold" stone of PETCO Park's support buildings. "It reminds me of a wedding, something old, something new, and all these blue seats."

PETCO Park wasn't at the forefront of the wave of new ballparks opening in the major leagues, but it was unique—featuring an openness that was San Diego and a building that serves as the left-field foul pole. Outwardly, the Western Metal Supply Company building and the Park at the Park are what set PETCO Park apart from the rest. But the $453.4 million project also features support buildings semi-detached from the main structure, leaving the steel support beams for the ballpark's superstructure exposed.

The brick-faced Western Metal building was built in 1909–1910 at the corner of Seventh Avenue and K Street in the heart of what was San Diego's industrial district. The original business of Western Metal Supply was to support San Diego's blacksmiths and carriage makers. Over the years, Western Metal Supply distributed everything from irrigation equipment to roofing supplies to engine parts. That building is the largest of a dozen historic structures inside the Ballpark District, but it's the only one incorporated directly into the ballpark. Many of the inner workings of the building are prominently displayed, including the original, manually operated freight elevator, boilers, safes, and huge exposed beams used in the original construction.

The main concourse for PETCO Park flows through the Western Metal building, as does a museum that includes pictures and artifacts of the area dating back to the 19th century. The building also hosts two floors of party suites (several of which actually jut out into fair territory in left field), a restaurant, and the Padres team store.

Prominent on the roof—which is 80 feet above the playing field and offers views of San Diego Bay to the west as well as the mountains to the east—are two areas, one for group parties and the other for standing-room-only viewing.

TRIVIA

What player was the last Padre to homer at Qualcomm Stadium in 2003 and the first to homer at PETCO Park in 2004?

Answers to the trivia questions are on pages 219–220.

The Park at the Park is another unique feature that features a grassy knoll just beyond the bleachers in right center. The 2.7-acre park is the first attached to a major league ballpark since Pittsburgh's Forbes Field closed in 1970.

The Park is open to all during the day. On game nights, Park at the Park tickets—which also allow for viewing from other standing-room-only areas around PETCO Park—go for $5, with fans allowed to bring blankets to place on the ground. Park at the Park visitors are supported by a video board on the back of the Batter's Eye structure in center. And in one corner of the Park at the Park is a youth baseball diamond. On some nights, members of the Padres bullpen, including Trevor Hoffman, have been known to come out and play with the children of Padres fans. The Park at the Park lends a mystery to PETCO Park. The bowl has 42,445 seats. But the ballpark's actual capacity rises and falls based on how many tickets are available on any given night at the Park.

TRIVIA

Who scored the first run at PETCO Park?

Answers to the trivia questions are on pages 219–220.

The total cost of the ballpark was $453.4 million. The actual construction cost was $298 million, with $104 million spent on land acquisition and $51.3 million for infrastructure work. The Padres footed approximately $200 million of the total bill.

Through 2033, PETCO Park is owned 70 percent by the city and 30 percent by the Padres. After 30 seasons, San Diego becomes the sole owner of the ballpark.

There have been several cosmetic changes made to the facility since it opened in 2004. The original Batter's Eye—dubbed the "green monstrosity"—was widened and painted a dark blue to match the color of the seats and predominant trim after the first season. And before the Padres third season at PETCO Park, the distance to the right-field power alley was shortened nine feet to 402 feet. More modifications to the right-center seating area will likely be made following the 2007 season.

In the meantime, it is possible to reach the stands at PETCO Park. If a right-handed hitter pulls the ball toward the left-field corner, the drive almost seems to be sucked in by the Western Metal Supply building. If a left-handed hitter pulls the ball, there is a short porch down the line in right. And the 396-foot porch in straight-away center is reachable from either side of the plate. But the more-distant power alleys are a different story.

"I think it makes the ballpark," Padres general manager Kevin Towers said of PETCO Park's multiple personalities.

It certainly makes for lively debate.

Back to the Top

There were high expectations as the Padres headed to PETCO Park to start the 2004 season. And not just from the Padres.

Since the subject of the new ballpark was first raised, Padres fans had heard promises that things would be different once the team got into its new home. The fans took that to mean better players and better fans. And they expected immediate rewards. After all, the fans of San Diego had voted in favor of the ballpark. And they had ridden out five long years waiting for the project to be completed. Everything the Padres had asked for had been granted. Now the fans wanted to share in the rewards. They wanted a winner.

"The message from our fans was pretty clear," said general manager Kevin Towers. "Now that we were in the ballpark they had helped us build, they expected results."

And the Padres delivered...sort of.

The first three seasons in PETCO Park also marked the first time that the team had three straight winning seasons. And the Padres won the National League West title in both 2005 and 2006—marking the first time the club advanced to the playoffs in back-to-back seasons. But both trips to the playoffs resulted in quick elimination at the hands of the St. Louis Cardinals. The Padres were swept in 2005, and they won only one game in 2006.

What followed caught almost everyone by surprise. Manager Bruce Bochy was advised there would be no immediate extension of his contract, which was due to expire at the end of the 2007 season. In addition, Padres CEO Sandy Alderson gave the Padres manager of 12 seasons permission to speak to other clubs. Bochy jumped and became the manager of the division rival San Francisco Giants. The

Padres, in turn, signed Bud Black, who was once a teammate of Tony Gwynn's at San Diego State, as their 16th manager.

"It's been a whirlwind," said Towers.

And while he was talking about the weeks immediately following the 2006 season, he could have been talking about the Padres' first three seasons at PETCO Park. Even before the Padres made their debut downtown, it became obvious the keys to success at the new park were going to be pitching, defense, and speed. Which created a problem.

The Padres team that completed its run at Qualcomm Stadium was a station-to-station club. And its two main sources of power, Ryan Klesko and Phil Nevin, were given to driving the ball toward right-center—which would become known as "Death Valley" at PETCO Park.

General manager Kevin Towers did start the needed overhaul going into the 2004 season. On November 26, 2003, the Padres acquired catcher Ramon Hernandez and outfielder Terrence Long from Oakland for center fielder Mark Kotsay. Then they signed center fielder Jay Payton and Japanese relief pitcher Akinori Otsuka as free agents. The coup came on January 6, 2004, when the Padres signed left-handed starter David Wells under the noses of the New York Yankees.

The 40-year-old Wells, who was raised in San Diego, had agreed to accept a minor league contract with the Yankees after undergoing back surgery in early December. Despite posting a 15–7 record during the 2003 regular season with New York, Wells's career appeared in jeopardy after back problems forced him out of Game 5 of the World Series.

Wells was anxious to prove he was still a front-line starter. And he liked the idea of continuing his career in his hometown. Rather than reporting to the Yankees with a minor league contract, he accepted an incentive-laden contract from the Padres.

"One of the best contracts I've ever drawn," Kevin Towers would say. "It benefited both David and us every time he went out there."

The 2004 season turned out to be a banner season for the Padres. PETCO Park was a smash hit. A regular-season, franchise record 3,016,752 fans passed through the turnstiles—not only to see the new downtown ballpark but to see the most improved team in baseball.

Although they finished third in the National League West, the Padres' 87–75 record represented a 23-game improvement over 2003—marking the biggest single-season gain in franchise history as well as the most positive forward swing in the major leagues for 2004.

Only one small problem: the Padres were a better team on the road (45–36) than at home (42–39).

That, and the Padres' key power threats—Klesko and Nevin—complained about the dimensions of PETCO Park deep into the season to the disgust of club officials. Bouncing back strongly from the injuries that plagued him the previous two seasons, Nevin returned to first base in 2004 and had productive numbers—a .289 average while leading the Padres in both homers (26) and RBIs (105). But his continued grousing about PETCO Park created a rift that resulted in a clubhouse shouting match between Nevin and Towers late in the summer. In the meantime, Klesko, who was returning from shoulder surgery and was back in left field, hit .291, although his power totals dipped to nine homers and 66 RBIs. For one reason or another, Nevin and Klesko were no longer the cornerstones of the franchise.

The hitter to watch was second baseman Mark Loretta, who had one of the greatest offensive seasons in Padres history. Loretta had career highs with a .335 average, 208 hits, 47 doubles, 16 homers, 76 RBIs, and 108 runs scored. He became the first Padre—and, remember, this is the team of Tony Gwynn—to have 200 hits, 100 runs, and

By the NUMBERS

2—Padres shortstops who have hit more than 10 homers in a season, Steve Huntz (11 in 1970) and Khalil Greene (who hit 15 in 2004, 2005, and 2006).

3.87—Padres ERA in 2006, marking the first time they led the National League in ERA.

7—Triple plays turned by the Padres in their history.

13—Straight times that outfielder Brian Giles reached base in 2005, a Padres record.

22—Wins in May of 2005, a Padres record for most wins in any month.

75 RBIs in the same season. Loretta's hit total was the fifth-highest in Padres history. The four players ahead of him are all named Tony Gwynn.

"One of the best seasons I've ever seen," said none other than Gwynn. "Mark kept us going," said Bochy. "It was not just one or two streaks, it was day-in, day-out production. If he was leading off, he got on. If we had a runner at third, he got him in."

On top of everything else, Loretta had 16 sacrifice flies—the fifth-highest total in major league history.

"What can I say? It was just one of those magical seasons," said Loretta, who was a unanimous pick as the Padres Most Valuable Player in 2004. "It was extremely rewarding for me. To come into a new park with all the enthusiasm of the city and have a season like that, it would be a dream come true for any player."

Loretta wasn't the only Padre to have a "magical season." Twenty-three-year-old right-handed pitcher Jake Peavy led the major leagues with a 2.27 earned-run average and posted a 15–6 record. Over the course of 27 starts, Peavy held opposing hitters to a .236 average. Peavy's ERA was the third-lowest in history for a Padres starter. He was the youngest pitcher to win the National League ERA title since 21-year-old Dwight Gooden in 1985 and followed club legend Randy Jones as only the second Padre to win the ERA title. Overnight, the humble Loretta and emotional kid from Alabama had become the Padres' stars.

Clearly, this was a new age.

Peavy was far from the only pitcher who had a notable season for the Padres. Sinker-ball specialist Brian Lawrence also won 15 games with a 4.12 ERA. Adam Eaton had 11 wins.

Wells won 12 games and deserved to win more. Throughout the season, he seemed to be the only Padres starter failed by the otherwise stellar Padres bullpen. Trevor Hoffman rebounded strongly from the shoulder surgery that had wiped out his 2003 season. He had 41 saves and a 2.30 ERA. Plus, right-handed setup specialists Scott Linebrink (2.14 ERA) and Akinori Otsuka (1.75 ERA) both appeared in 73 games.

"I think it was personal," joked Wells, who lost as many as six wins because of the bullpen's inability to hold leads on his behalf. All four of Hoffman's blown saves, for example, came at the expense of Wells.

What the Padres lacked on the mound was a fifth starter—and it cost them a shot at the National League pennant.

Offensively, the Padres were far more dangerous on the road (.288 average, 5.4 runs a game) than they were at home (.256 average, four runs a game)—and this would become a puzzling trend for the club over their first three seasons.

Loretta was the lone Padre to hit better than .300. Brian Giles (23) was the only hitter besides Nevin to hit more than 20 homers. Shortstop Khalil Greene's all-around play at short (.273 with 15 homers and 65 RBIs plus dazzling plays in the field) made him a Rookie of the Year candidate until his season ended early in September with a fracture to his right index finger.

Elsewhere, however, there were holes. Ryan Klesko, Jay Payton, and Terrence Long didn't give the Padres the defense the club needed in left and center, considering the dimensions of PETCO Park. Young third baseman Sean Burroughs hit a "soft" .298 (two homers, 47 RBIs in 523 at-bats).

More changes would be needed to fit the Padres to their new home.

The Padres entered the 2004–2005 off-season seeking to upgrade their defense and starting pitching. To improve the defense in center, San Diego prep product and Boston postseason hero Dave Roberts was acquired from the Red Sox for outfielder Jay Payton and utility infielder Ramon Vazquez. Four years after losing right-handed starter Woody Williams to the Cardinals in the ill-fated deal for outfielder Ray Lankford, the Padres re-acquired Williams as a free agent after losing David Wells through the same process. And in an attempt to fill the hole at the number five slot in the rotation, the Padres traded outfielder Terrence Long to Kansas City for left-handed pitcher Darrell May.

The result was the Padres' fourth National League West title in 2005.

But the first title at PETCO Park didn't exactly excite Padres fans. The National League West was down, and the Padres won the title with an 82–80 record—the worst by a division champion. After

The opening of PETCO Park in 2004 signaled a new beginning for the Padres. Such newcomers as shortstop Khalil Greene, standing at left discussing hitting with Ryan Klesko, helped turn the Padres into a winning team. And in 2005–2006, the Padres advanced to the playoffs for the first time in back-to-back seasons.

winning the division, the Padres were swept out of the playoffs in three games by the St. Louis Cardinals.

Most of the season's excitement came in May when the Padres produced the greatest single month in franchise history—22–6. Starting pitchers Adam Eaton (5–0) and Jake Peavy (3–0) were undefeated in May. Closer Trevor Hoffman had 12 of his season total of 43 saves. Brian Giles hit .364 with four homers and 21 RBIs. Dave Roberts, who had missed the season's first two weeks with a groin strain, hit .290 in May and reached base 40 percent of the time in the leadoff slot. Shortstop Khalil Greene batted .311. May shot the Padres to the top of the National League West.

But perhaps an omen of what was to come came in the ninth-inning on June 1, in a home game against Milwaukee. The Padres were trailing 5–2 with the bases loaded and two out when Geoff

Blum launched a drive that appeared to all of the 27,692 fans at PETCO Park to be headed for the right-field stands and a walk-off grand slam. But the thick marine layer seemed to grab the ball. Down it came short of the seats.

The Padres lost. They would lose 16 more times in June.

TRIVIA

Who hit the Padres' first grand slam at PETCO Park?

Answers to the trivia questions are on pages 219–220.

And as the season went on, injuries and slumps would become the norm. The Padres had an early warning when Roberts opened the season on the disabled list with the groin strain. And Roberts's replacement, Eric Young, suffered a dislocated shoulder in the first inning of the first home game when he crashed into the center-field fence at PETCO Park.

Shortstop Khalil Greene would make the first of his two trips to the disabled list in April with a fractured finger. Starting pitchers Woody Williams and Tim Redding would both go on the disabled list in May. And near the end of the Padres' record month, second baseman Mark Loretta would go on the disabled list for almost two months for a strained left thumb.

Matters would get worse during the summer. Right-handed pitcher Adam Eaton appeared headed for the All-Star Game and perhaps a 20-win season when a tendon problem in the right finger of his pitching hand essentially wiped out the second half of his season. Catcher Ramon Hernandez would make two trips to the disabled list, once for surgery.

Plus, the discord over the dimensions of PETCO Park continued until it reached the breaking point on July 30, when the Padres traded the disgruntled Phil Nevin to the Texas Rangers for the equally unhappy right-handed pitcher Chan Ho Park.

The trade of Nevin, who was hitting .256 with nine homers and 47 RBIs in an injury-interrupted season, stunned many of his teammates. Nevin ended his Padres career ranked second on the club's all-time list in homers (156) and third in RBIs (573).

If you look at the Padres' final statistics rather than the standings, it would be impossible to spot the 2005 club as a division champion. Ryan Klesko led the Padres with 18 homers. Brian Giles was the RBI leader with 83. Giles was the lone Padre to hit .300—.301, to be exact—although a league-leading 119 walks did give him a .423 on-base percentage. Only two regular starting pitchers—Jake Peavy and Adam Eaton—had winning records or as many as 10 wins.

As the season progressed, the Padres not only replaced Nevin at first, but they opted to go with Joe Randa at third rather than former first-round draft pick Sean Burroughs.

It was the bench—led by Mark Sweeney, Damian Jackson, Miguel Olivo, Geoff Blum, Eric Young, Robert Fick, Xavier Nady—who somehow found a way to get the Padres through to the division title.

"In some ways, 2005 was one of the toughest seasons we've had," said Bochy. "In other ways, it was one of the most rewarding. Every day, it was someone else stepping up. And I mean every day."

Giles was the only Padre to start more than 120 games at his position. Roberts was the only regular to start more than 80 games at his spring-assigned spot in the batting order.

Alas, the Padres limped into the playoffs. And they were hurting more than anyone knew. Jake Peavy, who had a National League–leading 216 strikeouts while posting a 13–7 record with a 2.88 ERA during the regular season, was given the assignment of starting the playoff opener in St. Louis. Unknown to almost everyone, Peavy had suffered a rib injury on September 28 during the Padres' raucous celebration after they clinched the National League West title.

Peavy had the worst outing of his career, giving up eight earned runs on as many hits in 4⅓ innings. Peavy was done for the game as well as the rest of the playoffs. Essentially, the Padres were also done.

The Cardinals took advantage of Pedro Astacio's wildness to win the second game in St. Louis 6–2, then flew to San Diego to close out the Padres two days later in the first playoff game at PETCO Park. St. Louis would jump out to a 7–0 lead before the Padres rallied to cut the final deficit to 7–4.

Neither the Padres nor their fans were pleased with the 2005 season. More changes would follow. The Padres would make two of the more significant trades in franchise history during the ensuing offseason. On November 18, 2005, San Diego finally found the needed center fielder to patrol the spacious outfield at PETCO Park. Mike Cameron was acquired in a trade from the New York Mets for Xavier Nady, who had started everywhere from center to first to third as a Padre. And on January 6, 2006, the Padres acquired right-handed power pitcher Chris Young and first baseman Adrian Gonzalez, plus outfielder Terrmel Sledge, from the Texas Rangers in a 3-for-2 steal for right-handed pitchers Adam Eaton and Akinori Otsuka.

Padres general manager Kevin Towers also made two other trades that led to controversy during the 2006 season. Although Mark Loretta was one of the more popular players in the clubhouse, as well as with the fans, Towers dealt the second baseman to Boston for catcher Doug Mirabelli. Towers viewed the trade as essential because the Padres wanted rookie Josh Barfield to play second and desperately needed a catcher after having lost Ramon Hernandez to free agency. But the fans hated the deal.

The faithful's rancor with the deal only grew when Mirabelli made it clear that he would rather be in Boston than playing backup in San Diego to future Hall of Famer Mike Piazza, who the Padres had signed as a free agent just two weeks before the opening of spring training.

There are times when need and opportunity create fateful events.

Without Mirabelli, the Red Sox assigned Josh Bard to catch knuckleballer Tim Wakefield. Bard struggled. He had 10 passed balls in three games while catching Wakefield.

The Red Sox called Towers, seeking the return of the unhappy Mirabelli. The Padres not only got Bard in return, they also obtained relief pitcher Cla Meredith.

So the Loretta-for-Mirabelli trade would essentially become Loretta-for-Bard and Meredith—no longer that one-sided. Bard would hit .338 with nine homers and 40 RBIs in 231 at-bats as Piazza's backup. The submarining Meredith would have a 1.07 ERA and a 5–1 record in 45 relief appearances as a Padre—a run that included a franchise record 33⅔-scoreless-inning streak over 28 appearances between July 18 and September 12.

Both Bard and Meredith would play major roles in the Padres' run to a second straight National League West title. Vinny Castilla would—but in a different way. Having given up on Sean Burroughs, the Padres had a void at third. Towers decided to acquire Mexican icon Castilla from Washington for right-handed pitcher Brian Lawrence.

Castilla was extremely popular with the fans across the international border just south of San Diego. He was also extremely popular in the Padres clubhouse. But there was little left in Castilla's tank. Shortly after turning 39, the Padres decided to release him. It was not a decision popular with Padres players or manager Bruce Bochy. At the time, the team had no other third baseman. When they first filled Castilla's spot weeks later, it was with second baseman Todd Walker, who was then asked to play out of position.

The front-office decision to release Castilla created friction between the players and the executives and was the first hint that Bochy and club officials, other than Kevin Towers, were not on the same page.

For the second straight season, the Padres took control of the National League West race with a strong May (19–10). And for the second time in three seasons, they played better on the road (45–36 with a .279 batting average) than at home (43–38, .245). In fact, the Padres scored 100 more runs on the road than they did at PETCO Park and had to win 10 of their last 11 games at home to post a winning home record.

In the meantime, newcomers Cameron and Gonzalez became both offensive and defensive leaders. Despite starting the season on the disabled list, Cameron hit 22 homers and shared the team RBIs lead with Brian Giles at 83. Not only did Cameron become only the seventh Padre to have 20 homers and 20 steals in the same season, he led the Padres with 65 extra-base hits and 88 runs scored, and

DID YOU KNOW . . . That Rudy Seanez set a record with the Padres in 2006 when he started his fourth separate stint with the Padres? Thirty-six players have had at least two different tenures with the Padres, including five who have been Padres on three different occasions.

posted career highs in doubles (34) and triples (nine). And after a slow start, Gonzalez finished the season with a .304 average, a team-leading 24 homers and 82 RBIs. Plus, it's impossible to calculate the number of runs Cameron and Gonzalez saved with their play in the field. Gonzalez, 24, who was raised in San Diego County, was named the Padres MVP. Cameron was a close second in the balloting.

"They pulled together the entire defense," Bochy said of Gonzalez and Cameron. The addition of Cameron also allowed Roberts (.293) to slide over to left and improve the defense there as well.

Although Klesko missed almost the entire season following early-season shoulder surgery, the Padres closed the power gap that had existed since they moved into PETCO Park. Three Padres topped the 20-homer mark (Mike Piazza hit 22), and San Diego was out-homered by only a 176–161 count on the season.

Barfield hit .280 as a rookie with 13 homers and 58 RBIs. Brian Giles hit a subpar .263, but reached base 37 percent of the time with 104 walks.

As the season entered the stretch, Bochy mix-and-matched his personnel at third (Todd Walker and Russell Branyan) and second (Barfield and Walker), and had Geoff Blum delivering at short as Khalil Greene missed the end of a third straight season with injury problems.

Walker and Branyan weren't the only players the Padres added down the stretch. David Wells returned home from Boston on August 31 and made five starts.

The 2006 season was, of course, the year during which Trevor Hoffman passed Lee Smith as the game's all-time saves leader—and his 46 saves during the season was also the second-highest total of his career.

While Jake Peavy (11–14, 4.09 ERA) hit a bump in his brilliant career, Woody Williams (12–5, 3.65 ERA), Chris Young (11–5, 3.46 ERA), and sinker-baller Clay Hensley (11–12, 3.71) more than picked up the slack.

Young was 6–0 on the road with a National League–leading 2.41 ERA. He took a no-hitter into the sixth three times and had pitched 8⅓ innings of no-hit ball September 22 at PETCO Park against Pittsburgh before giving up a pinch-hit, two-run homer to Joe Randa.

After winning their second straight N.L. West title, the Padres entered the playoffs with high expectations—before again being eliminated by the Cardinals, this time in four games. The disappointment was palpable in the Padres' offices. The team had been thinking in terms of the National League pennant and a third World Series visit.

In the wake of the playoff loss, Bochy was told he could listen to offers from other teams. Padres CEO Sandy Alderson told everyone not to make too much of that permission. He had granted Kevin Towers the same opportunity following the 2005 season, and Towers remained with the Padres after interviewing with the Arizona Diamondbacks.

But Bochy—as did most outsiders—took Alderson's invitation as a sign the manager's days could be numbered in San Diego. Offered a multi-year contract by the Giants, Bochy quit the Padres.

Signing Bud Black as the manager to replace Bochy was far from the only change made by the Padres immediately following the 2006 season. Although he had a strong rookie season, second baseman Josh Barfield was traded to Cleveland for rookie third baseman Kevin Kouzmanoff, whose projection as a pull-hitter with power played into the Padres' plans for PETCO Park.

The Padres also bid farewell to pitcher Woody Williams, leadoff-hitting left fielder Dave Roberts, and catcher Mike Piazza as free agents before signing future Hall of Famer Greg Maddux to a two-year contract as a free agent.

"We're not finished," said Padres general manager Kevin Towers.

Jerry Coleman

Tony Gwynn is Mr. Padre, but the Hall of Famer might not be the most endearing figure in Padres history.

"Jerry Coleman is now and forever will be the sound of this ballclub," Padres owner John Moores said in 2005 as Jerry Coleman prepared to enter the Hall of Fame.

But Jerry Coleman is far more than the voice of the Padres. Coleman is the club's enduring connection to a community that loves and respects the man who serves the Padres and the community with the dedication that he served his country in two wars.

"He is the most respected man I have ever known," said Ted Leitner, who has shared the Padres radio booth with Coleman since 1981. "People love this man. And they should. He's a good, decent man."

Coleman's connection with San Diego might best be defined by a segment of every Padres broadcast that includes Coleman. Leitner will simply ask, "Jerry, what did you do today?" and Jerry Coleman will describe part of his day. It might be a walk with his beloved dog. Or an ice cream cone that melted quicker than expected. Or anything. Nothing major, mind you. Just an unscripted snippet from his life that day delivered from the heart.

"I know," said Leitner, "that there are people out there who tune in just to hear Jerry's day."

A big part of Jerry's day is Padres baseball. And it's not restricted to the broadcasts. Coleman has long been the Padres' most popular public speaker. He is the Padres' ambassador to the city.

It's been that way ever since he broadcast his first Padres game in 1972. By that time, Jerry Coleman was 48 and had already spent 30 years around professional baseball. He was 80 in 2005 when he was honored as the 29th recipient of the Ford C. Frick Award and inducted into the broadcasters' wing at Cooperstown. Several years later, he's still going strong...albeit with a reduced schedule.

"I like telling people that I've been in the Padres booth since 1972, but that's not right," said Coleman with a touch of the self-effacing humor that San Diegans covet. "There was that year."

It was the 1980 season, in fact, when Coleman was called down from the broadcast booth to succeed Roger Craig as the Padres manager.

"'What am I doing?' might be the question I should have asked myself," joked Coleman. "The second question should be, 'What were they thinking?'"

The truth is, the Padres showed improvement under Coleman—hustling the way Coleman did as a second baseman with the New York Yankees. Coleman played on four World Series champion teams and played on six pennant winners in a nine-year career with the Yankees—a career that was both delayed and interrupted by service in World War II and Korea as a Marine Corps fighter pilot. In fact, he is the only major league player to have fought in both World War II and Korea.

Gerald Francis Coleman was born September 14, 1924, in San Jose and graduated from Lowell High School in San Francisco in 1942. Days after his graduation, Coleman signed with the Yankees and began his professional baseball career in Wellsville, New York.

On October 23, 1942, Coleman placed his baseball career on hold, enlisting in the Marine Corps as a naval aviation cadet. He won his wings on April 1, 1944. From August of 1944 through the end of World War II, Coleman flew 57 combat missions out of Guadalcanal, the Solomon Islands, and the Philippines as the pilot of a dive bomber.

He resumed his baseball career in 1946 and reached the major leagues with the Yankees in 1949. Coleman was the Rookie of the Year in 1949 for hitting .275 with two homers and 42 RBIs. The following season, he hit .287 with six homers and 69 RBIs, was named an American League All-Star, and was the Most Valuable Player of the World Series.

Jerry Coleman entered the Hall of Fame in 2005 as the Ford C. Frick Award winner for broadcasting. But Coleman's contributions went far beyond the radio booth. The only major league player to fight in both World War II and Korea—as a Marine pilot—Coleman had a distinguished playing career with the Yankees and managed the Padres in 1980.

In May of 1952, Coleman was called back into the Marine Corps and flew 63 combat missions in Korea, mostly in a ground-support capacity. As a Marine pilot, Coleman was awarded two Distinguished Flying Crosses, 13 Air Medals, and three Navy Citations.

Coleman returned to reserve status in August of 1953—he would eventually retire from the Marine Corps in 1964 as a Lt. Colonel—and immediately rejoined the Yankees. A month after arriving back in the United States, the Yankees honored Coleman with Jerry Coleman Day at Yankee Stadium.

Coleman's playing career ended four years later with a .263 lifetime average.

Coleman planned to remain in baseball as a member of the Yankees' front office and served two years as the player personnel director. "It was the toughest job I ever had," said Coleman. "I was on

the road all the time, something like 246 days one year. The travel was killing me."

It was a strange twist that turned Coleman into a broadcaster. Following the 1959 baseball season, Coleman was offered a position with the Van Heusen clothing company to be its western regional sales manager. "I loved the opportunity because it gave me a chance to return to the West Coast," said Coleman.

Within days of accepting the Van Heusen position, however, Coleman was approached by Bill MacPhail, the head of CBS Sports, about the possibility of becoming a broadcaster and serving as the pregame host of the national *Game of the Week* telecasts featuring Dizzy Dean and Pee Wee Reese.

Coleman respectfully declined because he had given his word to Van Heusen. But when officials of the clothing firm heard of the offer, they liked the idea of having one of their representatives on television.

"If Van Heusen said no, and they had every right to, we wouldn't be talking about any of this today," said Coleman. "This career is really amazing when you think about how I got here."

The CBS gig led to seven seasons working on Yankees broadcasts. After the 1969 season, Coleman again decided to head west. He applied to both the San Francisco Giants and expansion Padres in 1969 as a play-by-play announcer—and got neither job.

"It forced me to take a non-baseball job with KTLA in Los Angeles," said Coleman. "I did everything from boxing to bowling to wrestling. I was even the voice of UCLA basketball for a season. Those two years proved to me I was a baseball man."

TRIVIA

What was the Padres' record in 1980 under Jerry Coleman?

Answers to the trivia questions are on pages 219–220.

Late in 1971, he re-applied for the again-vacant Padres radio play-by-play job. This time he got it. "They must have lowered the standards," Coleman jokes.

Almost immediately, Coleman's two catch phrases— "Oh! Doctor" and "Hang a Star"—became part of the San Diego jargon.

"Everyone thinks I picked up 'Oh! Doctor' from Red Barber," said Coleman. "Red was a great teacher and really helped me out when I

239—Bases stolen by the 1980 Padres to lead the major league.

was starting out in New York. But 'Oh! Doctor' really originated with Casey Stengel. I never heard Red say it."

As for the "Hang a Star" call to highlight defensive gems, Coleman says it dates back to his childhood.

"In junior high, we'd have these spelling tests, and the best spellers would get gold stars," said Coleman. "I never got one. But kids in the class would be talking about hanging stars on their tests, and that always stuck with me as the epitome of excellence."

But what is endearing to Padres fans as much as Coleman's trademark phrases are his malaprops. There are San Diegans who have spent more than three decades building a list of what are affectionately known as "Colemanisms:"

- "He slid into second base with a stand up double."
- "Rich Folkers is throwing up in the bullpen."
- "Dave Winfield's head is bouncing off the wall and rolling back toward second."
- "It's a sunny afternoon here in San Diego tonight."

Those are but a few.

"Yes, I said them," says Coleman. "I make mistakes. I talk fast. Sometimes, it just happens. Some of them I don't remember at all. But if they've made people laugh, it's another good part of bringing the game to the fans."

What has been lost at times in the humor of Coleman's delivery is the depth of his knowledge and his ability to present the game. "I don't think I've ever heard anyone say anything negative about Jerry," said Jeff Torborg, a former major league player who worked alongside Coleman for five seasons in the CBS booth.

"Home-spun humility with a laugh," is how Joe Garagiola, also a Hall of Fame broadcaster, described Coleman.

Coleman's partners over the years in the Padres booth have included Ted Leitner, Dave Campbell, Charlie Jones, Bob Chandler, Rick Monday, and Tim Flannery.

For more than a third of a century, Coleman has ridden shotgun for San Diego motorists stuck in traffic and has been the last voice heard by many a shut-in at the end of a long day.

"I love this job," said Coleman. "I love this team and this city. I've never taken myself seriously. At the same time, I've never lost my love and interest in the game.

"Honestly, it took me a long time to feel accepted as a broadcaster. It didn't happen until my third or fourth season with the Padres. And it happened because of the fans here. We built something between us."

All-Time Padres

Any discussion of the greatest player to wear a Padres uniform starts and ends with Tony Gwynn.

He is number one. End of discussion.

Then comes Trevor Hoffman at number two.

Number three? That's where the debate starts with Padres fans.

Some would say Dave Winfield, who played eight seasons with the Padres before opting for the bright lights of New York. He was, after all, the first player to wear a Padres cap into the Hall of Fame.

Others would argue that number three should be Randy Jones, who was the first Padre who fans turned out in large numbers to see.

You could make an argument for Ken Caminiti, the only Padre to be named the National League's Most Valuable Player—and, at that, a unanimous selection in 1996.

Plus, don't forget Ozzie Smith, who was amazing fans with his fielding prowess in San Diego long before he was known to the Cardinals.

Steve Garvey might be deserving of the honor off that one home-run swing in the 1984 NLCS against the Chicago Cubs.

So we've discarded the idea of ranking our favorite Padres. Instead, what follows is the all-time Padres team—twenty-five players, including five starting pitchers and five relievers.

Starting Lineup

Tony Gwynn, Right Field, 1982–2001
Although he seldom batted in the leadoff slot during his playing career, Gwynn would have been a natural, given his .338 career batting average and .388 career on-base percentage. Plus, in his

prime, Gwynn could run. He is the Padres all-time leader with 319 stolen bases with a single-season high of 56 in 1987. "Mr. Padre" and Honus Wagner are the only players to win eight National League batting titles. In 20 seasons with the Padres, Gwynn was named to 15 All-Star teams. His career batting average is the highest in the major leagues since Ted Williams and the fifth-highest career mark since the 1930s. Gwynn had 3,141 hits in 2,440 games with the Padres and is one of only 17 players in major league history to spend an entire career of 20 or more seasons with the same team. In addition to his hitting skills, Gwynn also won five Gold Gloves for his outfield play. He leads the Padres in almost every offensive category except homers, where he ranks fourth.

Steve Finley, Center Field, 1995–1998
Finley filled this exact role in two of the Padres' five National League West championship seasons, including the National League pennant run of 1998. He holds the Padres' record for runs scored with 126 in 1996. He averaged 106 runs a season in his four years with the Padres and is the only Padre to score at least 100 runs in three separate seasons. Finley has two of the four 40-doubles seasons in Padres

TOP 10

Career Batting Average Leaders

	Player	Average
1.	Tony Gwynn	.338
2.	Bip Roberts	.298
3.	Ken Caminiti	.295
4.	Gene Richards	.291
5.	Phil Nevin	.288
6.	John Grubb	.286
7.	Dave Winfield	.284
8.	Ryan Klesko	.279
9.	Steve Finley	.276
10.	Steve Garvey	.275

history. Despite playing only four seasons in San Diego, Finley ranks among the top 10 in most of the Padres' career offensive categories, including sixth in triples (28), seventh in doubles (134), eighth in runs scored (423), ninth in homers (82), and 10th in batting average (.276). Finley was named to the 1997 All-Star team.

Dave Winfield, Left Field, 1973–1980
Winfield came straight from the University of Minnesota to the Padres' starting lineup as San Diego's first-round pick in the June draft of 1973. He played his first eight seasons with the Padres before he departed as a free agent. Although his final days in San Diego as a player were tumultuous, he won back the critics by deciding to wear a Padres cap upon his induction to the Hall of Fame in 2001. Winfield represented the Padres in four straight All-Star Games, starting in 1977, and was the first Padre voted to the starting lineup in 1979—a season in which he led the league with 118 RBIs and finished third in the MVP voting. Winfield led the Padres in home runs five times (1976–1980) and led the team in RBIs six times (1974–1975 and 1977–1980). He was also named the team MVP in 1978 and 1979. With the Padres, Winfield hit .284 with 154 homers, 626 RBIs, and 133 stolen bases. He ranks second among the all-time Padres leaders in RBIs and runs scored (599) and third in homers, games played (1,117), doubles (179), hits (1,134), triples (39), and walks (463).

Ken Caminiti, Third Base, 1995–1998
Caminiti had the greatest single season in Padres history in 1996 when he was the unanimous selection as the National League MVP. Caminiti hit .326 with 40 homers and a club-record 130 RBIs. He was also spectacular in the field. On August 18, 1996, Caminiti became a Padres icon. During the Padres' historic trip to Monterrey, Mexico, Caminiti fell ill before a game against the Mets. Because he was extremely dehydrated, Caminiti was receiving fluids through an IV while lying on a table in the training room as the first pitch approached. Caminiti refused to be scratched from the starting lineup. Downing a Snickers bar in the dugout just before the first pitch, Caminiti scrambled to his position. He homered in each of his first two at-bats before leaving the game. Like Finley, Caminiti played only four seasons with the Padres.

Yet, he ranks in the top 10 of many career statistical charts, including sixth in homers (121) and first in slugging percentage (.540). Sadly, Caminiti, who admitted using steroids after his career ended, died on October 10, 2004, of a drug overdose.

Nate Colbert, First Base, 1969–1974
To fully appreciate the exploits of Nate Colbert, one has to remember the dimensions of San Diego Stadium during the Padres' formative years. There was no interior fence. And to hit a homer, the ball had to clear the 17-foot walls. Colbert cleared that wall 73 times in his six seasons as a Padre. No other Padre hit that many homers at San Diego/Jack Murphy/Qualcomm Stadium, even with the shortened walls. Overall, Colbert remains the Padres all-time home-run leader with 163. He ranks only fifth in RBIs (481) largely because the Padres of that era seldom got on base in front of Colbert. The first baseman was a Padres original, coming from Houston with the 18th pick of the 1969 expansion draft. Colbert led the Padres in homers in each of their first five seasons and in RBIs in four of the first five seasons. He made history on August 1, 1972, when he hit five homers and drove in a major league record 13 runs in a doubleheader against the Braves.

TRIVIA

Who is the only Padre to have 200 hits, score 100 runs, and drive in 75 runs in the same season?

Answers to the trivia questions are on pages 219–220.

Mark Loretta, Second Base, 2003–2005
You can make strong arguments for other second basemen. Roberto Alomar launched his career as a homegrown Padres prospect. Alan Wiggins was the trigger for the Padres' offense in 1984, stealing a franchise-record 70 bases and scoring a then club-record 106 runs for the Padres' first National League champions. Trouble is, second base has been a revolving door. Over 38 seasons, the Padres have had 25 different second basemen on Opening Day. No one has lasted longer than four seasons. Alomar was traded away to Toronto, where he became a star. Wiggins's career—and life—was shortened by drugs. So why Loretta? His 2004 season was one of the greatest in Padres history. He hit .335 with 208 hits and 47 doubles, the best

TOP 10

Career RBI Leaders

	Player	RBI
1.	Tony Gwynn	1,138
2.	Dave Winfield	626
3.	Phil Nevin	573
4.	Ryan Klesko	493
5.	Nate Colbert	433
6.	Garry Templeton	427
7.	Terry Kennedy	424
8.	Ken Caminiti	396
9.	Benito Santiago	375
10.	Carmelo Martinez	337

marks in Padres history for someone not named Tony Gwynn. In three seasons with the Padres, Loretta hit .310 and was voted to the 2004 All-Star team.

Garry Templeton, Shortstop, 1982–1991

No, your eyes aren't playing tricks. Hall of Famer Ozzie Smith spent his first four seasons making magic in the field for the Padres. But Templeton was the captain of the 1984 National League champions, and his bat gave the Padres a weapon that they lacked with Smith. On the Padres' all-time lists, Templeton is second to Gwynn in hits (1,135), doubles (195), and games played (1,286) and sixth in runs scored (430) and RBIs (427). Templeton and Smith are forever linked in Padres history. It was Templeton who came to San Diego from St. Louis in exchange for Smith. At the time, Templeton had a strained relationship with the Cardinals—and Smith longed for a bigger stage. The trade seemed to benefit all sides.

Benito Santiago, Catcher, 1986–1992

Santiago now says that if he had to do it over again, he would never have left San Diego. "I think I could have played there for a long time," said Santiago, who beat Padres opponents with his bat and arm.

Padres fans still talk about Santiago's ability to throw strikes to second from his knees. He was the unanimous National League Rookie of the Year pick in 1987 and finished with a .300 average, 18 homers, and 79 RBIs—capped by a 34-game hitting streak that still ranks as the longest ever by 1) a Padre, 2) a catcher, and 3) a rookie. On top of everything else, Santiago could run, stealing a career-high 21 bases as a rookie. Santiago finished with a career .266 as a Padre. He ranks seventh on the all-time Padres list in homers (85) and ninth in RBIs (375) and hits (758).

Bench

Terry Kennedy, Catcher, 1981–1986

"Dependable" is a word former Padres manager Dick Williams used to describe Kennedy, which, given the source, is high praise. Kennedy was constant behind the plate—he expertly handled the young starting rotation that led the Padres to the 1984 pennant—as well as at it. He ranks slightly ahead of Santiago in most Padres career statistical categories—tied for fifth in doubles (158), sixth in hits (817), seventh in RBIs (424) and games played (835), and 11th in batting average (.274).

Phil Nevin, First Base/Third Base, 1999–2005

The former collegiate Golden Spikes Award winner and number-one draft pick was one of the Padres' most successful reclamation projects. He had already bounced through three teams when the Padres acquired him from Anaheim for utility infielder Andy Sheets just before the start of the 1999 season. By mid-season, Nevin had become the Padres' regular third baseman. In 2001 Nevin hit .306 with 41 homers and 126 RBIs—both ranking as the second-highest single-season marks in Padres history. Nevin had 72 homers and 233 RBIs in his first two full seasons before injuries started taking a toll. He wasn't a great fielder at third or first, but he is second on the Padres' all-time list in homers (156) and slugging percentage (.503), third in RBIs (573), and fifth in batting average (.288).

Ryan Klesko, Outfield/First Base, 2000–2006

Klesko was the perfect left-handed–hitting compliment to Nevin. And just as productive until injuries—in this case surgeries to both shoulders in 2003 and 2006—slowed him, too. Over his first four seasons with the Padres, Klesko averaged 26½ homers and 92 RBIs a season. Klesko has the fifth-highest on-base percentage (.381), third-highest slugging percentage (.491), and eighth-highest batting average (.279) in Padres history. Only Tony Gwynn drew more walks as a Padre. Klesko is fifth on the Padres home-run list (133) and fourth in doubles (176), RBIS (493), and runs (449).

TRIVIA

Who was the first Padre to homer into the third level of balconies at the Western Metal Building at Petco Park?

Answers to the trivia questions are on pages 219–220.

Gene Richards, Outfield, 1977–1983

His 193 hits in 1980 was a Padres single-season record until Tony Gwynn arrived. One of the fastest players to wear a Padres uniform, Richards led the National League with 12 triples in 1978 and stole a then–club record 56 bases in 1977. He finished only six hits shy of being one of four players with 1,000 hits as a Padre and twice led the Padres in runs scored. He ranks second on the Padres' all-time stolen-base list (242) to Gwynn, fifth in games played (939), third in runs scored (484), and fourth in batting average (.291).

Khalil Greene, Shortstop, 2003–Present

This is part production, part projection. Ozzie Smith is the superior fielder, although Greene is also capable of making the highlight shows. And Greene has hit 15 homers in each of his first three full seasons, although he has already made four trips to the disabled list. As a Padre, Greene is the much greater force as an offensive player. He is one of only two Padres shortstops to reach double digits in homers for a season.

Steve Garvey, First Base, 1983–1987

Need a big hit? No one has delivered a bigger one than Garvey's homer against the Cubs in the fourth game of the 1984 NLCS. That one swing earned Garvey a spot in the hearts of Padres fans and a spot in the Padres Hall of Fame. Garvey was on the downside of his career when he joined the Padres. Still, Garvey has the 10th-highest career batting average in Padres history (.275). He led the Padres in RBIs (86) during their 1984 championship season...and then came that big homer.

Ozzie Smith, Shortstop, 1978–1981
Okay, you need a glove on the bench. In this case, probably the greatest glove ever to field a ball. The Wizard was one of the first Padres to attract national attention. His diving stop of a Jeff Burroughs rocket still demands television time. Smith was promoted from Class A to the Padres in 1978 at the age of 23. He hit better than .230 only once as a Padre, developing his offensive skills as a member of the St. Louis Cardinals.

Starting Pitchers
Randy Jones, Left-handed, 1973–1980
Clearly the Padres' first superstar, Randy Jones is the Padres' first 20-game winner and their first Cy Young Award winner. More than that, he attracted fans to San Diego Stadium when no one else did. Attendance would soar on nights when the 6', 175-pound sink-baller would work. Fans would rise section by section and welcome Jones with a standing ovation as he made his way to the mound from the bullpen following his pregame warm-up. Jones was 8–22 in 1974. The following season he was 20–12 and had cut his ERA almost in half to 2.24. And in 1976 Jones went 22–14 with a 2.74 ERA and led the National League in games started (40), games completed (25), and innings pitched (315⅓). Added plus: Jones was also one of the fastest workers in Padres history.

By the NUMBERS

1—Ken Caminiti, in 1996, is the only Padre ever named the Most Valuable Player of the National League.

25—Complete games pitched by Randy Jones in 1976, a Padre record and the most in the National League that year.

1,027—Straight games played by Steve Garvey, the third-longest streak in major league history, when he dislocated his left thumb sliding into home July 29, 1983, against Atlanta.

TOP 10

Career ERA Leaders

	Pitcher	ERA
1.	Trevor Hoffman	2.69
2.	Greg Harris	2.95
3.	Dave Roberts	2.99
4.	Dave Dravecky	3.12
5.	Craig Lefferts	3.24
6.	Bruce Hurst	3.27
7.	Randy Jones	3.30
8.	Jake Peavy	3.51
9.	Andy Benes	3.57
10.	Bob Shirley	3.58

Jake Peavy, Right-handed, 2002–Present
At the age of 25, Peavy in 2006 became the seventh-winningest pitcher in Padres history with 57 victories. Peavy led the National League with a 2.27 ERA in 2004 (15–6). A year later, he led the league in strikeouts (216). He finished second in strikeouts in 2006 (215), although his record slipped to 11–14 with a 4.09 ERA. Peavy's career ERA of 3.51 is the eighth-lowest in Padres history while his 8.85 strikeouts per nine innings is second to Trevor Hoffman. Peavy already ranks fourth in career strikeouts (850), and his 15 games with at least 10 strikeouts ties Andy Benes for the most in Padres history. Peavy appeared in his first All-Star Game in 2005.

Eric Show, Right-handed, 1981–1990
The Padres' only 100-game winner was also one of the more interesting characters in team history. He also became a spokesman for conservative political causes and was a talented musician. He led the 1984 National League championship team with 15 wins and set a career-best 16 wins in 1988. Show ranks second on most Padres career pitching tables, including games started (230), innings pitched (1,603⅓), complete games (35), strikeouts (951), and losses

(87). Still, he had a winning record (100–87) at a time when most Padres starters had career losing records.

Andy Benes, Right-handed, 1989–1995

The 6'6", 240-pound Benes could be physically intimidating. In 1994 he became the first Padre to lead the National League in strikeouts, with 189. He is the Padres' all-time leader in strikeouts (1,036), and his 7.55-strikeouts-per-nine-innings ratio is the second-best in Padres history among starting pitchers. Benes was a horse. He made more than 30 starts in four straight seasons (1990–1993) and pitched at least 223 innings in three straight seasons (1991–1993). Benes's eight shutouts is the fifth-highest total in Padres history. His 3.57 ERA ranks ninth. Opponents hit only .242 against Benes when he was with the Padres, the lowest average against a Padres starter.

Bruce Hurst, Right-handed, 1989–1993

The last spot in the rotation was difficult. One could argue that Kevin Brown deserved it off his 1998 season (18–7, 2.38 ERA in a league-leading 35 starts) that led the Padres to the National League title. Or that the nod should go to Gaylord Perry, who won the 1978 Cy Young Award off a 21–6 campaign. But Brown was a Padre for one season, and Perry two. If Gary Sheffield and Fred McGriff didn't serve enough time to be ranked among the position players, Brown and Perry don't qualify either. Hurst reached double figures in wins in each of his four full seasons with the Padres and led the National League with 10 complete games in 1989 and four shutouts in 1990. In fact, 10 of Hurst's 131 Padres starts resulted in a complete-game shutout. Hurst's 3.27 career ERA is the sixth-lowest in Padres history and his .591 winning percentage is the franchise record.

Bullpen

Trevor Hoffman, Right-handed, 1993–Present

The entrance of Hoffman in a save situation at PETCO Park is an event unto itself. The crowd rises to its feet with the first note of AC/DC's "Hells Bells." In trots Hoffman, head down—on September 24, 2006, Hoffman recorded the 479th save of his career, passing Lee Smith as the game's all-time leader in that category. Hoffman also holds major league records for eight 40-save seasons and 11 30-save seasons. His National League–leading 46 saves in 2006 was the second-highest total of his career, and his 2.14 ERA equaled the second-lowest of his career. His 89.6 percent career conversion rate is also the highest for all closers with more than 190 saves. Hoffman has made 793 appearances with the Padres, dating back to 1993, and all but two of his saves have come in a San Diego uniform.

Goose Gossage, Right-handed, 1984–1987
Gossage is the only closer besides Hoffman to work a postseason game for the Padres. Although their title is the same, the job description of the closer changed considerably during the five-plus seasons between the departure of Gossage and the arrival of Hoffman. It wasn't unusual for Gossage to work two or three innings to get a save. At other times, he might come on in the middle of the ninth only for the final out. Gossage also entered tie games. "I got called sometimes when we were behind by a run," he said. "I was there on a for-need basis." Gossage appeared in 197 games in four seasons with the Padres and recorded 83 saves with a 2.99 ERA over 298 innings.

Rollie Fingers, Right-handed, 1977–1980
Like Gossage, Fingers was a long-haul closer who built his reputation with the world champion Oakland A's before coming to the

Although all-time saves leader Trevor Hoffman is usually the first Padres relief pitcher who comes to mind, the Padres have always been deep in closers. Future Hall of Famer Rollie Fingers, and his distinctive handlebar moustache, twice led the National League in saves while pitching four seasons for the Padres. Goose Gossage and 1989 Cy Young Award winner Mark Davis were other Padres closers.

Padres in 1977 as one of the club's first major free-agent signees. Fingers ranks second on the Padres all-time list with 108 saves and led the National League in saves in back-to-back seasons in 1977 (35) and 1978 (37). He also led the league in games in 1977. His 78 appearances ranks as the second-highest total in Padres history. Fingers appeared in 265 games in four seasons with the Padres—the fourth-highest total in club history—with a 3.13 ERA.

TRIVIA

Who is the Padres all-time leader in grand-slam homers?

Answers to the trivia questions are on pages 219–220.

Mark Davis, Left-handed, 1987–1989

Before Hoffman, Davis had the greatest season by a closer in Padres history, winning the Cy Young Award in 1989 when he saved 44 games (out of 48 chances) with a 1.85 ERA. Opposing hitters batted only .200 against Davis that year, and he had 92 strikeouts in 92⅔ innings while issuing only 30 non-intentional walks. The previous season, Davis had 28 saves and a 2.01 ERA as the closer successor to Gossage. Davis ranks fourth on the Padres' all-time saves list (78), although he was with the Padres for only 2½ seasons before signing with Kansas City as a free agent after his Cy Young season. Davis's ERA during his first tour with the Padres was 2.23 over 175 games. He returned briefly in 1993–1994.

Craig Lefferts, Left-handed, 1984–1987, 1990–1992

"Lefty" was one of the more durable and versatile pitchers in Padres history. He began his career as a setup man for Gossage on the Padres 1984 National League champions and was both the club's closer and a starter during his second tour in San Diego. He still holds the Padres record with 83 appearances during the 1986 season. His 375 career appearances ranks second on the Padres career list to Hoffman. Lefferts had a hand in 105 Padres wins—64 saves (the fifth-highest total in club history) and 42 wins. After making his first 348 Padres appearances out of the bullpen, Lefferts started 27 games for the Padres in 1992 and was 13–9 with a 3.69 ERA.

Manager

Bruce Bochy

It's hard to believe that Bruce Bochy and the Padres split company after the 2006 season. When the Padres released Bochy from the final season of his contract so that he could manage the division-rival Giants, it ended a 24-year run for Bochy in the Padres organization as a player (1983–1987), minor league coach and manager, major league third base coach (1993–1994), and climaxing with 12 seasons as the Padres manager (1995–2006). During Bochy's reign, the Padres won 951 games, four National League West titles (1996, 1998, 2005, 2006), and the 1998 National League pennant. Bochy's win total is only three less than the combined total of the next three managers on the Padres' win chart. He was the National League Manager of the Year in 1996. Bochy is also the only man to be in uniform during all five Padres trips to the playoffs. He was a backup catcher on the 1984 National League pennant winners.

ANSWERS TO
TRIVIA QUESTIONS

Page 4: Randy Jones won the Cy Young Award in 1976, Gaylord Perry in 1978, and closer Mark Davis in 1989.

Page 11: By innings, the two longest games in Padres history have gone to 21. The Padres scored an 11–8 victory at Montreal in 21 innings on May 21, 1977, and lost a 2–1 decision to Houston in San Diego on September 24, 1971 (in the first game of a doubleheader). In terms of time, it took the Padres six hours and 17 minutes to lose a 3–1 decision to Houston in San Diego on August 15, 1980.

Page 12: Atlanta's Dale Murphy ranks second for the most homers hit against the Padres with 60.

Page 17: Bruce Bochy is the only Padre to reach the postseason all five times. He was a backup catcher on the 1984 Padres that reached the World Series. He was the manager of the 1996, 1998, 2005, and 2006 Padres clubs that won the National League West. The 1998 team also won the National League pennant.

Page 20: Randy Jones (1975–1977 and 1980) and Eric Show (1984, 1986–1987, 1989) both made four starts on Opening Day for the Padres.

Page 29: San Francisco outfielder Ollie Brown was the Padres' first pick in the 1968 expansion draft.

Page 55: Randy Jones was the first Padre to lead the National League in earned-run average in 1975 with a 2.24 ERA.

Page 64: Dave Winfield in 1978 and 1980 and Ryan Klesko in 2000 and 2001 are the only two Padres to have two 20/20 seasons.

Page 73: Gary Sheffield won the National League batting championship in 1992 with a .330 average.

Page 82: Marvell Wynne, Tony Gwynn, and John Kruk connected off San Francisco's Roger Mason to become the first players in major league history to open a game by hitting back-to-back-to-back homers.

Page 91: Pitcher La Marr Hoyt was the only Padre named the Most Valuable Player of the All-Star Game, in 1985.

Page 94: Fred McGriff and Gary Sheffield went back-to-back in both the first and second innings, setting a major league record by hitting back-to-back homers in back-to-back innings.

Page 101: Jackson had 49 RBIs in 1991.

Page 106: Yuma in the southwest corner of Arizona was the Padres spring training home from the club's birth in 1969 through 1993. The Padres moved their spring camp to Peoria, Arizona, in 1994 to be closer to the other teams training in the Phoenix area.

Page 133: Bob Skinner won his only game as interim manager—the only one in Padres history—in between John McNamara and Alvin Dark in 1977.

Page 137: Sparky Anderson was a coach with the 1969 Padres and went on to win World Series titles as the manager of Cincinnati's famed Big Red Machine and the 1984 Detroit Tigers.

Page 138: Six of the team's 15 managers through 2006 have been replaced mid-season if you include Dick Williams, who "mutually" departed on the eve of spring training in 1986. The others were Preston Gomez (1972), John McNamara (1977), Larry Bowa (1988), Jack McKeon (1990), and Greg Riddoch (1992).

Page 140: The Padres record for runs scored in a single game was made in a 20–12 victory over Florida on July 27, 1996.

Page 145: Ken Caminiti became was the first switch-hitter in major league history to homer from both sides of the plate in the same game three times in a season. He did it in back-to-back games on September 16 and 17, 1995, and again on September 19.

Page 165: Brian Lawrence became the 36th pitcher in recorded major league history to strike out the side on nine pitches against Baltimore on June 12, 2002, at Camden Yards in Baltimore.

Page 168: Henderson broke two records as a Padre in 2001. He drew the 2,063rd walk of his career on April 25, 2001, to pass Babe Ruth. And on October 4, 2001, he scored his 2,246th run (on a homer against the Dodgers) to top Ty Cobb's major league record.

Page 172: Rickey Henderson doubled off Colorado's John Thomson in his first at-bat in the 2001 season finale at Qualcomm Stadium to become the 25th member of the 3,000-hit club.

Page 185: Mark Loretta was the last Padre to homer at Qualcomm Stadium in 2003 and the first to homer at PETCO Park in 2004.

Page 186: Khalil Greene scored the first run at PETCO Park from second on a ground rule double by Sean Burroughs on April 8, 2004.

Page 194: Khalil Greene hit the Padres' first grand slam at PETCO Park on September 17, 2005.

Page 203: The Padres' record in 1980 was 73–89.

Page 209: Mark Loretta had 208 hits, 108 runs, and 76 RBIs in 2004.

Page 212: Khalil Greene became the first Padre to homer into the third level of balconies at the Western Metal Building on August 4, 2002.

Page 217: Phil Nevin had six grand slam homers, one more than Nate Colbert.

San Diego Padres
All-Time Roster
(through 2006 season)

* Player still active in Major League Baseball

A

Shawn Abner (OF)	1987–91
Ed Acosta (P)	1971–72
Jon Adkins* (P)	2006–Present
Mike Aldrete (OF)	1991
Manny Alexander * (IF)	2005–Present
Dusty Allen (OF)	2000
Carlos Almanzar * (P)	1999–2000
Bill Almon (SS)	1974–79
Roberto Alomar (2B)	1988–90
Sandy Alomar Jr.* (C)	1988–89
Matty Alou (OF)	1974
Gabe Alvarez (3B)	2000
Larry Andersen (P)	1991–92
Dwain Anderson (IF)	1973
Jose Arcia (SS)	1969–70
Alex Arias (IF)	2001
George Arias (3B)	1997–99
Steve Arlin (P)	1969–74
Mike Armstrong (P)	1980–81
Randy Asadoor (3B)	1986
Andy Ashby (P)	1993–99, 2004
Tucker Ashford (IF)	1976–78
Pedro Astacio* (P)	2005
Rich Aurilia *(IF)	2004
Brad Ausmus * (C)	1993–96
Oscar Azocar (P)	1991–92

B

Carlos Baerga (3B)	1999
Chuck Baker (IF)	1978, 1980
Jack Baldschun (P)	1969–70
Josh Bard * (C)	2006–Present
Josh Barfield* (2B)	2006–Present
Kevin Barker (1B)	2002
Marty Barrett (2B)	1991
Bob Barton (C)	1970–72, 1974
Randy Bass (1B)	1980–82
Rich Batchelor (P)	1997
Jason Bay* (OF)	2003
Trey Beamon (OF)	1997
Billy Bean (OF)	1993–1995
Rod Beck (P)	2003–04
Glenn Beckert (2B)	1974–75
Derek Bell (OF)	1993–94
Mark Bellhorn* (IF)	2006
Andy Benes (P)	1989–95
Gary Bennett* (C)	2003
Sean Bergman (P)	1996–97
Victor Bernal (P)	1977
Andres Berumen (P)	1995–96
Jim Beswick (OF)	1978
Kurt Bevacqua (IF)	1979–80, 1982–85
Dann Bilardello (C)	1991–92
Dennis Blair (P)	1980
Willie Blair (P)	1995–96
Curt Blefary (OF)	1972
Geoff Blum* (IF)	2005, 2006–Present
Doug Bochtler (P)	1995–97
Bruce Bochy (C)	1983–87
Brian Boehringer* (P)	1998–2000

Ricky Bones (P)	1991
Juan Bonilla (2B)	1981–83
Greg Booker (P)	1983–89
Bret Boone (3B)	2000
Dan Boone (P)	1981–82
Rob Bowen * (C)	2006
Jason Boyd (P)	2002
Darren Bragg (OF)	2004
Russell Branyan* (3B)	2006–Present
Angel Bravo (OF)	1971
Dewon Brazelton (P)	2006
Craig Breslow (P)	2005
Dan Briggs (1B)	1979
Doug Brocail* (P)	1992–94, 2006–Present
Jim Brower (P)	2006
Bobby Brown (OF)	1983–85
Chris Brown (3B)	1987–88
Emil Brown (OF)	2001
Jarvis Brown (OF)	1993
Kevin Brown (P)	1998
Ollie Brown (OF)	1969–72
Jim Bruske (P)	1997, 1998
Brian Buchanan* (OF)	2002–04
Al Bumbry (OF)	1985
Sean Burroughs (3B)	2002–05
Terry Burrows (P)	1997
Randell Byers (OF)	1987–88
Mike Bynum (P)	2002–04

C

Mike Caldwell (P)	1971–73
Mike Cameron (OF)	2006–Present
Ken Caminiti (3B)	1995–98
Dave Campbell (IF)	1970–73
Mike Campbell (P)	1994
Chris Cannizzaro (C)	1969–71, 1974
Javier Cardona (C)	2002
Buddy Carlyle (P)	1999–2000
Joe Carter (OF)	1990
Dave Cash (2B)	1980
Scott Cassidy* (P)	2005–Present
Vinny Castilla (3B)	2006

Tony Castillo (C)	1978
Andujar Cedeno (SS)	1995–96
Mike Champion (IF)	1976–78
Floyd Chiffer (P)	1982–84
Archi Cianfrocco (IF)	1993–98
Jeff Cirillo* (3B)	2004
Jack Clark (1B)	1989–90
Jerald Clark (OF)	1988–92
Jermaine Clark (OF)	2003
Phil Clark (OF)	1993–95
Horace Clarke (2B)	1974
Matt Clement* (P)	1998–2000
Pat Clements (P)	1989–92
Mike Colangelo (OF)	2001
Nate Colbert (1B)	1969–74
Keith Comstock (P)	1987–88
Clay Condrey (P)	2002–03
Scott Coolbaugh (3B)	1991
Danny Coombs (P)	1970–71
Joey Cora (2B)	1987, 1989–90
Mike Corkins (P)	1969–74
Pat Corrales (C)	1972–73
John Costello (P)	1991
Mike Couchee (P)	1983
Cesar Crespo * (OF)	2001–02
Jack Cust (OF)	2006
Deivi Cruz * (SS)	2002
Will Cunnane* (P)	1997–2000
John Curtis (P)	1980–82
Eric Cyr (P)	2002

D

John D'Acquisto (P)	1977–80
Paul Dade (OF)	1979–80
Mike Darr (OF)	1999–2001
Doug Dascenzo (OF)	1996
Jerry Davanon (IF)	1969
Tom Davey (P)	2000–02
Ben Davis (C)	1998–2001
Bill Davis (1B)	1969
Bob Davis (C)	1973, 1975–78
Gerry Davis (OF)	1983, 1985

John Davis (P)	1990
Mark Davis (P)	1987–89, 1993–94
Storm Davis (P)	1987
Willie Davis (OF)	1976
Roger Deago (P)	2003
Tommy Dean (SS)	1969–71
Marty Decker (P)	1983
Rob Deer (OF)	1996
Kory De Haan (OF)	2000–02
Luis DeLeon (P)	1982–85
Matt DeWitt (P)	2002
Jim Deshaies (P)	1992
Miguel Dilone (OF)	1985
Glenn Dishman (P)	1995–96
Pat Dobson (P)	1970
Brian Dorsett (C)	1991
Paul Doyle (P)	1970
Dave Dravecky (P)	1982–87
Tom Dukes (P)	1969–70
Mike Dunne (P)	1990
Mike Dupree (P)	1976

E

Adam Eaton * (P)	2000–05
Dave Edwards (OF)	1981–82
Juan Eichelberger (P)	1979–82
Dave Eiland (P)	1992–93
Donnie Elliott (P)	1994–95
Randy Elliott (OF)	1972, 1974
Alan Embree * (P)	2002, 2006–Present
Todd Erdos (P)	1997, 2000
Shawn Estes * (P)	2006
Mark Ettles (P)	1993
Barry Evans (3B)	1978–81
Leon Everitt (P)	1969

F

Bill Fahey (C)	1979–80
Brian Falkenborg (P)	2005
Paul Faries (2B)	1990–92
Tony Fernandez (SS)	1991–92
Al Ferrara (OF)	1969–71

Robert Fick* (C)	2004–2005
Jeremy Fikac (P)	2002
Rollie Fingers (P)	1977–80
Steve Finley * (OF)	1995–98
Mike Fiore (1B)	1972
Steve Fireovid (P)	1981, 1983
John Flaherty* (C)	1996–97
Tim Flannery (IF)	1979–89
Bryce Florie (P)	1994–96
Rich Folkers (P)	1975–76
Alan Foster (P)	1975–76
Jay Franklin (P)	1971
Dave Freisleben (P)	1974–78
Danny Frisella (P)	1975
Tito Fuentes (2B)	1975–76

G

Oscar Gamble (OF)	1978
Ron Gant (OF)	2002
Carlos Garcia (IF)	1999
Jesse Garcia (IF)	2005
Ralph Garcia (P)	1972, 1974
Jeff Gardner (2B)	1992–1993
Wes Gardner (P)	1991
Steve Garvey (1B)	1983–87
Rod Gaspar (OF)	1971, 1974
Clarence Gaston (OF)	1969–74
Bob Geren (C)	1993
Rusty Gerhardt (P)	1974
Justin Germano (P)	2003–2005
Brian Giles* (OF)	2003–Present
Ed Giovanola (IF)	1998–99
Joe Goddard (C)	1972
Chris Gomez (SS)	1996–2001
Pat Gomez (P)	1993
Adrian Gonzalez * (1B)	2006
Alex Gonzalez (SS)	2004
Fernando Gonzalez (2B)	1978–79
Tony Gonzalez (IF)	1969
Wiki Gonzalez* (C)	1999–2003
Tom Gorman (P)	1987
Rich Gossage (P)	1984–87

Mark Grant (P)	1987–90
Gary Green (SS)	1986, 1989
Khalil Greene (SS)	2003–Present
Brian Greer (OF)	1977, 1979
Bill Greif (P)	1972–76
Mike Griffin (P)	1982
Tom Griffin (P)	1976–77
John Grubb (OF)	1972–76
Ricky Gutierrez (SS)	1993–94
Freddy Guzman* (OF)	2004–05
Domingo Guzman (P)	1999–2000
Doug Gwosdz (C)	1981–84
Chris Gwynn (OF)	1996
Tony Gwynn (OF)	1982–2001

H

Luther Hackman (P)	2003
Don Hahn (OF)	1975
Joey Hamilton (P)	1994–98
Atlee Hammaker (P)	1990–91
Chris Hammond (P)	2005
Dave Hansen (IF)	2003–04
Larry Hardy (P)	1974–75
Mike Hargrove (1B)	1979
Gene Harris (P)	1992–94
Greg A. Harris (P)	1984
Greg W. Harris (P)	1988–93
Andy Hawkins (P)	1982–88
Ray Hayward (P)	1986–87
Rickey Henderson (OF)	1996–97, 2001
George Hendrick (OF)	1977–78
Clay Hensley* (P)	2005–Present
Ron Herbel (P)	1970
Matt Herges* (P)	2003
Dustin Hermanson* (P)	1995–96
Carlos Hernandez (C)	1997–2000
Enzo Hernandez (SS)	1971–77
Jeremy Hernandez (P)	1991–93
Ramon Hernandez* (C)	2004–05
Junior Herndon (P)	2001
Kevin Higgins (C)	1993
Dave Hilton (3B)	1972–75

George Hinshaw (OF)	1982–83
Sterling Hitchcock (P)	1997–2001, 2004
Trevor Hoffman * (P)	1993–Present
Ray Holbert (SS)	1994–95
Mike Holtz (P)	2002
Ben Howard (P)	2002–03
Thomas Howard (OF)	1991–92
Jack Howell (3B)	1991
La Marr Hoyt (P)	1985–86
Walt Hriniak (C)	1969
Trenidad Hubbard (OF)	2002
Randy Hundley (C)	1975
Steve Huntz (IF)	1970, 1975
Bruce Hurst (P)	1989–93
Tim Hyers (1B)	1994–95
Adam Hyzdu (OF)	2005

I

Dane Iorg (1B)	1986
Mike Ivie (C)	1971, 1974–77

J

Damian Jackson* (IF)	1999–2001, 2005
Danny Jackson (P)	1997
Darrin Jackson (OF)	1989–92
Roy Lee Jackson (P)	1985
Chris James (OF)	1989
Kevin Jarvis* (P)	2000–03
Stan Jefferson (OF)	1987–88
Garry Jestadt (IF)	1971–72
John Jeter (OF)	1971–72
D'Angelo Jimenez * (IF)	2001–2002
Brett Jodie (P)	2001
Ben Johnson * (OF)	2005–Present
Brian Johnson (C)	1994–96
Jerry Johnson (P)	1975–76
Jonathan Johnson (P)	2002
Mike Johnson (P)	1974
Jay Johnstone (OF)	1979
Bobby J. Jones (P)	2001–02
Bobby M. Jones (P)	2002
Chris Jones (OF)	1997

Jimmy Jones (P)	1986–88
Randy Jones (P)	1973–80
Ruppert Jones (OF)	1981–83
Von Joshua (OF)	1980
Wally Joyner (1B)	1996–99

K

Fred Kahaulua (P)	1981
Randy Keisler (P)	2003
Dick Kelley (P)	1969–71
Van Kelly (3B)	1969–70
Fred Kendall (C)	1969–76, 1979–80
Terry Kennedy (C)	1981–86
Jason Kershner (P)	2002
Mike Kilkenny (P)	1972
Dave Kingman (OF)	1977
Gene Kingsale (OF)	2002
Dennis Kinney (P)	1978–80
Clay Kirby (P)	1969–73
Ryan Klesko* (1B)	2000–2006
Jon Knott * (OF)	2004, 2006
Brandon Kolb (P)	2000
Mark Kotsay* (OF)	2001–2003
Marc Kroon (P)	1995, 1997–98
Bill Krueger (P)	1994–95
Chris Krug (C)	1969
John Kruk (1B)	1986–89
Ted Kubiak (3B)	1975–76

L

Tom Lampkin (C)	1990–92, 2002
Rick Lancellotti (1B)	1982
Mark Langston (P)	1998
Ray Lankford (OF)	2001–02
Joe Lansford (1B)	1982–83
Dave LaPoint (P)	1986
Greg LaRocca (IF)	2000
Brian Lawrence* (P)	2001–05
Bill Laxton (P)	1971, 1974
David Lee (P)	2001
Derrek Lee* (1B)	1997
Leron Lee (OF)	1971–73

Mark Lee (P)	1978–79
Joe Lefebvre (OF)	1981–83
Craig Lefferts (P)	1984–87, 1990–92
Dave Leiper (P)	1987–89
Justin Leone (3B)	2006
Jim Lewis (P)	1991
Jim Leyritz (C)	1998–99
Sixto Lezcano (OF)	1982–83
Francisco Libran (SS)	1969
Derek Lilliquist (P)	1990–91
Scott Linebrink* (P)	2003–Present
John Littlefield (P)	1981
Scott Livingstone (IF)	1994–97
Keith Lockhart (2B)	1994, 2003
Gene Locklear (OF)	1973–76
Carlton Loewer (P)	2001, 2003
Mickey Lolich (P)	1978–79
Tim Lollar (P)	1981–84
Joey Long (P)	1997
Terrence Long* (OF)	2004
Luis Lopez (IF)	1993–94, 1996
Rodrigo Lopez* (P)	2000
Mark Loretta* (2B)	2003–05
Gary Lucas (P)	1980–83
David Lundquist (P)	2001–02
Fred Lynn (OF)	1990

M

John Mabry (OF)	2000
Shane Mack (OF)	1987–88
Mike Maddux (P)	1991–92
Dave Magadan (3B)	1999–2001
Jerry Manuel (IF)	1982
Dave Marshall (OF)	1973
Al Martin (OF)	2000
Carmelo Martinez (OF)	1984–89
Jose Martinez (P)	1994
Pedro Martinez (P)	1993–94
Don Mason (2B)	1971–73
Roger Mason (P)	1993
Julius Matos* (IF)	2002
Mike Matthews* (P)	2003

Gary Matthews Jr.* (OF)	1999, 2003
Dave Maurer (P)	2000–01
Tim Mauser (P)	1993–95
Darrell May* (P)	2005
Jim McAndrew (P)	1974
Paul McAnulty* (OF)	2005–Present
Alvin McBean (P)	1969
Billy McCool (P)	1969
Willie McCovey (1B)	1974–76
Lance McCullers (P)	1985–88
Ray McDavid (OF)	1994–95
Chuck McElroy (P)	2001
Fred McGriff (1B)	1991–93
Joe McIntosh (P)	1974–75
Marty McLeary * (P)	2004
Kevin McReynolds (OF)	1983–86
Brian Meadows * (P)	2000
Jose Melendez (P)	1991–92
Luis Melendez (OF)	1976–77
Paul Menhart (P)	1977
Donaldo Mendez (SS)	2001, 2003
Cla Meredith * (P)	2006
Lou Merloni * (IF)	2003
Butch Metzger (P)	1975–77
Dan Miceli * (P)	1998–99
Jason Middlebrook* (P)	2001–02
Bob Miller (P)	1971, 1973
Ed Miller (OF)	1984
Doug Mirabelli * (C)	2006
Kevin Mitchell (3B)	1987
Sid Monge (P)	1983–84
Willie Montanez (1B)	1980
John Montefusco (P)	1982–83
Steve Montgomery (P)	2000
Jerry Morales (OF)	1969–73
Rich Morales (IF)	1973–74
Keith Moreland (1B)	1988
Jose Moreno (OF)	1981
Juan Moreno (P)	2002
Jerry Moses (C)	1975
Jose Mota (2B)	1991
James Mouton (OF)	1998

Sean Mulligan (OF)	1996
Jerry Mumphrey (OF)	1980
Steve Mura (P)	1978–81
Dan Murphy (P)	1989
Heath Murray (P)	1997, 1999
Ivan Murrell (OF)	1969–73
Greg Myers (C)	1998–99
Randy Myers (P)	1992, 1998
Rodney Myers (P)	2000–02

N

Xavier Nady* (OF)	2000, 2003–05
Charles Nagy (P)	2004
Blaine Neal (P)	2004
Rob Nelson (1B)	1987–90
Phil Nevin* (3B)	1999–2005
Graig Nettles (3B)	1984–86
Marc Newfield (OF)	1995–96
David Newhan* (2B)	1999–2000
Kevin Nicholson (SS)	2000
Doug Nickle (P)	2002
Joe Niekro (P)	1969
Melvin Nieves (OF)	1993–95
Wil Nieves (C)	2002
Eric Nolte (P)	1987–89, 1991
Fred Norman (P)	1971–73
Jose Nunez (P)	2001–02
Gary Nyman (P)	1970

O

Miguel Ojeda* (C)	2003–05
Miguel Olivo*(C)	2005
Mike Oquist (P)	1996
Eddie Oropesa (P)	2004
Jesse Orosco (P)	2003
Jimmy Osting (P)	2002
Al Osuna (P)	1996
Antonio Osuna (P)	2004
Akinori Otsuka* (P)	2004–05
Bob Owchinko (P)	1976–79
Eric Owens (OF)	1999–2000
Chris Oxspring (P)	2005

P

Mike Pagliarulo (3B)	1989–90
Vicente Palacios (P)	2000
Lowell Palmer (P)	1974
Mark Parent (C)	1986–90
Chan Ho Park* (P)	2005–06
Bob Patterson (P)	1985
Jay Payton* (OF)	2004
Jason Pearson (P)	2002
Jake Peavy* (P)	2002–Present
Alex Pelaez (1B)	2002
Roberto Pena (SS)	1969
Oliver Perez* (P)	2002–03
Santiago Perez (OF)	2001
Broderick Perkins (1B)	1978–82
Sammy Perlozzo (2B)	1979
Gaylord Perry (P)	1978–79
Roberto Petagine* (1B)	1995
Adam Peterson (P)	1991
Gary Pettis (OF)	1992
Mike Phillips (2B)	1981
Tom Phoebus (P)	1971–72
Mike Piazza* (C)	2006
Kevin Pickford (P)	2002
Joe Pittman (2B)	1982
Phil Plantier (OF)	1993–95, 1997
Johnny Podres (P)	1969
Jim Presley (3B)	1991
Brandon Puffer (P)	2004
Tim Pyznarski (1B)	1986

Q

Paul Quantrill* (P)	2005
Humberto Quintero* (C)	2003–04

R

Doug Rader (3B)	1976–77
Mario Ramirez (SS)	1981–85
Roberto Ramirez (P)	1998
Joe Randa * (3B)	2005
Dennis Rasmussen (P)	1983, 1988–91
Eric Rasmussen (P)	1978–80

Randy Ready (3B)	1986–89
Frank Reberger (P)	1969
Tim Redding* (P)	2005
Jody Reed (2B)	1995–96
Steve Reed * (P)	2002
Desi Relaford * (SS)	2000
Merv Rettenmund (OF)	1976–77
Carlos Reyes (P)	1998, 1999, 2000
Dennys Reyes * (P)	2005
Don Reynolds (OF)	1978–79
Ken Reynolds (P)	1976
Ronn Reynolds (C)	1990
Gene Richards (OF)	1977–83
Adam Riggs (2B)	2001
Mike Rivera (C)	2003
Roberto Rivera (P)	1999
Ruben Rivera (OF)	1997–2000
Joe Roa (P)	2003
Dave A. Roberts (P)	1969–71
Dave R. Roberts* (OF)	2005–Present
Dave W. Roberts (3B)	1972–75, 1977–78
Bip Roberts (OF)	1986, 1988–91, 1994–95
Dave Robinson (OF)	1970–71
Kerry Robinson (OF)	2004
Rafael Robles (SS)	1969–70, 1972
Aurelio Rodriguez (3B)	1980
Edwin Rodriguez (IF)	1983, 1985
Rich Rodriguez (P)	1990–93
Roberto Rodriguez (P)	1970
Ron Roenicke (OF)	1984
Mandy Romero (C)	1997–1998
Vicente Romo (P)	1973–74
Steve Rosenberg (P)	1991
John Roskos (OF)	2000
David Ross * (C)	2005
Gary Ross (P)	1969–74
Jerry Royster (IF)	1985–86
Sonny Ruberto (C)	1969

S

A. J. Sager (P)	1994
Luis Salazar (3B)	1980–84, 1987, 1989

Reggie Sanders* (OF)	1999
Scott Sanders (P)	1993–96, 1998
Benito Santiago (C)	1986–92
Al Santorini (P)	1969–71
Rick Sawyer (P)	1976–77
Pat Scanlon (IF)	1977
Mark Schaeffer (P)	1972
Calvin Schiraldi (P)	1989–90
Don Schulze (P)	1989
John Scott (OF)	1974–75
Tim Scott (P)	1991–93, 1997
Rudy Seanez* (P)	1993, 2001, 2005, 2006
Todd Sears (1B)	2003
Dick Selma (P)	1969
Frank Seminara (P)	1992–93
Dan Serafini (P)	2000
Wascar Serrano (P)	2001
Al Severinsen (P)	1971–72
Dick Sharon (OF)	1975
Andy Sheets (IF)	1998
Gary Sheffield* (3B)	1992–93
Darrell Sherman (OF)	1993
Jason Shiell (P)	2002
Craig Shipley (IF)	1991–94, 1996–97
Bob Shirley (P)	1977–80
Eric Show (P)	1981–90
Terry Shumpert (IF)	1997
Paul Siebert (P)	1977
Sonny Siebert (P)	1975
Candy Sierra (P)	1988
Brian Sikorski* (P)	2006
Steve Simpson (P)	1972
John Sipin (2B)	1969
Tommy Sisk (P)	1969
Don Slaught (C)	1997
Terrmel Sledge* (OF)	2006
Ron Slocum (IF)	1969–71
Heathcliff Slocumb (P)	2000
Ozzie Smith (SS)	1978–81
Pete Smith (P)	1997–98
Frank Snook (P)	1973
Elias Sosa (P)	1983

Stan Spencer (P)	1998–2000
Ed Spiezio (3B)	1969–72
Dan Spillner (P)	1974–78
Ed Sprague (3B)	2000
George Stablein (P)	1980
Larry Stahl (OF)	1969–72
Fred Stanley (IF)	1972
Dave Staton (1B)	1993–94
Tim Stauffer * (P)	2005–Present
James Steels (OF)	1987
Phil Stephenson (1B)	1989–92
Todd Steverson (OF)	1996
Kurt Stillwell (2B)	1992–93
Craig Stimac (C)	1980–81
Bob Stoddard (P)	1986
Tim Stoddard (P)	1985–86
Ricky Stone (P)	2004
Brent Strom (P)	1975–77
Champ Summers (1B)	1984
Gary Sutherland (2B)	1977
Brian Sweeney* (P)	2004, 2006
Mark Sweeney * (OF)	1997–98, 2002, 2005
Rick Sweet (C)	1978
Steve Swisher (C)	1981–82
Jason Szuminski* (P)	2004

T

Jeff Tabaka (P)	1994–95
Dennis Tankersley (P)	2002–04
Jim Tatum (3B)	1996
Kerry Taylor (P)	1993–94
Ron Taylor (P)	1972
Tom Tellman (P)	1979–80
Gene Tenace (C)	1977–80
Garry Templeton (SS)	1982–91
Walt Terrell (P)	1989
Tim Teufel (2B)	1991–93
Bob Tewksbury (P)	1996
Derrel Thomas (2B)	1972–74, 1978
Jason Thompson (1B)	1996
Michael Thompson* (P)	2006
Dickie Thon (SS)	1988

Mark Thurmond (P)	1983–86
Ron Tingley (C)	1982
Bobby Tolan (OF)	1974–75, 1979
Fred Tolliver (P)	1989
Brian Tollberg (P)	2000–03
Brett Tomko* (P)	2002
Dave Tomlin (P)	1974–77
Hector Torres (SS)	1975–76
Bubba Trammell (OF)	2001–03
Rich Troedson (P)	1973–74
J. J. Trujillo (P)	2002
Jerry Turner (OF)	1974–81, 1983

U

John Urrea (P)	1981

V

Ismael Valdez* (P)	2004
Rafael Valdez (P)	1990
Wilson Valdez (SS)	2005
Bobby Valentine (OF)	1975–77
Fernando Valenzuela (P)	1995–97
John Vander Wal (OF)	1998–99
Ben VanRyn (P)	1998
Jim Vatcher (OF)	1991–92
Greg Vaughn (OF)	1996–98
Ramon Vazquez* (IF)	2002–2004
Jorge Velandia (IF)	1997
Guillermo Velasquez (1B)	1992–93
Dario Veras (P)	1996–97
Quilvio Veras (2B)	1997–99
Shane Victorino* (OF)	2003
Brandon Villafuerte* (P)	2002–03
Ron Villone* (P)	1995–96
Joe Vitiello (1B)	2000
Ed Vosberg (P)	1986, 1998–99

W

Kevin Walker* (P)	2000–03
Pete Walker (P)	1996
Todd Walker* (IF)	2006
Donne Wall (P)	1998–2003

Gene Walter (P)	1985–86
Dan Walters (C)	1992–93
Kevin Ward (OF)	1991–92
Mark Wasinger (3B)	1986
Steve Watkins (P)	2004
Ramon Webster (1B)	1970–71
Dave Wehrmeister (P)	1976–78
Chris Welsh (P)	1981–83
David Wells (P)	2004, 2006
Don Wengert (P)	1998
Matt Whisenant (P)	1999–2000
Rondell White (OF)	2003
Wally Whitehurst (P)	1993–94
Matt Whiteside* (P)	1999–2000
Ed Whitson (P)	1983–84, 1986–91
Alan Wiggins (2B)	1981–85
Mark Wiley (P)	1978
Jim Wilhelm (OF)	1978–79
Rick Wilkins (C)	2001
Bernie Williams (OF)	1974
Brian Williams (P)	1995
Eddie Williams (1B)	1990, 1994–95, 1998
George Williams (C)	2000
Jim Williams (OF)	1969–70
Randy Williams (P)	2005
Woody Williams* (P)	1999–2001, 2005–06
Scott Williamson* (P)	2006
Ron Willis (P)	1970
Earl Wilson (P)	1970
Dave Winfield (OF)	1973–80
Rick Wise (P)	1980–82
Jay Witasick* (P)	2000–01, 2003–04
Kevin Witt (1B)	2001
Ed Wojna (P)	1985–87
Tim Worrell* (P)	1993–97
Jaret Wright* (P)	2003
Marvell Wynne (OF)	1986–89

Y

Chris Young* (P)	2006
Eric Young* (IF)	2005–06